RODNEY MARSH: I WAS BORN A

Loose Cannon

with Brian Woolnough

RODNEY MARSH: I WAS BORN A

Loose Cannon

with Brian Woolnough

Optimum
PUBLISHING SOLUTIONS

First published in hardback in Great Britain in 2010 by:

Optimum Publishing Solutions, OPS LLP, Partnership Registered Number OC347586.

The Cottages, Regent Road,

Altrincham, Cheshire WA14 1RX.

www.optimumpublishingsolutions.uk.com

ISBN 978-0-9563274-2-0

This book was printed in the UK, saving the environmental cost of long distance transportation to major markets. The printing facility has all its operations under one roof and employs many local people. It is certified to ISO 14001 and is working to achieve carbon neutrality. It was printed using 100% vegetable based inks on Magno Matt Satin FSC paper which is produced from 100% Elemental Chlorine Free (EFC) pulp that is fully recyclable. It has a Forest Stewardship Council (FSC) certification and is produced by a mill which supports well managed forestry schemes.

Mixed Sources
Product group from well-managed forests and other controlled sources
www.fsc.org Cert no. SGS-COC-005091
© 1996 Forest Stewardship Council

To my Grandson, Addison Marsh.

Acknowledgement

I have known Brian Woolnough for over thirty years, and when we first started the planning stages of this book, he was my first choice as co-author – thankfully, he agreed! Brian is a renowned journalist and television presenter and I am delighted that he could take time out of a ridiculously intense schedule which included the 2010 World Cup. Thank you for the many enjoyable hours we spent together, reminiscing. Further, I would like to thank Ian Cheeseman for working with me to collate the Manchester City chapter; and also Jim Holden and Rui Farias for their help with the chapters on America.

This was certainly not an easy project to pull together in terms of research and editorial, especially the American portion of the book. Accordingly, I would like to thank my daughter Joanna Olszowska for all her time and efforts with moving this book forward. Also Mike Jones of Optimum for making this happen; and Gail Cooke and Melina Galley, also of Optimum, for their dedication and determination to make this a quality read. A 'big thank you' goes to the team who supported Gail with the editing and creative for this book, in particular Suzanne Jones, Clive Jones, Lauren Hughes and photographer Maria Rushton.

Finally, I'd like to say thank you to all my family for their continued support.

I hope you enjoy the book.

Contents

Foreword

I first met Rodney Marsh in London's King's Road. Well, you would, wouldn't you? The Duke of Wellington pub was a favourite watering hole for players from Fulham and Chelsea in the early 70's. It was an era when newspaper reporters were allowed to mix with players and form friendships involving trust, and it was the start of a relationship between Rodney and I that has lasted more than 35 years. Rodney is a bit like Marmite; you either like him or you don't, understand his sense of humour or find it offensive, find him compelling company or walk away. It was the same when he played. He either drove you mad, or you marvelled at his skill and his obsession with wanting to produce tales of the unexpected on the pitch. Some managers and team mates couldn't cope, failed to understand that here was someone who only comes around every so often. A rebel in boots, a fairytale you have to believe in, a talent that you couldn't ignore. A character; how we could do with more like him in today's game. I've always liked Marmite, and I've always liked Rodney Marsh. He is my kind of footballer and person. He tells it like it is, doesn't suffer fools, hates being told what to do and, most significantly, is good company. He makes you laugh. He played and has lived his life with a public smile. What word best sums him up? Unpredictable.

When we first met, he had just played for Fulham during his second spell at Craven Cottage. I had finished my report and been invited along to meet the great men by Jeff Powell, then Football Correspondent at the Daily Mail. Rodney was sitting with Bobby Moore and George Best. Not a bad hat-trick, and certainly a special moment for a junior reporter in his early days at the Sun Newspaper. It is amazing when I look back on those times; three of the biggest names in English football, sitting in a pub sipping beer and talking football with members of the public and reporters. No bodyguards, no 'yes men,' no mobile phones, no agents and no worries. Just conversation until they threw us out. What was born that night was trust.

Over the years Marsh, Moore and Best told me things I have never repeated and never will. It was an era when you could talk to managers and players, and they knew that it wouldn't go any further. What would have been the point? Had I let Rodney down over the years, I wouldn't be writing this book and certainly would not have sat for hours with him recording the story of his life.

Trust in journalism is an unwritten law and, sadly, is broken too many times today. Such is the pressure on journalists to produce exclusive stories, the pressure on them from Sports Editors worried about protecting their own backs. Such is the circulation war in these times of internet information and other electronic media. Rodney once told me something and I still can't bring myself to repeat it. It was so controversial that it would have produced a week's worth of back-page headlines for me. He asked me not to tell anyone, and that was the bond so many journalists shared with their friends and contacts in the past. Rodney was always controversial and a reporter's dream when in full flow. There were times when he needed protecting for his own sake, and isn't that part of the trust? Maybe I'm old school. I once advised Arsenal and England fullback Kenny Sansom not to go ahead with an article in which he heavily criticised his then manager George Graham. Sansom wanted a better contract than Arsenal were offering, so we did a 'back me or sack me' interview. "If we go ahead with this, Kenny," I said, "George will be furious." Sansom wanted to do it, so the article appeared in The Sun on a Saturday, twenty-four hours before The League Cup Final against Liverpool. Kenny rang me at lunchtime to say he had been stripped of the armband and that Tony Adams was taking over. There have been times when I have held back quotes or stories to protect Rodney, and other times when I have been amazed and indeed grateful at his determination to go the whole hog. There is one thing about Rodney Marsh, and that is he isn't scared to say what he believes.

Football has always needed and wanted stars, players who get the fans on their feet and make things happen. Heroes. Today in England, it is Wayne Rooney, Carlos Tevez, Didier Drogba, Cesc Fabregas and others. Thirty years ago it was men like Marsh. Testimony to his impact on the game is that he has remained a household name. His mouth has kept him in the face of the public, with his outrageous comments as a pundit. Marsh has never been afraid to say what he believes and he often says what you, the fan, thinks. Marsh is the man in the pub with a platform to voice his opinion.

How Marsh and others like Moore and Best would love to have played today, with wonderful surfaces to perform on and protection from referees, not to mention the huge riches thrown at all players. Marsh earned £500 a week at Manchester City.

His equivalent today in the blue shirt of City, Emmanuel Adebayor, gets £120,000 a week. Rodney, of course, would have been the same person had he been playing today, refusing to accept authority, ignoring tactics and scoring wonderful, unexpected goals. Driving people mad, yet providing entertainment. And that has been a hallmark of his career. Doing the unexpected.

Football needs public heroes and it's sad that today, so many of the stars have become untouchable. Out of reach for the common man, surrounded by agents and club officials, job's worths who act like star-struck fans. When I was learning my trade as a football journalist you mixed with the players, called them at home for a chat to discuss stories you wanted to write, and if they told you not to publish something, you didn't. Of course today there are exceptions, although across the board there is a natural distrust, created by the 'them and us' atmosphere between players and the media. Call a player today, and nine times out of ten he will tell you to speak to his agent or demand to know where you got his number from. Do an interview with Manchester United and England star Wayne Rooney, and you will need to provide his agent with a list of questions and submit the article for approval. Even with England, players are protected by the system and everything is organised for you, and that is not reporting as I knew it. I was brought up on players like Marsh, Moore and Best. Then Hoddle, Robson and Gascoigne. When they enjoyed a 'craic' with journalists. You felt part of them, not as if you were looking in from the outside, waiting for a quote to fall or for someone to say, "He'll see you now." At the 1990 World Cup in Italia, England captain Bryan Robson and a few of the players like Paul Gascoigne, Chris Waddle and John Barnes, often used to stroll down to the media hotel for a chat and a drink. That would not happen today. The fact that Gazza went missing after one such 'afternoon off' is another story. Gascoigne was a character and it's so sad to see him looking completely lost today.

Marsh remains a character of the English game. Walk down any high street and ask a person about Rodney Marsh, they will have an opinion. It may not always be complimentary but they will react. Whether they think of him as an outrageous football pundit or the man who went into the jungle on 'I'm a Celebrity get me Out Of Here,' as the player who made them smile or drove them crazy with frustration, Marsh always generates debate.

The title of this book sums Rodney up perfectly. Loose Cannon. It is what he is and always has been. Controversial, outspoken, someone who has said things that have lost him his place at football clubs and, yes, with England. Sometimes he's had no idea why he's made such comments and that, of course, is what a Loose Cannon is all about. That is Marsh. This book gives you more, much more of Marsh. This is an icon laid bare, and never before has he been so honest with himself as he takes us inside the public figure. This is a story of brutal soul-searching and in this book, Rodney has revealed things about himself that have sat uncomfortably with him since he was a boy. It is a story that he has always wanted to tell. It will upset some, hurt others and amuse many of you. His story reflects his life not just as a player for Fulham, Queen's Park Rangers, Manchester City, England and his career in America, but as Rodney the person. Some of his revelations will shock you. Just when you think there is nothing more to come from him, he delivers another story out of the blue. Just like the goals he scored, his book creates the feeling of 'where did that come from?'

He doesn't have one regret in his life, and why are we not surprised by that? He has made mistakes, many of them, and admits that some things he has done were wrong. It is a controversial book and when you read it, it will remind you of how Marsh played, off the cuff and unpredictable, yet always with a smile on his face.

The first thing Rodney said to me was, "All is well," a catchphrase he took from Bobby Moore and still uses every day now. And all was well, and has been ever since. 'Life is for living' has been his motto.

The day after our first meeting, I called him at home and we talked about Fulham and football and arranged to meet up again. That is what we have been doing for years, because that is what journalists and footballers should do; build a relationship of trust. Some of the things in this book, Rodney has never spoken or opened up about before in public. He admits that throughout his life he has built a wall around him, a protection that has kept things inside, and that he has allowed no one to break it down. That is dismantled in this book. It is a story he wanted to tell and, for so many reasons, had to.

Brian Woolnough

Introduction

It's Friday lunchtime at the Player's Bar and Restaurant, at the popular Marriott Hotel near Manchester Airport. The wine is flowing as quickly as the conversation, and three Manchester City Legends are talking about Rodney Marsh and the 'good old days.' Marsh is there too, listening, correcting and regularly telling Francis Lee, Mike Summerbee and Tommy Booth what bollocks they are uttering. It's a good craic and we go on until early evening, doing what footballers and journalists do best, talking, rowing, and then agreeing about the game they love. Conversation turns to Marsh as the subject, because it's time to get a view of the team mates he joined in 1972 when he arrived from QPR. The year City should have won the old First Division, only to blow it. Marsh has often been accused of being the reason City slumped, allowing Derby to overtake them.

Marsh kicks off what becomes a lively debate, remaining adamant that he was to blame, that his signing disrupted the team and blew them off course. "If Manchester City had not signed me in that year, would we have won the Championship?" he asked the others, "I believe the answer is yes." After all these years he wanted an honest opinion from people he respected. Clearly, it had been bugging him.

Lee was first to react with, "I would answer that by saying probably, yes, we would have been Champions. That, though, is the easy answer because we did have to change the team and alter the way we played. There were, I believe, other reasons. We played Stoke and battered them, only for Gordon Banks to have one of the games of his life. He was incredible that day, making save after save. Let me tell you something else about that season. We should have had a blatant penalty at Ipswich, when Mick Mills palmed the ball over the bar and for some reason it wasn't given. We should also have had a penalty at Arsenal when Jeff Blockley clearly tipped Rodney's shot over the bar. It was a terrible decision by referee Gordon Hill and we chased him all the way back to the halfway line. Apart from you joining, everything that could have gone wrong did.

Ipswich were mid-table and we battered them. How we didn't win, I'll never know. They did strong arm us, and our centre forward, Wyn Davies, got twenty stitches in his face after someone butted him. I will take a lot of convincing that they were not taking a special bung from somewhere. I can't prove that, but I still believe something was up in that game. Leeds were top of the old First Division going into their last game, at Wolves. Leeds had to win to be Champions and Bill McGarry, the manager of Wolves, told his team to go and fight for their lives and win because everyone would be watching their performance. Wolves beat Leeds, and Derby won the League. Typical of Derby manager, Brian Clough, he was on a beach somewhere when they were crowned. It should have been us."

Summerbee had a different theory as to why City lost that title, saying, "I can't blame Rodney, although I do believe he wasn't fit enough when he joined City. We'd done months of what Malcolm Allison called 'power training' and we were super fit. Rodney took some time to catch up with us. You could see he was struggling, and perhaps Malcolm put him into the side too early. We had to change our style and that didn't help. We were a quick, attacking team with the ball pinging around between us. Rodney's inclusion inevitably changed that. It slowed us down, and that is nothing against his ability on the ball. Rodney wanted to hold the ball up and that wasn't our style. It is a little unfair, though, to say that he lost us the title that year."

Lee added, "Wyn Davies was centre-forward and I played off him. It worked and we were six points clear when Rodney arrived. To accommodate Rodney, they dropped Wyn and moved me back to centre-forward. The way we'd been playing became disrupted, although that is no excuse because professional players should not need an excuse. We were five or six points in front of everyone with three games in hand (when it was only two points for a win) at Easter, and I believe the only reason we lost is because we ran out of luck. When it goes against you, it goes against you big time."

There were many stories that some City players were against the signing. Marsh was certainly Coach Malcolm Allison's man, while manager Joe Mercer was not in favour of the £200,000 deal. However, Lee was not one of the players who did not welcome Marsh and added, "No, we were delighted when Rodney joined because he was in the England squad and had great skill. We'd seen him play in the League Cup Final and on TV, and the only thing that worried me was that he couldn't run to save his life. I said to Malcolm two days before he arrived, "He's not the quickest runner in the world." Marsh, with a huge grin on his face, said, "The wine's talking Franny!"

Lee continued, "The training was severe in those days and Allison had all sorts of professional athletes organising us, including one of England's best, Derek Ibbotson. Our pre-match meal was cornflakes and honey, toast, jam and tea, but that was it. At half time he gave us a Gatorade drink, which no other club had heard of. People say the drink has only arrived on the market in the last five years, yet we had it in 1972. That was Malcolm for you. We were so far ahead in our thinking. Me, I don't care what people eat. They can go into the toilet just before a kick off and do what is good for them, for all I care. Our winger Tony Coleman, and Arsenal forward Charlie George were two players who made themselves sick just before the kick off. It was so important in those days to be in the team, because an appearance meant your money, £70, went up to £140. That was the incentive and why you played week in and week out. There was never any thought of missing a game with a tweak or minor injury, not like today."

Booth agreed, saying, "I travelled with the City first team recently and not one of them had a drink after the game. They all carried bottles of water. If that had been us after a match, whatever the result, we would have raided the nearest bar." Lee agreed, commenting, "I honestly believe drinking after a game is good for you and relaxes the body, brings you back down after such an adrenaline rush. Surely you're entitled to have a drink after a game. When you play, millions of thoughts go through your mind. You can't just switch off like that and go to sleep; you need something to calm you down. When I played for Derby, I employed a driver and went out with the lads until at least midnight, then got him to drive me home. It's hugely different today because there is a different mind-set. Remember all the running we did in training? At Salford University, we were wired up and they took blood and did tests on us, even cut our ears to take a sample. But take the three fittest players in the City team then, and compare them with three today and there would be fuck all between us. We were fit."

Marsh said, "They used to take tests on how far we ran in games, and Colin Bell did eleven miles while I did three!" Lee responded, saying, "You would have done more than that Rodney, three miles in an hour and a half; you must have walked through every game. Our three fittest players in those days were Bell, Mike Doyle and you, Mike. Malcolm was a great coach and I got on with him well. His ideas were new to me because I came from Bolton where we didn't even have a coach, only a PT instructor. He used to scream, "Go, go, go," before every training session and that was it. "Go, go, go," and we did. Malcolm eventually left us and he definitely took the easy way out. When things were not going well he ducked out. Malcolm's problem is that he wanted to be the President, Chairman, Manager and Coach all in one. He wanted to do everything. If he couldn't do it, he walked away. He was a bright guy, but coaching was his limit. He finally left because he was in love with a girl called Serena Williams, who was the head bunny at London's Playboy Club. Why doesn't that surprise me?" Marsh thinks back to the time Allison left him behind at City, recalling when he came to him and said, "I'm thinking of leaving to go to Crystal Palace." Marsh was shocked and said, "I've only been here for five minutes and you're going?" He said he wanted to talk to him about it. "Rodney," he said, "I'm telling you the truth because I'm in love." Lee added, smiling, "What kind of manager discusses his future and private life with one of his players? Shouldn't it have been the other way around?"

Booth joined in, saying, "He was an extraordinary character who never did things normally. After training one day he was in the bath with us and he suddenly said, "Asa, (Hartford) how do you fancy joining Nottingham Forest?" What a way to treat a player? He just came out with it and Asa was just as shocked as the rest of us. When he was coach, he always went out with the lads and the board thought he was the be all and end all." Lee added, "There were four or five board members and they all copied Malcolm, even leaving their wives like him. They started drinking champagne and smoking big cigars. They thought, "This is the life.""

The conversation then switched back to Marsh and the impact he had on the club, with Lee saying, "When Rodney arrived there was no problem. He was one of us apart from the fact he was wearing no shoes when he first walked into Maine Road, plus being a scruffy bugger. We were smart, and he was like a disciple when he first arrived. Like us, though, all he wanted to do was play."

Booth added, "There were one or two players who turned up their noses up at Rodney and what he stood for. Their attitude was "Oh, well we just have to get on with it." "Name names!" ordered Marsh, to which Booth confessed, "Mike Doyle, and Big Joe Corrigan were not exactly fans. Doyle was always looking to blame someone. If we conceded a goal he would look round and blame the youngest one or the new arrival."

Lee went on to say, "There were a couple of cliques in the team but, for heavens' sake, we were a team and you needed to gel. We were the daft bunch, dedicated during the game, but as soon as it was over we enjoyed ourselves. If there was something going on against Rodney, I didn't know or hear about it. He could be an infuriating bugger, mind you. I remember once him dribbling across the goalmouth when I was waiting for a pass to score, but he never gave me the ball and the chance was gone. At half time, I laid into him and said, "Why didn't you pass?" to which he replied, "I couldn't hear you because I'm deaf in one ear." "Forget about your hearing," I said, "you must have lost your eyesight too!" Summerbee piped up, saying, "I think the deafness thing was a load of bollocks. He used it as an excuse. I used to spend so much time on the pitch shouting "Yoo hoo!" trying to catch his attention, and I never did unless he thought the time was right. Or he would benefit if he actually got rid of the ball!"

Lee went on to say, "We were a great team, and had it not been for all the troubles and changes in the boardroom, we could have taken over the old First Division and dominated for years. After United had gone down in 1974, City had the chance to become so big, but they blew it. If we had not had the boardroom coup and take-overs, and not brought Malcolm in then who knows? The new people all loved Malcolm, but I believe they should have kept Joe Mercer in charge. It wasn't long before Malcolm buggered off to Crystal Palace anyway. As I see it, Peter Swales manipulated his way in as mediator and saw a gap to become Chairman. The first thing he did was to try and get the players to condemn manager Ron Saunders so he could sack him. That's how messy it became. I said at a meeting, "If you want to criticise the Manager get him in here, because I am not saying anything about him behind his back," then walked out. I knew that was me finished. Swales sold me to Derby to buy Asa Hartford."

Summerbee commented, "It's interesting, because when I signed Malcolm didn't want me but Joe did, the opposite way around to Rodney. It wouldn't be City without the conflict and the unrest. It wasn't great for me but I came through. Rodney was always an oddity to most people because he did things differently from the norm. He wasn't a problem to me, and it was always his skills and ability that people loved and concentrated on. He was a character, a personality and had a huge following within the City supporters. We were a great team when he joined, although a few of us were coming to the end of our careers, and maybe Malcolm wanted to freshen things up. It's difficult to come into a club that was sitting on top of the First Division and try to improve it. Rodney was always a popular person and became a favourite. Everything he did was controversial and the public loved him for that. The way he played and talked drew attention. We were an exciting side, and in many ways he added to that. It's just that you never knew what he would do next, on and off the pitch. Diplomatic, he wasn't. He was a showman and that sums him up perfectly. He was a character, and there are not enough of them today. Marsh would be huge in today's game because we cry out for people who stand out, who can play but who can also say what they feel and believe. Players and characters like him are a rarity. He talked bollocks half the time, but it didn't matter. If he had ever gone into politics, we'd be in World War Three by now, because he could never control his tongue. Mind you, all politicians talk bollocks, don't they? There were many times I wanted to smack Rodney because he could be so infuriating. That doesn't mean to say I didn't like him, or that I didn't appreciate his skills. We all liked Rodney even if he was a smart Alec. We got used to the crap he came out with. In my opinion, he didn't play enough for England and that may not have been his fault. I only played eight times for my country and only once did Alf Ramsey play me in my proper position of wide on the right. That was in Wales at Ninian Park when I crossed for Rodney to score his only goal for England. Needless to say, I have reminded him of that fact about a million times! He was certainly unpredictable, and one of his most unexpected acts has cost me a fortune. He stayed with us for the first three days when he arrived from London, and when he walked in for the first time he handed my wife, Christine, the biggest bunch of flowers I have seen. My wife was so impressed and gave me a look of "why don't you ever buy me flowers?" I've bought her flowers every Friday since, shamed into it by Rodney Marsh! It must have cost me thousands!"

It was gone eight o'clock when we finally got up from the lunch table, after seven hours of talking Marsh, City and football. We could have gone on through the night, because these are three subjects that provoke debate and argument. Everyone has an opinion on Rodney Marsh, and Lee, Summerbee and Booth, three of his team mates and friends, provided an insight into one of the most extraordinary characters the English game has known.

At the end we raised a glass to him, to City and to football. It was the evening before the Manchester derby in April 2010, the biggest clash between the bitter rivals since 1968, when both clubs were going for the title. It was one of the biggest matches in City's history and should have represented the confirmation of a new era; new owners, new manager and a new belief. They all predicated a City win. United won 1-0 and afterwards Summerbee said, "That's the trouble with City; you never know what's going to happen next."

1

I was Born a Loose Cannon

My name is Rodney Marsh. I'm 65 years old and a Loose Cannon. Always have been, always will be. I was born one.

How do you describe a Loose Cannon? That's easy: someone who doesn't really care about anything except the things they love. Say what you think, do what you believe in and live with the consequences. I have taken that motto with me through a wonderful life in football.

I have upset people including the people I love and in return they have angered me. I have fallen out with managers, officials and opponents, and been in the company of all different types of characters and celebrities. All the way through I have been me, and that has been important: the very key to my existence. My life has been a roller coaster and sometimes I have not been in control of the ride.

I have been a Loose Cannon from the day I blinked sunlight. A uncompromising upbringing in Bygrove Street, Poplar, in the East End of London before moving to Stoke Newington, (I was actually born in Hatfield, Hertfordshire on October 11th, 1944, where my mother, Lillian, was sent to give birth to me as an evacuee, but three days later we were back in Poplar.) I was surrounded by violence, and that's the way it was on my street in those days. You had to live on your instinct and wits. As kids, we all learned how to look after ourselves. We were all rascals.

What I learnt from my parents was not to cry or show emotion, to put a barrier up around me and not allow anyone inside. That tough, unbreakable coating has stayed with me throughout my life. I don't have close friends, apart from my family, especially anyone involved in football, and there really are very few people who understand the real Rodney Marsh. Who is he and what does he stand for?

Hopefully, you will become a little closer to me as you read my story. As you probably already realise, I am going to try to be brutally honest about myself, the game and those I have met and mixed with. Life is what it is and I can't regret a decision I have made or anything I have said and done. This attitude is me and has made me who I am, the good, the bad and the ugly. Love me or hate me, I wouldn't be me if I hadn't screwed up along the way. Mistakes are part of life. I can say I have never done anything intentionally to hurt anyone.

People ask me if I miss playing and my answer is "I am still playing. Just take a look at The Premier League every week, can't you see, it's me? I'm Wayne Rooney. The passion, the fire, the love of football, the kid off the street living the dream. It's me. Entertaining, bringing people to their feet, doing the unexpected, it's me. Roooooney, Rooooooney . . . . Rodneeeeey, Rodneeeeey . . . . it's me."

Rooney is a throwback to my era. He just wants to play. There is a saying they use in America, "you can take the boy out of the country but you can never take the country out of the boy." They have been using that phrase about the East End in London for fifty years and it's true. I, like Rooney, will never forget my roots. Straight off the streets into dream land. You have to put so much in before you can take so much out.

Rooney will enjoy the spin offs and the riches it brings him, but we are not talking about a David Beckham brand here. We are talking about raw talent whose first priority is to get out there on the grass and play. He hates it when Manchester United manager Sir Alex Ferguson, his mentor and father-figure at Old Trafford, tells him he needs a rest and leaves him out of a game. I was like that; I just wanted to play day in and day out. It was my stage, my release, my everything. To score a goal for the people, to entertain them and, yes, to be loved, something I never experienced at home. Scoring goals and winning football matches changes people's lives; yes it is that important.

Rooney will go down in history as a proper footballer. We will not be talking about his money or what he achieved outside the game; he will be remembered for what he did with United and England. So much of what Rooney does on the pitch comes from his own vision. I can relate to that and when I see him I get excited, I'm rolling back the years myself. He spots something and does it. He sees something and does it. He has been born with a wonderful gift, and I suspect he's now doing things on a football pitch he used to practice on the street outside his Merseyside home or with his mates in the park.

Instinctive is a great word in football. You play off the cuff; I used to and so does Rooney. I didn't run back and defend my own area like he does; Rooney's work rate is phenomenal. He has something unique and his career will evolve from now onwards. What a great future he has and what a talent he is.

Rooney is currently the best header of the ball in the World when he gets into his opponents' six-yard box. How does that happen at five foot seven inches and against top, taller defenders? Instinct, the gift of being in the right place at the right time and an uncanny ability to read the game. Plus, of course, desire. It is such a great feeling when opponents don't know what you are going to do next, when you surprise them with talent you have been gifted with.

He will just love it when he crosses that white line and steps into his arena, where he can make things happen his way. People will no doubt point at me; accuse me of not working hard enough or of losing interest in matches. Not true. I am not comparing myself to Rooney as a footballer, just in terms of the passion, love, attitude and commitment to entertaining.

Whatever people may think of Rodney Marsh the player, I always did everything I could to win the game. My managers and coaches didn't always appreciate what I was trying to do, although deep inside I had so much desire and passion to achieve. Yes, doing things differently and, yes, as a Loose Cannon. But, like Rooney, I was a winner.

There were only a couple of occasions when I ran onto the pitch and felt out of place. One has stuck in my memory forever and that was a match in the early sixties at Leeds. I was only eighteen, in the Fulham first team, and walking into Elland Road and then onto the pitch didn't feel right for me. Funny, isn't it, how mood and the psychological effect can take over in sport. I felt out of my depth. In the same season we went to Anfield to play Liverpool and, in contrast, I immediately felt like a million dollars. It was after that game that the late, great Liverpool manager Bill Shankly said in an interview in the Sunday newspapers that Rodney Marsh should be a Liverpool player. I took that as a huge compliment.

How other clubs would love to have Rodney Marsh in their team, Shankly said. He added that there are other players who grab as many headlines and yet who don't compare with the attitude, skill and love of the game that Marsh possesses. This was how to handle me, by understanding my philosophy and outlook on football. I wanted to be the Great Entertainer. The line that I trod throughout my career, indeed my life, was a thin one. I was like a trapeze artist, swaying one way and the other, but never quite falling off, always willing to have a go at a new challenge.

There will always be opposites. Take Cristiano Ronaldo, the most expensive player in the World who went from Manchester United to Real Madrid for a staggering £80 million, and Nicolas Anelka, who has played for so many clubs, as two good examples of the opposite of Rooney. In my opinion, they are not in love with the game and are in it for what they can take out.

Yes, Ronaldo is a wonderful talent and I enjoy watching him play, but Rooney is like a great band you pay to watch, he gets lost in the music and enjoys what he does. The others are not in love with the sport. Rooney, when he closes his eyes, is back on the street, playing with his mates.

Many years ago, I was lying in a grim bedsit, staring at the ceiling. The room was covered with reindeer wallpaper and a million things went through my mind. "The reindeer, Rodney, are on the march," I kept saying to myself as I fought sleep. Where were these Reindeer going to take me? I have been carried to more places, mental and physical, than I could have imagined.

From a small boy surrounded by violence I always dreamed of better things, a better life. Being a professional footballer has taken me to all corners of the globe. Marsh the player and Marsh the person have clashed many times and demons have been fought and beaten. But I have always been me, the Loose Cannon against the rest of the world.

Come with me and I'll take you where I have been, battles fought, victories won, the amazing characters I have met, and how I came out the other side. It's my story in its rawest form, and if you don't agree with anything, do you know what, you can please yourself.

2

Triumph and Tragedy

When you have represented your country, played at all the great stadiums in the world, scored fabulous goals and met so many different people from all walks of life, how do you select a best moment from a career spanning fifty years? It didn't take me too long to choose, with my mind often slipping back to a fabulous afternoon at Wembley Stadium in 1967. The day Third Division Queen's Park Rangers came from 2-0 down at half-time against First Division favourites West Brom to win the first League Cup Final at Wembley 3-2.

It was the game that signalled the arrival of QPR as a proper football club, the greatest achievement in the clubs long history.

We were a family at QPR, and I had a special attachment to them due to the way their former owner, the late Jim Gregory, took me under his wing. He became a father-figure, he had faith in me when others didn't, and it was at Loftus Road in West London that my career took off and blossomed. I grew into the real me. Thrown out by Fulham, I turned my career around with help from Gregory and the manager, the late Alec Stock. I was encouraged to play the game my way, off the cuff, and it was at QPR that I experienced hero worship for the first time. The Rangers fans loved me, and it was here that the chant "Rodneeeeee" was born.

When I equalised at Wembley in the final to make it 2-2, every one of the near-capacity 100,000 crowd knew we would win. It was a 'meant to be' moment. I am a great believer in fate and in the different cards dealt to you along life's path. This was one of them. Rangers were 2-0 down and on the floor, but came back to win 3-2. Someone somewhere was looking after us.

I have re-lived the goal thousands of times and it always brings a smile to my face. I picked up the ball forty yards out, controlled it, first with my left boot and then my right, wandered around, looked up, saw an opening and drove it into the gap I spotted at the far post. Two goalkeepers could not have saved it, and from that moment I was in a dream. The noise was fantastic, "Goal, goal, Rodneeeee, Rodneeee!" Smiling, happy people everywhere, it was exactly what I played for.

The fact that we were 2-0 down at half-time can probably be related to what happened the night before.

It is usual ahead of a big cup final for a team to go away for a few days and prepare. Jim Gregory said that a trip to the coast for a week's preparation would prove to be a bit expensive, and so he decided instead to spend the night before the final in a top Mayfair, London hotel. One of the squad was Bobby Keetch, a larger than life character who lived life to the full with fine wines, beautiful women and anything else he could get his hands on, couldn't believe it. He loved a gamble and was man about town at the London casinos. With a huge smile on his face he immediately announced to the players he was having £900 on West Brom to win at 4 / 9 on.

Feeling confident, Keetchy, who sat on the bench for the final, then sent a secret message to the rest of the squad on that Friday night. He had set up a card table with drinks in his room, 402, if anyone fancied a nightcap and a few bets. Yes, this was the night before a cup final and, no, it couldn't happen today. But this was the sixties when things were changing in the big, bad world and Bobby Keetch was the kind of person not to conform. He loved the new 'carefree' atmosphere that was growing in the country, especially around London. A little bookie friend of his even came to the room to collect his bet! Incredibly, eight of us playing the next day went to his room and were still dealing cards and drinking at three o'clock in the morning. Irresponsible, yes, breaking curfews, no, because there weren't any. These were the underdogs enjoying themselves and, twenty-four hours later, how we celebrated.

At half time and 2-0 down it had been different, with long faces and a realisation that we were probably facing a stuffing. Manager Alec Stock tried his best to lift the players' spirits, while Keetchy, trying hard not to look cocky and say 'I told you so' attempted to make contact with his bookie to double his bet on West Brom!

Funnily enough, I didn't accept the game was over because that is me, ever the optimist. When there is a game to be played, I have always felt the unexpected could happen. It did. We had never been to a Cup Final and, as the underdogs, didn't feel the pressure of defeat. We were new to the experience, and the more we talked in the dressing room, the more a feeling that we had nothing to lose grew. West Brom were confident going into the second half, while we just went out to carry on playing and to enjoy ourselves. How we enjoyed ourselves.

The winning goal should never have been allowed, however, because the player who created it, Ronnie Hunt, a five foot nine inch centre half, who was one of the hardest players I ever came across, should have been sent off in the build up. After tackling their centre forward, the ball ran loose and Ron went after it. He must have run thirty yards before working a one-two with Mark Lazarus. Then he over-hit the ball and it spun towards their goalkeeper. Ron didn't pull out and, despite the 'keeper being favourite to collect it, Hunt, with studs up, launched himself at the ball and went right through the keeper. A definite foul. The ball spilled out and Lazarus tapped it back over the line. We all thought the goal would be disallowed but the referee gave it. Today, it would have meant a red card for Hunt and no goal. Yet, in those days, what you could, and did get away with was incredible. And wrong.

The controversy was soon forgotten, with the huge surge of joy and happiness our victory brought to so many people. It was a private moment for a small family club. We were all together and part of something special. Alec Stock was a picture in the dressing room afterwards, trying desperately to control his emotions and maintain his dignity. His favourite saying was always "It's a funny old game," and he must have repeated it more than a hundred times as he moved around the players. At least he could abandon all the lucky charms he either wore or carried with him throughout the cup run, like always wearing one blue sock, and the small bell in his pocket he turned over in his fingers.

Alec was a one off and he refused point-blank to allow us to play in all red kit at the final. His superstition wouldn't allow it. Because both teams wore blue and white it was compulsory for both teams to change strips. Our second strip was all red, yet Stock said no, even though it's what we wore in the semi final away leg. Instead we went out to win the final, for the first time ever in QPR history, in all white. I don't believe Rangers have ever used the kit again since. Amazingly, West Brom wore all red. When you have a wily old fox like Alec Stock around anything can happen.

How Alec loved to talk. He almost made us miss the kick off of the semi-final first leg against Birmingham at St. Andrews, another First Division side who were favourites to beat us. At our team meeting he went through the tactics and told us the first leg didn't really matter because we could beat anyone back at the Bush. "Keep it tight," he said, "to lose 1-0 would not be a disaster. We'll beat them back at the Bush, funny old game football, funny old game." It was, and by half time we were 4-1 up and dear old Alec was beside himself with pride. "Told you, told you," he repeated, "funny old game football." He didn't have a clue how it happened, the fact we were on the way to Wembley. What a priceless character.

I was recently offered £25,000 for the signed number ten shirt I wore at Wembley for that League Cup Final. That is how much it meant to a QPR fan, but I had to tell him that I no longer had it. Never did, in fact, after simply tossing it into the laundry basket in the dressing room after the game. Collecting memorabilia and the money it generates today simply didn't exist in those days. I have never been one to keep and collect any of my football stuff, apart from my England caps. Memories are enough for me, and I will never forget that QPR dressing room following our victory. It was a wonderful place to be with so many smiles, apart from Keetchy, that is, who had just lost £900.

For the record, the QPR team that day, and I will never forget them, was: Ron Springett, Tony Hazell, Jim Langley, Mike Keen (capt.), Ron Hunt, Frank Sibley, Mark Lazarus, Keith Sanderson, Les Allen, me and Roger Morgan. West Brom's Clive Clark had put West Brom 2-0 ahead with goals in the seventh and thirty sixth minute and we responded with Morgan, 63 minutes, me, 75 and the winner from Lazarus nine minutes from the end. The rest is history.

The worst moment of my career is just as easy to recall: the day Manchester City manager Tony Book ended my days at Maine Road. He cut my legs off in my prime and sent me to train with the injured players. Yes, my Loose Cannon reputation had struck again, although it was so harsh of Book. He was supported by the club's late chairman, Peter Swales, and I was run out of town. I had been playing the best football of my career but that didn't appear to matter to them. Clearly, I was too big, powerful and outspoken for the two men who ran the club. I still see Book today, and when we had a cup of tea and a chat recently, he insisted that he did what was best for the club and that he still sticks by his decision. I have to respect that even though, after all these years, I continue to believe he was wrong.

The end at Maine Road came for me just when I believed City were on fire, with players like Dennis Tueart, Colin Bell and Asa Hartford. We had just beaten Norwich in the quarter final of the League Cup 6-1, and were at home in the next game to Burnley in the League. We never seemed to play badly or lose at home. It turned into a terrible game, and it wasn't long before the coach under Book, a big, passionate Scotsman called Ian MacFarlane, started ranting and raving on the touchline. His language was appalling. He never let off and eventually I went over and told them both to calm down and that they were not being of any help to the team. They didn't like it one bit, but this was me again, saying and doing what I thought best.

You will hear more about this story later in this book. To conclude for now, I told Tony Book I stood by everything I had said and he told me he did too. So that was it, a wonderful career at City over and what next for Rodney Marsh? Although, once more, if you are a Loose Cannon you say what you feel, and why not? Surely no one could condone MacFarlane's behaviour, so I was completely in the right to say what I did. Someone had to stand up to his bullying ways.

What killed me and became the lowest point of my career was being forced to train with the injured players. As captain, I was sent out every day with the walking wounded. It was nothing compared to the wound in my heart. I had been at City for four years and was a dead man walking. I was kept in that situation for three months and it felt like an eternity. They wouldn't even let me play in the reserves, despite me begging for a game. Book stayed firm and said that I was out and would never play for City again.

There was interest from Aston Villa, Birmingham, Crystal Palace and Anderlecht in Belgium, where my wife Jean and I visited. I said no to them all because it didn't feel right. City were paying me something like £400 a week to do nothing and it was a crazy situation. I took a phone call from Cork Hibs in Ireland, who had heard of my problems and asked me to go on loan for six matches at £1000 a game. It was too good to turn down, and 5,000 people turned out to watch me in the first match. I felt wanted again. The whole City situation was nonsense and I got low and depressed. I started drinking too much, at lunchtime and in the evenings, and I became a mess. Swales told me later he had seven thousand letters of complaint, and still they didn't change their minds. What a way to run a football club, an asset sitting around doing nothing. I believe it was spite against someone they couldn't or wouldn't try to understand. I was never on the same wavelength as Book and Swales.

The match before Norwich, and my ban had been at Arsenal, where I scored the winning goal with a diving header. From that high to the lowest low. In the same period City also lost legend Colin Bell with a horrific injury that ended his career. So, the club had their captain suspended and the best player injured and out. Not even Bell's injury would persuade them to recall me. It was stubbornness taken to the extreme.

I had many nights out in London with Malcolm Allison during my low period. It was the only thing that kept me sane, talking to a football person who was actually making sense. My professional life was a mess; I was drinking too much and living in Manchester, where I didn't want to be because of City's attitude. I thought about my family a lot at that stage and got more and more down. I realised how much they meant to me.

It is no stretch of the imagination to say that at this point in my life I did consider ending it all. I never locked myself away in a darkened room and took an overdose, but the thought of ending it all passed through my muddled mind more than once. One night I was driving along the Cromwell Road in London at three in the morning, worse for wear from a long session at Tramp's nightclub, and I remember thinking that it would not bother me if I died. A mug I know, but that's the way a twisted mind works sometimes. I was a footballer and a proud man, but I was a mess mentally. City had cut my legs from under me, and I didn't know what to do. It just shows how the mind works in mysterious ways when you are lost as a person.

Amazing things have happened to me in my life and career. There have been many unexpected situations, and one such moment helped rescue me from my City nightmare. One day the phone rang and it was Elton John's agent, and he told me that he had been talking to Terry O'Neill, the iconic 60's photographer, and Ken Adam, a friend who became my agent, and they had given him my number. "What are you up to?" He asked. I told him fuck all, and related the story that had driven me into a corner. He said the reason he had made contact was that he was working for Elton John, who was buying into the North American Soccer League in Los Angeles. He said that if my spirits needed a lift how about playing for the Aztecs? Why not, I thought, a new challenge and everyone had heard about Pelé joining the American dream. Why not indeed, especially when he said that Elton was putting on an all-expenses trip to the US on his private plane.

So a few days later there I was, with twenty five other invited guests, including film director Bryan Forbes on one side, his wife Nanette Newman on the other, sipping champagne on the way to the US. I was thirty-one years old, at the peak of my career in England, heading for the unknown in America. As I have said many times, you couldn't make up my career.

At the Dodgers Stadium, we watched an Elton John concert, spoke to the great man, and inevitably I ended up drinking more in LA than I had been in London. Through all the haze of that trip I remember one night we went for a Chinese meal with Elton and Ray Cooper and the gang and I began to relax and enjoy myself. City, Book and Swales were a distant memory, even if the club were still paying me. After that particular meal, Elton invited me to his private trailer before the LA concert where we sat down and shared a glass with the great actor Cary Grant. Me, who a few weeks earlier had contemplated ending it all, Elton John, Ken Adam and Cary Grant drinking and chatting. Now that's my kind of hat-trick.

Two days later my life took another twist when I took a phone call from a character called Beau Clare Rogers IV. "Rodney," he boomed, "before you sign for Elton I want you to come and see me as the owner of Tampa Bay Rowdies." "Where is it?" I asked. "Florida," he said, and I thought again "Why not?" Nothing ventured, nothing gained. He sent a couple of plane tickets, first class and no expense spared, and so I went. The moment I set foot in Tampa I knew I had reached the next stage of my career. It felt right, something came over me, you know those feelings you get you can't explain. Fuck off City, this is my new life.

No one knew me from a bar of soap and yet there were hundreds of people at the airport, including a whole team of media outlets and TV stations. At air side there were a series of press conferences set up and the first question I was asked was: "You are described as the white Pelé, is that true?" "No," I said, "he is the black Rodney Marsh." The Loose Cannon strikes again. All hell broke loose and suddenly I was in the headlines once more, for all the wrong reasons. They even got the racist card out on me after that one.

Going to Tampa was a real turning point in my life and I still live there today. It felt like home the moment I stepped off that plane. Their motto in those days was 'Soccer is a kick in the grass' and that seemed appropriate for me.

In England, and at City, I had fallen from grace. I soon became a King in Tampa and America changed me and my life.

I have to couple my worst moment with one of my best memories at Manchester City. When I joined City I wasn't really fit; I had been struggling with a groin injury and it took me a few weeks to reach the level of fitness that coach Malcolm Allison demanded. After about six weeks with me in and out of the team we went to Manchester United for a midweek game, and what an atmosphere. It was drizzling with rain, freezing cold and you couldn't have got another body inside Old Trafford. It was jam-packed. I was on the bench and Malcolm, being the flamboyant character he was then, had all the substitutes dressed in state of the art bright yellow tracksuits. You can imagine the stick we took, especially me. "You great Southern softie, Marsh," they screamed and "Marsh is a Wanker." As you can imagine I took it lying down!

It was such a great City team, who played wonderful football under Malcolm. Both sides had five forwards, all Internationals, with one thing in mind. To play spectacularly, and to win the game. With thirty minutes left, it was 1-1 and I was told to warm up down the touchline. More stick from the United fans and I got mullered with cries like "Rodney is a fairy" and "Southern Arsehole" but I felt good inside my bright yellow weather suit with the hood zipped up. The sweat started to run down my back and the adrenaline enveloped me. I couldn't wait to get on.

Minutes after I trotted into the action, the ball fell between George Best and our Mike Summerbee, two great friends who were best men at each other's weddings. Mike went in high with his boot raised and caught George in the face with his elbow. Best went down and, incredibly the referee waved to play on. Today it would have been a red card. The United fans went mad and you just sensed that something big was going to happen. Summerbee sprinted down the right, and crossed it back into my path and, in one moment, I drilled the ball with my instep, past Alex Stepney into the bottom corner. I can still feel the rain exploding from the netting as the ball went in; funny the little things you remember, isn't it?

The crowd went mad again, and that's nothing to compare to the spite when Francis Lee made it 3-1 a few minutes later. Then, with two minutes left to play, I was played into the corner and, knowing the clock was ticking, put my foot on the ball to waste time. The United fans around me could hardly contain their anger and out of the corner of my eye I saw Nobby Stiles, I think it was, flying towards me with only one thing on his mind, to bury me and give the crowd what they wanted, me in a heap. At the last moment I moved the ball and myself out of the way and watched Nobby scream past me and end up under one of those benches alongside the pitch. As he picked himself up I smiled and tapped an imaginary watch on my wrist at the crowd and mouthed "How long to go?" Christ Almighty, I have never known such abuse come my way. That is me, love it or hate it, you get what you see.

Malcolm Allison, of course, was a picture of pride after the game. How he loved moments like that. His team, his tactics, his planning, getting the better of City's fiercest rivals. As a coach, I never worked with anyone better. He understood more about the game than most and was way ahead of his time, I'd say thirty years beyond other people in the game.

Arsenal manager Arsene Wenger is acknowledged as the coach who changed so much in English football, with his foreign knowledge of fitness, food, tactics and how to get the best out of players. Malcolm was doing things Wenger is doing now back in the seventies. On match days we went to the ground at noon, three hours before kick off, and that had never been heard of before. He had all the best gear ordered and he made you feel like an Olympic athlete, with smart tracksuits, training regimes and fitness centres. Like Wenger, he made sure the players had no excuse if things went wrong. There was always a long table of food before games, the kind of things footballers never used to eat before games, like honey, pasta, cereal, jams and food he had researched that was good for the body. Remember, this was in the sixties and seventies. It was all part of his mental games with the players.

Allison was a one off and I would say something of a fraud. Not as a coach but as a man. I believe he was a fraud to himself, someone who was self-loathing and football was his escape from things he couldn't cope with. His precarious nature, the women, the flamboyant lifestyle, the bottles of expensive champagne he drank, hid much deeper problems; Malcolm had issues he couldn't cope with. He and I were friends although never close. You didn't get near to Allison's inner feelings, and I suppose you can say the same about me. He was happiest as a coach, mixing with players and, boy, did he build a team and a half at City in those golden days. He was a complex character few understood, and this is perhaps why professionally he and I got on so well. I tried to figure him out and him me.

One last story about City here and, again, it relates to the good and bad moments of my career. This one was the most bizarre and ridiculous. One of the greatest players in that City team, and indeed one of the most underrated ever, was Colin Bell, an International who was never praised by enough people for what he contributed. You had to play with Bell to appreciate how good he was. They called him Nijinsky after the famous racehorse because he never stopped running.

When City went to away games, the team coach picked us up on the way because Colin lived in Wilmslow and me in Prestbury. We parked our cars at a nearby hotel called Valley Lodge, and the coach dropped us off after the matches.

On the way back from one particular game, I was chatting with Joe Royle and Willie Donachie and a few others at the back of the coach, mainly about how well we'd done and before long it was time to get off.

Colin and I got off together and waved goodbye to the rest of the lads and it was on this occasion Colin and I went for a drink, whick I've talked about earlier. Of course I didn't mind having a drink with him, not in the slightest, but his invitation had come as a bit of a shock; it was so out of character for him.

It was the first time Bell had really spoken to me apart from on the pitch. Into the bar we went and he asked me what I would like to drink. I asked what was he having and the answer shook me, a double brandy. I had a Southern Comfort with ice. Before I had sipped mine, Colin had downed his in one and asked for another. He threw it back and went on ordering. He then said he needed someone to talk to, and that was a surprise in itself because Colin Bell didn't open up to anyone. He told me that his wife had just had an ectopic pregnancy. For an hour he poured out his heart and I listened to this wonderful footballer with problems that no one realised. It didn't affect him as a player, and here again is evidence that football allows so many people to escape from their 'other world.' It was one of the most poignant moments of my life because he chose me to offload onto. The brandy gave him confidence I guess, to say what he had clearly been bottling up and that is life, isn't it. How many people don't have the courage to say what they really think? I have never been like that. Say it how it is and you feel better for it.

It told me so much about him, as a person. He must of felt I was the only one he could have talked to about it. I just sat there by the bar listening. It made me feel good that I could be there for him.

When I saw him the next day, it was like it had never happened. He just carried on as normal.

Colin Bell was such a strange character. It was so hard to read him and Francis Lee, who would never let a team mate down and would go into battle for anyone on his side, tells extraordinary stories about our colleague.

Apparently while I was in the USA, Bell and Neil McNab, who were part of the coaching set up when Francis went back as Chairman, were always at each other's throats; they disliked each other intensely and one day McNab threatened to beat Bell up. It got that bad. Bell went to see Lee and told him he had to do something about McNab. Lee just said why didn't Bell take McNab into the dressing room, lock the door and have it out with him. If McNab continued to threaten him, just smack him one. Bell said he wasn't like that and Lee said do you want me to smack him for you? So what do you want to do about it, Lee asked, and he could see the situation was getting out of control. There was even talk of Bell going to an Independent Tribunal. Bell later wrote in his autobiography that Lee had refused to sort out his problem. It had been a terrible situation with the coaching set up, certainly a mess, and the club was left unable to attract young players.

When Frank Clark was appointed manager he brought in Alan Hill as his assistant, who had been Brian Clough's number two at Derby. Lee told him the situation behind the scenes was all wrong and that, somehow, they had to sort it out. When City tried to sign Gary Flitcroft's brother, it only confirmed how bad things had become behind the scenes. Flitcroft's father told Lee that City had got it completely wrong, that the atmosphere was bad and the club's training facilities were miles behind other clubs. Needless to say, Flitcroft didn't sign. Lee told Clark that City had to attract young players and to make his own investigation into what was wrong with the coaching set up. Clark wrote a dossier after weeks of investigation and it condemned McNab, Bell and a third member of the staff, Terry Farrell. It didn't make for nice reading.

Clark handed his report to the board, and when Lee read it he was completely embarrassed that his club could have so many problems. He had played with Bell for seven years at City and roomed with him at the 1970 World Cup with England. He therefore found it difficult to be impartial in a case involving Bell and other employees, since he had great affinity with Bell. At the board meeting to discuss the dossier, Lee explained to the Deputy Chairman, David Bernstein, that he would like to leave the room while it was discussed. In his absence the board decided unanimously that they all had to go. Sacked.

Lee knew that Bell had been a special player for the club and was popular with the fans, but the board were adamant that he had to go with the others. Francis told Clark to leave things on hold for three days while he took a short break with his wife. He was determined to find a place somewhere in the club for someone he still considered a friend. On his first day away he picked up a newspaper and was shocked and furious to read the headline 'What a way to treat a hero.' Bell had been sacked behind Lee's back. Francis rang Clark to demand what the hell was he thinking of, going against his wishes. Clark said the board wanted them out, and so he had sacked them. Lee discovered later it had been Hill who told Bell and the others to go because Clark, claimed Franny, couldn't make a decision to save his life.

When Lee got back the shit had hit the fan. The papers were full of Bell's sacking; it was huge news and to Lee's dismay, heading for a tribunal. The club's lawyers encouraged Lee to go to tribunal but he refused because he didn't want to go in front of a judge and get pilloried for sacking a Manchester City legend. He told the board to pay them all the maximum and so eliminate a tribunal. The club said that if the dossier was shown at the tribunal none of them would get a penny. Lee knew that, but didn't want Bell to suffer that kind of humiliation. He didn't want Colin laughed out of court. "Pay them the maximum and let's end this," said Francis. It wasn't the end of it.

Bell accused Lee of not having the guts to go to the Industrial Tribunal and what he doesn't know to this day, until now, is that Lee protected him from the contents of that dossier and potential public humiliation. It was Lee who got him a full pay-out instead of nothing at a tribunal. Lee paid McNab and Farrell to protect Bell.

Incredibly, Bell still doesn't speak to Lee. He says he will go to his grave hating Lee, and this certainly shows a weakness in his character. You just can't harbour that kind of bitterness when you don't know the real truth. I hope this brings him to his senses. He was protected from the dossier, a confidential report that remains in Lee's hands today, because it would have broken his heart.

Bell has been told that he was out of order many times by former team mates, but he just will not have it. He has got this deep-rooted problem with Francis. Tommy Booth once visited the boardroom with Bell and went to speak to Lee and Bell encouraged him not to go. Booth warned him "Don't go down that road, don't even think about it." That is how far this extraordinary situation has gotten out of hand.

Bell is such a difficult person to understand, as my 'drinks' story and Lee's problems with him prove. I once went to Bell and told him I wanted him to return a big favour. We had an unspoken gentleman's agreement after I had done him a huge turn, that he would help me out if I asked. When I confronted him thirty odd years later and told him it was time for the favour to be returned, he said no and that he couldn't do it. "Hold on," I said, "you owe me." He again refused and I walked away from him. I am not prepared to discuss what it was that he owed me.

He is so complex that he will not sign a City shirt if Lee's name is already on it. If the two of them are walking down a corridor at City's home Eastland's Stadium, Bell turns around or ducks into another room. What does this tell us? Apparently he tried to sue Martin Buchan eighteen months ago for finishing his career. That is how stupid, or indeed dangerous, this has become.

Lee sums Bell up like this. "A top notch player who would have been outstanding in the Premier League, a good European and International player, but someone with a weakness when the chips were down because you never knew if he would be on song or not." I disagree with Lee about this, although Franny is adamant and explains why.

When Lee made his England debut in 1969 against Bulgaria he roomed with Bell. His life's ambition was realised when he was picked for his country, and he talked to Bell excitedly about the game. Lee said to Bell that when he got the ball to immediately look for him. "Give me the ball" said Lee. Bell said no. "Why not," Lee said, "just do what we do every week; we know each other inside out. What is the difference? You get the ball and give it to me, simple", but Bell said no. Lee was amazed and disappointed when his team mate for years said "you play your game and I'll play mine."

Then, at the 1970 World Cup in Mexico, Bell came on as a substitute in the infamous game against Germany when England were 2-0 up and lost. Lee got hold of Bell as he trotted on, and explained that he was now the fittest bloke on the pitch because everyone else was knackered with no water allowed for players in those days and the humidity draining the body. The match was played in searing Central American heat and exhausting humidity. Lee told him to chase the ball and close down any German with it. "You can make sure we win this," he said. Bell took little notice according to Francis, and although he played well, in Francis' opinion, Bell could have done a lot more.

Lee couldn't understand his attitude and, indeed, never has. My own stories about Bell the person compare with Lee's. My drink with him in that hotel and the fact he would not return my favour have always confused me.

The thing that disappointed me most was that every time I go to City I have a chat with Belly, last time I said "I'm writing a book Colin" and asked him to phone me. "I'd love to hear what you have to say". He never called me.

I have told you my best and worst moments and Bell represents the strangest. In my opinion, a truly great footballer and yet such a weird character. For someone to harbour a grudge against a former team mate for all these years doesn't make any sense. He should have had it out with Francis a long time ago.

3

Loose Cannons and Celebrities

I love a Loose Cannon, don't you? It's the fact that they are so different. I hate boring players afraid to express themselves on or off the pitch. Loose Cannons make the world go round and it's amazing how they attract all sorts of characters. Personalities, celebrities, dodgy geezers, thugs, VIPs, they all like to attach themselves to football. It is usually the unpredictable character they want to be with the most.

They are not exclusive to football and there are loads in every walk of life, but the following is my all time, football Loose Cannon Top Ten in reverse order, see if you agree?

At No.10, BRUCE GROBBELAAR. I've always thought he was one card short of a full deck. You never knew what was coming next.

How many times did we see Bruce arrive out of his area to clear or suddenly appear alongside his own centre half? I lost count of the number of times Liverpool defenders looked sideways and saw Bruce. They had that 'what the hell are you doing here?' look. He kept goal outside the box more than inside.

One of the great images of Bruce came in the 1984 European Cup Final. Liverpool and Roma were locked at 1-1 after extra time and it went to a penalty shoot out. When Roma's Bruno Conti stepped up, Bruce walked into goal smiling confidently for the cameras and then bit the back of the netting as if it were spaghetti. Conti missed. When it was Francesco Graziani's turn Bruce stood on the line and made his legs go all wobbly as if he was scared. Again, Roma missed and Liverpool went on to win 4-2.

Earlier in that season he had rushed onto the pitch to bring down an invading fan and hold him until the police arrived to handcuff the offender.

They do say you have to be mad to be a goalkeeper. I think Grobbelaar's a loveable nutcase who entertained us for so long.

No. 9, CRAIG BELLAMY. I have watched him closely for about ten years and don't have a clue what is coming next. Whether he is scoring a wonderful goal, kicking the centre half, rowing with the referee, complaining to his manager or being sent off.

Bellamy is box office and, of course, like all Loose Cannons, he can play. I'd have him in my club every time.

I don't think he can control his tongue either and I identify with this. He says things before he thinks and it's often the stark truth. So many managers have bought him because they all believe they are the one who can tame the tiger. You never tame a Loose Cannon.

No. 8, JOHN TERRY. This choice will probably surprise a few of you, although what is there predictable about John Terry? He is easier to read on the pitch than off.

Losing the England captaincy over a private issue involving former teammate Wayne Bridge is so typical of a Loose Cannon. We are a dream for all headline writers.

What you see is what you get with Terry. He's either throwing his head into a melee in Chelsea's area or hitting the front pages of newspapers over something controversial. He is, of course, a born leader.

When Terry held a press conference on a dark day in South Africa before England played Slovenia, he believed he was talking on behalf of the whole team and that they would have a meeting to tell some home truths to the manager. This wasn't the case. Brilliant!

No. 7, FRANK WORTHINGTON. The Elvis Presley worshipper who dressed like the King and probably thought he was him. He once arrived at Tampa airport in leathers and a cowboy hat, with bottle of whiskey in his hand.

A wonderful character that had great silky skills and, like so many of us, never played enough times for his country. It was the late Joe Mercer, when he was caretaker manager of England following the exit of the late Don Revie, who encouraged his style on the international stage.

Others backed off him and that happens so often. Football is scared of controversial characters. Take Stan Bowles, Peter Osgood, Alan Hudson, Matt Le Tissier and Tony Currie. They were all discarded by England too soon.

Worthington was capable of scoring great goals and he could do anything with the ball. Frank was a real Maverick.

At No. 6, VINNIE JONES. From a bricklayer to a world-famous film star. That is some rise. In the middle, he was the cornerstone of the Wimbledon Crazy Gang.

Vinnie was the hard man of the side who took no prisoners. He, John Fashanu and the others would not get away with some of their antics today and you couldn't keep your eyes off Jones.

I once watched him in a game at Queen's Park Rangers and changed my mind about him. My initial impression was always that Vinnie couldn't play, although on this day he ran the midfield and hardly put a foot wrong. There was an underrated player inside the Loose Cannon skin.

His controversial moments are legendary, fights in bars and outside nightclubs, his physical rant at Alan Mullery in a hotel after 'Mullers' had criticised him on TV, and none more so than when he grabbed Paul Gascoigne's balls during a game with Newcastle at Wimbledon's old Plough Lane ground. That picture will forever tell the story.

No. 5, PAUL GASCOIGNE. Here is someone destined to be a footballer and nothing else. How Gazza loved every minute of his career and when it was over he simply couldn't handle it, but what a great footballer he was. I think it's why he went off the rails. Everything that has happened to him since he hung up his boots had been because of his frustration at no longer playing.

When he was at his prime with England and Spurs he was the clown everyone loved and people were always laughing at his antics. Whether he was pushing a pie into someone's face, eating worms and spitting them out on camera or belching into the mike, he was never fully under control. He even wore a pair of false tits once!

His story is one of highs and lows, pathos and pathetic moments. From crying at the 1990 World Cup, to beating up his wife, spending time at the Priory to delighting us with his skills, we will never forget Gazza.

He, more than most Loose Cannons, had the knack of upsetting the apple cart when everything seemed to be going well. It is inbuilt and hard to explain. You wake up and think everything is great, yet say to yourself "I don't deserve this." So you go and do something stupid. It is a self-destruct button that is so hard to control.

It is like being happy at a club and in the peak of condition and performance and asking for a transfer. Why? That my friends, is the million dollar question. If we Loose Cannons knew the answer to that we wouldn't be what we are. Nothing is normal.

No. 4, ROY KEANE. Loose Cannons are people you can't control and Roy Keane exemplifies this.

Throughout his career he was someone managers were wary of. Even as a manager he says what he thinks and doesn't care what others, even former teammates, think of him.

The best two examples are his four-letter tirade when he had a row with

Republic of Ireland manager Mick McCarthy in front of the other players that led to him walking out of the 2002 World Cup.

Then, his deliberate revenge attack on Alf-Inge Haaland when he was playing for Manchester United. There was an incident with Haaland in 1997 when Haaland played for Leeds, which put Keane out for the majority of a season. Keane has admitted he waited a long time to get his own back. In my opinion, to use a football phrase, Keane 'did him' in cold blood at Old Trafford one Saturday lunchtime in 2001. He then openly admitted what he had done.

Again, like other Loose Cannons, Keane was a brilliant leader and is the captain of my team. He was a winner at all costs and a player everyone looked up to.

He did some crazy things in his career. He's not alone there though.

No. 3, ERIC CANTONA. Anyone who can take out a fan with a two-footed kick over a barrier after being sent off is right up there in any Loose Cannon list.

Cantona's extraordinary reaction on that infamous night at Crystal Palace will go down in history. A world-class player whose fuse was tiny.

Another true leader and someone everyone at Manchester United looked up to. People like Cantona and Keane make others follow them, leading by example with their mental strength and ability to inspire.

You just never knew what was coming next with Eric, whether it was a wonderful goal with a deft chip or a flash of temper that resulted in a red card.

He was always wonderful entertainment and, like Vinnie Jones, has gone into the film industry. Pure box office, you see.

At No. 2, GEORGE BEST: I still think of him often. If ever there was someone who lived the life of a Loose Cannon then it is George Best. Booze, birds, gambling, late nights, not turning up, playing after no sleep, he did the lot and more.

He was so very special in every way and it is amazing that George was always forgiven, whatever he got up to. That was the man. He had an aura and magic about him. The greatest player in the world and people loved him. There were 130,000 at his funeral and that tells the story. They came from everywhere just to say goodbye and pay tribute. Women wanted him and men wanted to be him.

I was once with him in a Casino when he lost every penny. It was around £10,000 and that was a lot of money back then. As we left, he said 'There is always tomorrow Marshy,' and that was his motto. Yesterday has gone, tomorrow is yet to come, live for today!

This kind of character comes along once in a blue moon, but would he get away with his controversial lifestyle today? You bet he would because people will always forgive a genius.

And my number one all time Loose Cannon.

No. 1, MARADONA. Yes, number one and I doubt whether he will ever be overtaken in any list of Loose Cannons. If he was a painter he'd be Vincent Van Gogh. He is the original article in every way.

The Argentine superstar is someone who has never appeared to give a fuck about anything. He doesn't do authority. One of the greatest players the world has ever produced has lived a life of booze, drugs, women and fantasy football. A few years ago he almost died because of his body abuse. Again, we forgive him and, after everything he has been through, he turned up at the World Cup as his country's manager.

Even in South Africa he ran over a photographer and mimicked opponents in press conferences. On the touchline he never sat down and then, when his side were beaten by Germany, he looked a forlorn, lonely figure. It is all about the high and lows with these characters.

Maradona has always lived on the edge, wobbling from side to side as he went on his way. In 1986 he scored his infamous 'Hand of God' goal against England, and then followed that up with the greatest World Cup goal of all time, running from the halfway line and beating five England players. Just one of the moments from his life we will never forget.

The world has always loved a controversial, cheeky chappie, a character they wished they could be. Someone to play football they could only dream of and to say the things they wished they had the courage to utter.

I played for Queen's Park Rangers from 1966 to 1972, when England was alive with the air of the swinging sixties, and things were changing. I was in my early twenties and establishing myself as a top footballer. Rodney Marsh fitted the image of what was happening in the country: enjoyment, flamboyance and fun. A carefree attitude. What I quickly came to realise was that beneath the surface, football attracted some extraordinary characters. People who loved to attach themselves to the game, for all the wrong and right reasons. It was the greatest time for music, for rock and roll, and many people say the seventies were the wildest times ever.

For instance, a lot of people lived in fear of Jim Gregory, my Chairman at Rangers. Underneath the rough surface there was, however, a decent bloke and he and I always got on. I understood him for what he was and he appreciated me for bringing some glory and success to his football club.

A story I was told of Gregory's toughness came when he first started work at a fishmonger's in Fulham at eighteen years of age. Through the grapevine, he heard there was a bit of a 'naughty' car sale every Sunday morning in the West End of London, between eight and twelve o'clock, with stolen cars exchanging hands quickly. Jim thought he would have himself some of that, and so he got himself a Rolls Royce to take along the next Sunday. He got to there at six am and drove proudly into the best slot on the street. Two hours later 'the boys' arrived and asked Jim what he was doing parking in their place. In fact, they didn't ask, they said "What the fuck are you doing here? Move it or you'll get a fucking good hiding." Not one to be intimidated, Gregory told them to "fuck off," he had got there first, and was leaving his car exactly where he'd parked it. So they knocked him out and gave him a kicking as he lay on the street. They took the car keys, moved the Roller and told Jim never to return.

Next Sunday he was back again at six o'clock, two hours before anyone else and parked his car in exactly the same spot. "What the fuck are you doing?" he was asked as the same mob arrived. "Are we going to have to sort this out every fucking Sunday?" With that, Jim took out a plastic bag, produced a container of sulphuric acid and poured it over the three cars owned by the yobs who were confronting him. He just looked at them as he poured. Now that takes balls, and the guys who had kicked him half to death the previous week said, "Okay, let's work this out." Fear is a great leveller, I guess, when you have the bottle to confront dangerous situations.

This is how Jim got into the car business and how he got on in life. By having the guts to face up to people. He had rows, intimidated others and had a reputation of being someone not to mess with.

Characters like the ones Jim took on are what footballers then, and indeed today are surrounded by. Hangers on, manipulators and money-grabbers, those who like to be seen with the stars. They are mostly agents and friends of agents and friends of friends of agents. Of course, there are genuine people in there somewhere, although too often the 'shadows' are only there to get what they can out of being seen with celebrity footballers. There were, and still are, endless girls available and the WAG situation today has run out of control. It became an amazing way of life for me, and when you mixed with icons like George Best and Bobby Moore, what could you expect? They attracted 'hangers on' like no one else in the history of football.

My life also gave me the opportunity to be amongst many iconic figures from the 60's and 70's.

When George and I were at the height of our success with the road shows, I got a phone call from a television producer asking if I would play the cameo role of a character from the seventies in a Campari commercial they were making. "Why not?" I thought and went along to a big warehouse in Fulham. It was an impressive set up, all decked out with hundreds of production staff. Sipping a coffee and admiring what was going on around me, I was suddenly aware of a commotion at the end of the building. Two six foot, heavily set guys in suits were deep in conversation with the bosses and then, behind them, a figure dressed immaculately in dark blue appeared and looked around. It was the legend, Frankie Fraser, one of the most notorious men that ever lived. You could have heard a pin drop until he came over and whispered "Rodney, how you doing?" I had actually never met him before, and yet Frankie marched over, shook my hand and wanted to talk football.

It turned out he was a big Arsenal fan and his knowledge about them and the game was second to none. Here I was, talking football with one of the most dangerous men in England, and it's just amazing to see how this sport brings a complete cross-section of people together. It is a natural bond and will never change. Frankie kept going on about how Don Howe was so good at breaking down the wing and telling me about the games he would never forget. He was there to play his role in the commercial as part of London's underworld. I was now living a life I never expected, mixing with the super wealthy, famous and notorious.

One early morning in Tramps with George Best, the owner Jonny Gold brought someone over to our company who couldn't stop talking football. He asked George for an autograph, said he was a huge West Brom fan, and that he wondered how we thought they would do. George hadn't a clue who he was, but I sort of recognised the face and Aussie accent. It was Dennis Lillie, the famous fast bowler.

Tom Jones, the great Welsh singer and entertainer, once stopped a packed concert in London to introduce George to the audience. "Ladies and gentlemen, it is a privilege to have the greatest footballer in the world with us tonight." Hank Marvin of the Shadows was another who was dumbstruck by Best, along with the golfer Sam Torrance and so too the unlikely figure of actor Michael Caine.

After a Fulham game and an evening at the Duke of Wellington in Chelsea, George had moved on to Tramps. Again there was a crowd with George, his first wife Angela, Michael and his wife. "What about that goal you scored, and that one, and what about that run and pass at Old Trafford," Caine apparently said, and kept going on. George was getting bored with him and the conversation. Then Caine leant across the table and, with messy fingers, took some of Angela's chips from her plate. "Don't do that again Michael or I'll slap you," George said, but Caine took some more and so George got up, whacked him on the chin and knocked Caine off his chair. Picture the scene: one of the most famous faces in England spread-eagled across the floor covered in ketchup. Now, not a lot of people know that and how the incident was kept out of the newspapers I'll never know.

My mouth often got me into trouble, although on one occasion it brought a lovely connection with pop superstar Phil Collins. When I was working for Sky television on their incredibly successful Gillette Soccer Saturday special results programme, I was also contracted to appear on the late night phone-in called 'You're on Sky Sports.' After two years, I realised that some of the calls were from idiots who had come back from the pub and rang in just to slag me off. I got into a ritual of having a go back, there was a lot of banter and confrontational conversation and it became very funny and successful.

One night, a punter came out with the biggest load of bollocks and I just refused to talk to him. "Get him off!" I told the producer through his earpiece. It did get me thinking though, and the next night I brought a drinks tray and a tablespoon in with me and announced at the start of the show that anyone talking rubbish from now on would get gonged off. It was fun and, again, it worked.

Next week I got a phone call from an old mate, Danny Gillan, who was once actor Tony Curtis' minder. "Great show Rodney," he said, "and Phil loves the gong stuff." "Phil?" I said. "Phil Collins," he answered, "he never misses it living in Switzerland." Danny then said that Phil couldn't stand me banging the tray and would I like a cymbal from one of his drum kits to hit every time I wanted to gong a punter out. Two weeks later, a package arrived at Sky and inside there was a signed percussion gong from Phil Collins, and I banged away to my heart's content thereafter. When I was eventually sacked by Sky, I auctioned it off to raise money for my favourite charity, 'The Burned Children's Club.' Phil was delighted, and this millionaire pop star continued to enjoy watching 'You're on Sky Sports' from his home in Switzerland.

Just another example of football attracting the unexpected. In 1979 at the American Soccer Bowl Final, I was invited to the directors' suite and had the privilege of meeting Dr. Henry Kissinger. Yes, he wanted to talk football. However, despite being a person who spent his life as a peace envoy around the world, he turned out to be one of the most boring individuals I have ever met. After three minutes I made my excuses and left to go and talk to the tea lady instead.

An extraordinary life in football that embraced every walk of life. All they wanted was to be part of the beautiful game. They saw football as an escape. It didn't matter how much money they had, they needed to have one foot inside the game. It is the same today and it will never change. The bigger football becomes the more characters it attracts. They just love a Loose Cannon.

4

A Lasting Impression

In February 2010, a package arrived for me at my office in London. They opened it and it contained a letter from a lady in Devon. She said, in shaky handwriting, that she hoped I didn't mind her writing and that she had been trying to make contact and track me down for years. She had something for me, she said, and would like me to have the enclosed items.

In the package was a photo of my Dad, Bill, sitting on the guns of a ship he served on called HMS Rodney. The writer of the letter was, it seems, my Dad's sweetheart before he married my mother. They had been eighteen when they were together, and she had kept all the memories of her relationship with him before sending them on to me. We couldn't believe it, and I discovered things in that package and letter that I didn't know about my father.

The fact he was a Catholic, took Communion at thirteen years old, and that it was confirmed that I was named after the ship in the picture, hence Rodney (christened Rodney William Marsh). Fancy getting to sixty-five years old and finding out things about your parents you had no idea about. That, however, was my relationship with them. It was never deep, no real personal conversation and certainly not much love shown. In fact, I can't remember it existing.

I'm sure they loved me but it seemed we were never close to each other. I had a very difficult early life, being hit by a belt, witnessing terrible mêlées amongst family members and constant obscene language. There is no doubt that the memories of my early years will stay me with forever. These experiences damaged me, and led me to form a protective barrier around myself, just like my parents who didn't drop their guard when it came to showing emotions. My escape was clearly to be a bit of a clown. My old Fulham mate Bobby Keetch used to call me Tom Pepper, a fictional character who was always making up stuff to avoid reality. To fend for myself, to say what I thought and, yes, to be a Loose Cannon. My early character was formed in the streets of the East End of London.

My father supported me as a footballer, although he was never the loving dad all young boys crave. All my life I have had a problem telling anyone I love them, and that goes straight back to my parents.

When my father died in 1981 aged sixty-three, I was living and working in the US (my mum, Lillian, had died a year before). I had often invited Dad to come to America for a holiday, and he never accepted. So I visited him when I could, and on one particular occasion when I went to see him things were different. He looked so forlorn, lost, drawn, depressed and he had clearly been crying, which I had never experienced before. As I walked towards him in the small hallway of his North London home, he put both arms around me, cuddled me and said, "I love you son." I was shocked and confused because this was the first time I had heard him say this to me. I just couldn't bring my arms up to hold him, couldn't tell him that I loved him too, because the damage of years of spite and hate had already been done. It was a strange feeling, standing in the hall with my Dad holding onto me, not being able to respond. It was his fault and this was too late for emotion.

We talked for a while and I said that tomorrow, a Saturday, I would take him out for the evening. I stayed out on the Friday at a pal's flat after a night on the town and went to Queen's Park Rangers the following afternoon to watch the game. As I was parking my little Mini close to the ground, a policeman recognized me and waved me down. He asked if he could have a word. I thought he was after me for parking in the wrong place, but he said it was nothing to do with any offence and was sorry to have to break the news like this, but my father had died. "Dead?" I said, "I was only with him yesterday." He had been found at the bottom of the stairs of the house where we had stood the previous day, him clinging to me and me not knowing what to do, unable to respond. He'd had a stroke, fallen down the stairs and was discovered with his head on the front door.

I don't know why but I stayed and watched the first half of the game in a trance, didn't even know who was playing or what the score was. I needed time to think. Clearly, he had said those words, "I love you son," to me because he knew, deep inside him, that something was happening and he was going to die. No wonder my childhood was mixed up. As I sat and watched Rangers play, and win or lose, I still have no recollection, my mind was in turmoil.

I will try and explain what my Dad was like. He had been beaten by my grandad often and had no real relationship with him. He was proud of me and my success in football, but at the same time he was unable to bring himself to open up and be a real father. When I craved attention and affection, my Dad walked away or just wasn't there. No wonder my head has been messed up.

At college, Brook House Technical College in Hackney, London, I hated the science teacher. We had a tremendous anti-relationship, and every year he wrote on my report that I was a complete failure, whatever I did. He had the habit of throwing a piece of chalk across the classroom when he was annoyed with us, and on this particular day he threw it at a kid, missed and then came storming over. "What were you talking about?" he demanded, and my friend explained he had been telling me that he wanted to go to the toilet. "You took your time saying that?" he said and I, yes the old Loose Cannon struck again, explained sarcastically that my friend stuttered. With that he hit me on the side of the head with the board duster. Now, you couldn't get away with that today, and he didn't then either, because the next day my father marched into school and knocked him out cold with one punch.

That was dad, his hands were his voice. He couldn't communicate, and yet was loyal to the end and that action proved how much he loved me. But he just couldn't bring himself to say it.

I never spoke to that teacher again, although he continued to damage me whenever he could. On my last school report he took great delight in telling everyone that I was useless and would never make a go at any career I tried. "He wants to be a professional footballer," he wrote, "he will never make a living playing football."

If my dad was violent, his brother Albert, my uncle, was even worse. He was an Amateur Boxing Association champion who represented the Army. On one visit overseas, he was buried alive and suffered damage that affected him psychologically for the rest of his life. His personality changed dramatically and after that he was intimidating and scary.

When he came out of hospital after six years following his burial and rescue, he was clearly mentally damaged, a fit man whose escape and outlet was violence. He had fists like jackhammers. Amazingly though, he used to play the piano beautifully. Albert never had any lessons and it was just a natural gift, the beautifully soft music he played was a complete contrast to his darker side. Interesting, isn't it, how some people can be violent and yet also get lost as an artist. This was his secret life, a release. Who knows what goes on inside people's minds? It's scary.

When he had a pass out from hospital to spend some time at home with us, my grandmother bought him a piano for £5 from the local pub. Even when he was playing I was scared of him, and knew that nothing much would make him blow. I once saw him take a screwdriver to my grandfather and hang him on the kitchen door. My grandmother, on this day, brought him a cup of tea while he was playing and asked him gently why he didn't play another tune instead of playing the same one all the time. Albie, as we called him, stood up, picked up an ashtray and smashed it into her face. It was horrific and 'they' immediately took him back into an asylum in Tooting Bec. He never came out again and died in a psyche ward years later. All incidents like this formed my character. They left a stain that still remains today. I am sure I have an underlying psychological problem that is still dormant in me. I just had an unbelievably complicated upbringing, and you don't know what effect it has on you at the time, but I realise it now. The more and more I think about my childhood, the more I realise why I am the way I am.

Another story about my father, which explains a great deal: When he was twenty and living in a pre-fab home after the First World War, he had a midnight curfew issued by my grandfather. There was no electricity, only gas lights, and family rules were family rules. Dad had a few drinks that night and got in late. As he went to bed in the dark, my grandfather said, "Is that you Billy?" and put his hand on his face. Then he punched him hard in the nose for breaking the curfew. Six months later it happened again, only this time Dad reacted first and punched Grandad and knocked him out cold. Dad went to bed only to be woken by his own father smashing his son's knee with a large hammer. He broke his leg, and was left screaming in pain with Grandad leaving the bedroom saying, "Don't do that to your Dad again, will you son?" My dad often showed me his scarred knee, I think as a reminder of how to behave.

I was never really close to my mother either, and once, when Dad was away for eight months, I was never told why, although I think I know, apparently she had an affair with our postman. I was only about ten or eleven; I recall the postie being ginger-haired and coming round for tea in the afternoons. I never said anything, only listened, especially when I was ushered outside to play.

When my dad came back, my parents had a massive row and he went and found the postman and sorted it out. Why she did it, I'll never know. Maybe she did it on purpose to wind my dad up.

Oh, the memories of those days. Standing outside pubs while my parents were inside drinking, kicking a ball around with mates and waiting for Mum and Dad to emerge. Mum loved her gin and orange, flirting all the time until Dad got wound up. Was she seeking attention? Neither of them ever opened up in front of me, apart from during rows, and there was never any serious parent to son discussion. I have no idea what made them tick apart from rowing. It was their escape clause.

The other side of the family, my dad's mother's side, the Dredges, apparently were the same. I was told her brother was sentenced to fifteen years after hitting someone with an axe during a fight and people were afraid to go down those streets in fear of the violence.

I think a lot of my early family problems came at my birth. I was born and weighed in at 10lb 3oz and had a huge head. At that time, with no option of a caesarean delivery, my mother was in agony for days and was badly split. I found out, thirty years later from my aunt, that because of my birth, my mother never had sex again. So how did she have an affair with that ginger headed postman, and what kind affair was it? All these things, clearly, have been spinning around at the back of my head for my entire life. Did she resent me? It's hard to live with that.

Apart from a few teenage scraps, my life has not been physically violent. Playing football, I have been sent off for head butting, and once lost my rag at school and hit a boy with a cricket bat, but that's not me. It is probably because I had too much experience of it as a child growing up. The cricket bat incident came when I was asked to guest for Harrow against Eton Manor from the East End. I was the only cockney playing, and the other boys took the piss out of me all afternoon. I had the wrong shoes, the wrong kit and the wrong accent, so at tea amid the cucumber sandwiches I just swatted this one boy. It wasn't hard enough to really damage him, but it was one of the few times I lost control.

All these things in life have affected me. I like to think I've become a bit of a deep thinker and someone who likes to analyse. I had a lack of love and affection, it was just confrontation, and so the protective shield came up. When I look back, it was an incredible upbringing and I'm not surprised one bit to have turned out the way I have. My attitude and own safety valve have annoyed people along the way.

I became a rebel, someone who took the piss out of myself and others, giving and taking, chatting back and protecting myself against the world with what I knew best, being away from the mainstream. I was anti-establishment because of my parents, and this was the James Dean era, I was a rebel without a clue. I hate the 'establishment' telling me what I can and can't do. That was a challenge and always has been; I have been out to beat the system. In my opinion, I always knew better than most and was not slow to tell them, even if it was absolute bollocks. I became arrogant at times, a know all, and the mistakes I have made in my life have been my own fault.

Until now, in this book, I have never revealed such thoughts or talked about them so openly. But this is my story, warts and all. In 1983 when I was coach at Carolina in the States, I got extremely depressed and down and things began to get on top of me. I was successful and no one knew I had problems; it would be like Sir Alex Ferguson suddenly revealing to his Chairman that he needed mental help. I was upset, depressed and morbid. I went to the owner for help and he put me in touch with a psychologist at Duke University.

This guy concentrated on my mind and we got into some really deep personal and serious stuff. He listened to my childhood stories, I told him about my upbringing, and what I felt about certain issues. I only saw him three times but he diagnosed that I had developed multiple personality syndrome. He said that I was not damaged and that it wasn't the same as multiple personality disorder, but I had those tendencies and I resented change in myself. Sometimes I would laugh at things and then suddenly completely flip and be serious. He said I had a tendency to be different personalities. I trace it all back to my childhood and the damage it did to me.

I wear a mask that no one can see the real me hiding behind. It disguises a lot of things still going on inside.

As I grew older in my family home, it became increasingly obvious to me that I had to do something with my life. I used to tell myself over and over again "there has to be more to life than this." I lay in bed thinking that I couldn't stay there and go the same way as all the others, living a life of anger, frustration and not knowing anything else. I had to get out.

I'd played a lot of cricket at school and was a good all-rounder, but was especially talented as a fast-bowler. In those days, you either played football or did boxing in the winter, and then cricket when the evenings got warmer. I once had a bad experience whilst playing cricket, when I got hit in the face by a fast-bowler and it knocked the heart out of me. The damage was done, and from then on I concentrated on football.

At fifteen, West Ham asked me to go to trials and I had to make the decision whether to drop out of education and try to become a professional footballer. One night it just came to me, my love was football, and so Rodney Marsh went on to pursue his dream.

I had fantasised about being a singer when I was ten, when I wanted to be like Elvis and make a few bob down the local pubs. Be like Rod Stewart, the Yardbirds and Long John Baldry, who had all escaped from their own problems. I also trained for boxing and had two youth fights for Eton Manor although I never laid a punch on an opponent and got hammered in two under twelve bouts. My face was a mess, so that was definitely a non-starter. It was no to boxing or singing, and cricket was out after that blow to the face. So, it was football, my first love. Onwards and upwards.

My father was happy I chose football because he loved the sport. His favourite players were Len Shackleton and Jackie Milburn. He saw me as Shackleton and himself as Milburn. It was Dad who also helped me get my first break in joining Fulham.

I have no doubt that he was proud of me, although he never told me, never told me he loved me until it was too late. The day before he died. The damage had already been done as I grew up into a Loose Cannon. I'm sorry to go on about this and repeat myself but it's in my head all the time and its part of my story.

The controversial character formed as a child has been with me right through my career in football.

5

Fulham to the Rescue

I idolised Johnny Haynes. He was exactly what I was looking for once Fulham had rescued me from my young life of turmoil and solitude in the East End of London. It was his flamboyance, aura and relationship with the crowd that had such an impression on me. I identified with him and you could say I wanted to be him.

I cleaned his boots in my first years as an apprentice in the early sixties and once, after he returned from England duty at Wembley, I scraped the mud from his boots and put it into a matchbox to keep.

What was I looking for in this relationship with Fulham? A way out, that's what. A new direction. I'd been training with the youth team at West Ham where former players Malcolm Musgrove and Phil Woosnam were in charge. When the time came for West Ham to offer boys an apprenticeship contract, they pulled me to one side and explained that they had someone else who played in my position and was better than I was. "Who?" I asked. "A lad called Geoff Hurst," they said. "Who?" I carried on playing and attracting attention for the Joseph Priestly School and Alexander Boys Club in Stoke Newington until Fulham offered me the breakthrough I'd been searching for.

Everything Haynes did fitted me perfectly. It wasn't just his range of passing, it was his awareness of what was going on around him, the ability to make things happen and bring the crowd to their feet. There was a buzz when he got the ball, and that is what I wanted from my relationship with the game, to be someone. He had a knack of being part of the crowd when things went wrong or right, turning to them if a team mate like Maurice Cook or Tosh Chamberlain missed one of his inch perfect passes and throwing his arms into the air in exasperation. The crowd loved him and I looked on in awe. Here was a showman.

It was the way Haynes conducted himself. He was the biggest name in European football and it showed. Yet he was still dignified. He remains the best passer of a ball I have witnessed in my career and, like a lot of things in my early years; he had a huge effect on me. I worshipped him.

I only came into contact with him and the other first team players by standing around and watching them from the terraces. I would put their gear out, sweep Craven Cottage clean of rubbish and keep an eye on them in training. They were great days and I loved the time I spent there. I have a huge amount of fondness for my introduction to professional football at Fulham, my first job on six pounds a week.

Those first impressions also helped to create the image of Rodney Marsh. I joined Fulham as a kid on a mission. Not to conform, but to be different, and that was drummed into me as I watched Haynes the superstar. The clock was ticking and I refused to let it run down. I was about to take my place on the big stage.

Ironically, it was my father who helped me make the breakthrough and get to Fulham. A little guy called Bill Brown who once played for Spurs (not the famous goalkeeper) invited me to Fulham for a trial because I had been scoring a lot of goals in junior football, and before we started he asked me what position I played. "Inside left," I said proudly, "I wear number ten." "Okay," he answered, "start at right back." I got a roasting from the left-winger I was up against, which was not surprising. He was quicker and better than me. Not much was said afterwards and I went home with my tail between my legs. Five months later my Dad wrote again to Bill Brown, called him a twat and said I had scored another forty-eight goals since my last trial and told him to give me another go. I don't think there were any threats in the letter. Interesting character, my dad. He made such an effort to help his son when it came to football, and yet none at all over personal relations.

The same thing happened when I went for my second Fulham trial. Bill Brown asked me what position I played, but this time I said outside left. He actually started the trial with me there and I got a hat trick. They signed me, I dropped out of school and I was on my way at sixteen years old. It was football, football, football all the way and the door was finally open. I was going through it no matter what. I wanted to see what was on the other side, not just in terms of football but life itself.

That was my first thought when I signed, here was the opportunity I had been waiting for. My escape route. I had been given a chance. Within a week I had my first fight with a player called Freddie Callaghan, a character who later subsidised his pay by being a black cab driver around the London area. In a five-a-side game on the concrete car park behind one of the goals I nutmegged Callaghan three times and out of frustration, and because he wanted to teach me a lesson, he lamped me. I was young and fit but couldn't fight, and other players dived in to pull us apart. We were both fined by general manager Frank Osborne, the man who ran the club. A controversial start but I was happy.

My progress was quick because whichever club I'd played for, I'd scored goals. Fulham was no exception. I loved scoring, the buzz, the pride, the adulation, the thrill. It was something I discovered I could do from an early age. I liked to score outrageous goals, attempting the impossible, doing the mischievous on the pitch, never afraid to miss.

My goals took me through the youth team, through the reserves, and I was eventually handed my first team debut against Aston Villa at Craven Cottage when I was eighteen years old. To my great surprise I actually took the place of Johnny Haynes (no, manager Bedford Jezzard didn't drop him; Haynes tweaked a hamstring and failed a fitness test.) So I wore the great man's number ten shirt. In those days, players didn't have their own numbers and it was just one to eleven who ever played. In the sixty-first minute came one of the great moments of my career when George Cohen, Fulham's World Cup winning right back, crossed to the back of the area and I volleyed it into the net for the only goal of the game. My first goal on my debut; it doesn't get much better than that. How did I feel? Like a million dollars. "This, Rodney, is what you were waiting for," I told myself. All those nights lying in bed at home wondering what the future had in store exploded when my shot hit the back of the net.

I have been asked so many times what it feels like to score a goal. I'd like every football-loving fan to experience it, and then to try and describe the moment. I want everyone to smell it, taste it, especially at Wembley. The surge of adrenaline as you see the ball go in, the blood rushing into the veins in your neck, the power you feel, the colours of the grass, the taste of sweat in the mouth. The feeling is out of this world and never changes. That will stay with me forever. In so many ways it is what I lived for, to be the winner and the hero. That is how I felt after my first goal for Fulham.

The next match I was dropped, for Haynes. It was back to reality, although I'd had a taste and now I wanted more. Much more.

It was a good Fulham team to become a part of: Haynes, Cohen, Scottish International winger Graham Leggat, goalkeeper Tony Macedo from Gibraltar, Jim Langley, Bobby Robson and a strange character called Jimmy Hill. Jimmy thought he was superior to the rest of us and he was certainly the best talker I ever met. He never stopped, and it was mostly about him and how good he was. I remember him talking non-stop on the coach back from a 3-0 defeat about the runs he had made, the tackles and headers he won, and I thought to myself "If he was so good, how come we've just been thrashed?" Fulham eventually dropped Hill for me and I took over his number eight shirt.

My six pounds a week pay doubled when I got to the reserves and doubled again when I made it into the first team. There were crowd bonuses and extra money for winning, yet no reward for the goals I scored. That didn't matter because goals meant more to me than cash. They were priceless.

How I loved those early days at Fulham. I once nutmegged George Cohen in training and he kicked me so hard in retaliation and told me never to do it again. I didn't care; it was all part of growing up and the experience. And what experiences they were.

Bobby Keetch, the same guy who bet on West Brom in Queen's Park Rangers' League Cup winning triumph, was the first footballer I knew of taking performance-enhancing drugs. Before each game all the Fulham players used to go into trainer Frank Penn's room, where he would dish out a swig of scotch from a large bottle. "Warms the heart," he would say, "gets you going for the game." Everyone had a swig, except for Bobby, who was a law unto himself, and had his own stash that he popped ten minutes before kick off. I have no idea what it was and didn't ask. I loved Bobby and thought whatever it is, it must be right for him.

Our pre-match meal in those days was steak and potatoes at midday, three hours before kick off. How times have changed! It was the worst possible meal to play on. It was just tradition and no one knew any better. It still rattled around the stomach two days later.

It was Graham Leggat, our little winger, who taught me how to dive. I'd watched him closely from the stands in matches and could see he had this trick of kicking the back of his own heel and going down. I spoke to him about it and he said it was a wonderful way of conning the referee. "They hear a noise, see me go down," he explained, "and more often than not give a free kick or a penalty."

I mastered the art and dived throughout my career to beat the system. Why not? Defenders kick lumps out of talented forwards and get away with murder, and that's cheating, so why not do something to even things up? After Leggat, Francis Lee, the England International and my team mate at Manchester City, was the best diver I ever came across. In my opinion, Maradona, Pelé and Eusabio are all experts too. Look, cheating goes on in all sports, so don't get carried away with a few dives in football. Leggat's trick is used by many stars across the world today. Take a closer look at the Premier League, it happens all the time.

The greatest boxer of all time, Muhammad Ali, allegedly cheated when his corner said he had split his glove to buy time after being knocked down by Henry Cooper. Boxers hit low; cricketers don't walk when they know they have hit the ball, tennis players scream and shout when they know the ball is out, rugby players tackle high or put their finger into an opponent's eye. Footballers fake injury, dive, get into the face of the referee, and what about the rugby tackling we are seeing in the six-yard areas? At corners and free kicks when defenders manhandle forwards, that's cheating.

I spent my entire career being kicked by hatchet men, hard tacklers like Norman Hunter, Johnny Giles and Ron Harris without protection from referees, which in my opinion is cheating. So, what is wrong with diving to get your own back? I was brilliant at it, thanks to Leggat. If a defender brushed me in the area down I'd go, if I was being chased my heels would click and a penalty would be given. I got away with it hundreds of times and don't apologise for that. No way. It was my way of getting back.

I recall one important game at Plymouth that was a real battle, and stuck at 0-0 heading towards the final minutes. I went down for a penalty that never was, got it and we won. The Plymouth fans went berserk, and we needed a police escort out of the ground with stones and other objects being thrown at our coach, at me in particular. Through the window I was mouthing "you beauty" and putting my thumbs up. It's all part and parcel of the game. They kicked me and I dived for penalties and free kicks.

Most of the top players do it today, and don't believe anyone who says they don't. As I see it, Wayne Rooney has dived to get a penalty, and I can see it a mile off, as the goalkeeper comes rushing off his line to make the challenge. The forward knows what's coming, and just makes minimal contact with an arm or trailing leg of the goalkeeper, and goes down. Penalty. Nine times out of ten I can call it and ten times out of ten I know whether it was a penalty or not. How it would be great to play today with the wonderful surfaces instead of the mud heaps we used to play on. Also, the protection of the referee that exists today is so helpful to the forward. The talented player has the freedom to do what he likes and to win penalties. If defenders are not allowed to tackle as they would like, there are going to be more controversial incidents with referees trying to guess what happened; did he get the ball first or was there contact? It's a lottery at times. Had I asked for more protection from referees when I was playing they would have laughed in my face.

The more goals I scored, the more popular I became at Fulham. I was different, did things on the pitch that took the fans to fantasy land and, of course, I revelled in the acclaim and loved the spotlight. Who wouldn't? I had come from nowhere, a boy with nothing apart from his wits, talent in his feet and a brain that was working overtime to take him as far as he could go. But on his own terms.

They were fun days and things happened that you just couldn't make up. One day Johnny Haynes, after tweaking a calf muscle playing for England on a Wednesday afternoon, went into Craven Cottage at 8.30 on a Thursday morning for some treatment. Our trainer, Frank Penn, didn't know the captain was coming in and Haynes was bemused when he found the treatment room locked. "Frank? It's me, John, I need some treatment, open up," he said. This went on for about ten minutes. "Frank, what's going on? Come on, I need treatment!" Eventually the door opened slightly, just enough for John to put his head through. To Haynes' surprise, our trainer was treating a greyhound for a friend called Charlie Mitten. The dog was running in the 3.45 that afternoon at Stamford Bridge and had a leg-pull. Sheepish Frank, who earned hardly any money, was doing it for cash while the best player in Europe was waiting to be treated. Mad.

At Fulham, we had an initiation ceremony for every new signing, a bit like the Wimbledon Crazy Gang used to do. When one young lad joined, we put him in a cold bath, then whitewashed his bollocks and chained him outside to the pitch-side railings for an hour. Stupid, but in those days good fun, only this time the poor lad almost caught pneumonia. Another fine from Frank Osborne followed and we didn't complain because everyone was petrified of him.

There was an incident while playing for Fulham that stayed with me for the rest of my life. We were playing Leicester away and Johnny Haynes sent a good cross into the box. I saw the ball all the way and knew that it was mine. Up I jumped, hung in the air and as I powered my header towards the top corner their defender, John Sjoberg, came straight through me with a clattering challenge that saw his head butt the side of my face. The last thing I saw was the ball going into the net out of Gordon Banks' reach, before I was knocked out cold. I was stretchered off and taken to hospital where they diagnosed a fractured skull and damage to the left side of my face. From that day I lost all hearing in my left ear and, despite operations and consultations, no one has ever managed to return me to my normal hearing. I know he didn't mean to cause my deafness, but nothing will convince me that the tackle wasn't intentional. I was a target for all defenders.

My deafness has been no more than an irritant throughout my life, and certainly hasn't stopped me doing things I've wanted to achieve. There are times when I can't pick up things that people have said, especially at parties or in busy social situations where the acoustics are difficult.

The Loose Cannon reputation was actually grounded at Fulham and eventually saw me forced out of the club.

Manager Bedford Jezzard left and was replaced by a man called Vic Buckingham.

He came from Ajax, was half Dutch, thought he was a public schoolboy and was right up his own arse in every way. I was from the East End, a cockney, playing wonderful off the cuff football and scoring goals, yet he didn't accept me from day one. This was a working man's sport and yet he wanted to change my approach. No chance.

I immediately fell out with him and we had problems every single day. He called me a clown and a joker, even though I scored dozens of goals for him in his first six months. The more things I did on the pitch that outraged him, the more he treated me with contempt. The angrier he got, the more outrageous I became and the crowd loved it. That made Buckingham even more annoyed. In one game, a fan threw a newspaper onto the pitch and I picked it up, leant on the post, and read it. Buckingham went berserk after the game. Why? Didn't he realise that it takes all kinds of characters to make a successful football team?

I once scored a fantastic goal against Nottingham Forest, running the length of the pitch, beating defender after defender before slotting the ball in. I walked back to the halfway line and spread my arms in celebration as if to say 'how about that, Mr Manager?' I saw him shaking his head and that, my friends, was the beginning of the end.

On the Monday morning he called me into his office and said he was putting me on the transfer list. "You are not the type of person I want to work with, have around me or be part of this club," he said, "I like doing things a certain way," as he took out a handkerchief and mopped his brow. He then told me a story to try and make me understand why he was letting me go. "Rodney," he said, "you know some ships are called galleons. On those galleons they tied the guns down with ropes to stop them flying around the deck and becoming out of control and injuring the crew. They didn't want them to get loose or they had no control over them. I'd like to tie you down, Rodney, and have more control over you." What complete bollocks he was talking. I was nineteen, just a footballer scoring goals and entertaining the Fulham fans, and here was someone trying to rein me in. All I wanted was to train, play and go down the Wimpey Bar for a lunchtime burger and chocolate milkshake. That was my life, and this prat wanted to change me. Loose Cannons on a ship, what was he talking about? I guess that's where the saying came from.

I spent four years at Fulham, from 1962 to 1966, scored twenty-two goals in sixty-three appearances, and loved it until Buckingham arrived. He said I hurt the team, but how can you hurt a side when you are scoring so many goals? I never wanted to leave, and would happily have spent the rest of my career at Craven Cottage, playing for the fans, scoring goals and building my reputation. Ten years there and a testimonial would have done me.

I still love going back, the tearooms under the stand, the family atmosphere, walking through Bishop's Park to get to the ground, the Cottage sitting and looking out over the pitch. In those early days, the celebrities like Sean Connery, Honor Blackman, Michael Caine and Michael Crawford, used to flock to the Cottage to be part of something special. Buckingham ruined that for me.

It was a ridiculous situation, as I continued scoring goals despite knowing I was up for sale. By the time I left I had become a totally different animal to the one who had signed four years earlier. I was more confident as a player and as a person, back chatted everyone, even argued with Johnny Haynes. I wanted to prove myself to everyone, and I was sure of going all the way.

It was six months before Fulham sold me, and it was their local West London neighbours, Queen's Park Rangers, who provided my next challenge. It would prove to be a wonderful move for me and Loftus Road, close to the old White City, was where I turned into something special. I knew it was coming and here it was. "Rodneeeeeeeeeeeeee!"

6

Great to Feel Wanted

Am I envious or bitter about the huge salaries footballers earn today? No, not in the slightest. Just imagine what the late, great Bobby Moore or George Best would have commanded in today's market. That was then, and this is now. Good luck to any player who can demand £100,000 a week plus. I have never been an 'if only' man.

Top entertainers like Robbie Williams and Phil Collins are paid huge salaries, so why not footballers? I do have an issue with ordinary players getting over-paid, and I also worry whether clubs can actually afford these wages or if they just pay out to keep up with the huge pressure on them to succeed. That is another argument. Big money for big players is okay by me.

I have always looked after my money and thought of the future. I may have done outrageous things on the pitch, yet when it came to finances I've done the right things.

I was never someone who thought, "Sod this, let's go and blow the lot!" My first professional contract came at eighteen as a youth team player at Fulham, and I signed into a pension fund straight away. Most football clubs back then took money from salary into a pot and invested it for the players; I presume it is the same today. I still get paid from that pension fund. As I recall, I was on about £27.50 a week when I left Fulham, and Queen's Park Rangers gave me a rise to £35. That was good money, although you can't equate it to the salaries of today's players.

Life was so different when I was playing. Only the big players had agents or sponsorship deals, so it was just negotiations between the player and the club. Jim Gregory, the owner of Queen's Park Rangers, was a man I liked instantly. He was ambitious for his club and I was hell-bent on becoming a top star. My first thought when I met him was "He's just like me." Jim was straight and told it how it was; I respected that and I knew exactly where I stood with him. In so many ways he was like a father figure to me, and I could tell he wanted to take me under his wing.

In me, he saw what he wanted for his club: success and the spotlight. My signing was an inspiration for him to go and take Rangers into the big time.

How Gregory handled contract negotiations was unique. He was in control of all the finances, and it was him you talked to directly. This story sums up how he dealt with footballers he liked and wanted: My first season, 1966-67, was remarkable. It could not have gone better and I didn't do a thing wrong. Everything I touched turned to gold, and there was a huge amount of publicity being given to the club. We won the League Cup against West Brom at Wembley, got promoted and I scored forty-four goals. There was talk of England for me and for Gregory, and I knew he was delighted. Proud too.

At the end of the season, he called me in and we talked about what a wonderful season it had been. "You've been brilliant, son," he said. "I'm going to give you a pay rise." Jim offered me £60 a week, an increase of £25. I looked at him with surprise and disappointment etched into my face. "That's hardly fair," I told him, "I've just had the season of my life, scored so many goals, we've won promotion and a cup final, and you're only offering me £60?" He said he couldn't go any higher because it would break the club's wage structure, and I could see he was thinking of the bigger picture.

Gregory then said he was going public with his car company, Godfrey Davis I think, and that the company's shares would soon be worth triple their current value. "Just buy £500 worth," he said. I told him that I didn't want shares, just a better contract. "I'll take the £60, but I'm not happy," I replied and walked out. Jim, I felt, had let me down and I could see he was uneasy about the situation.

The following year, after we had been promoted again, this time to the old First Division following another great season for myself and the club, he called me into his office. He said QPR were now on the map, attendances were soaring through the roof, and the club was to build a new stand to meet demands. This time, he gave me a pay increase to £125 a week. Gregory then returned to the story of the previous year, when he had told me to buy shares in his company. "You said no to the shares, but I didn't" he said. I can't remember exactly how much the shares had gone up to, but he said "I bought them for you, and they're now worth a lot more." With that, he handed me the shares. I was gob-smacked, yet so grateful. I immediately went out, cashed them in and bought a house in Epsom, Surrey.

That is what I call brilliant man-management, and my respect for Gregory went through the roof that day. It was typical of him. If he was your enemy, look out, whereas if he liked you, he treated you like family. He was a tough, tough man who could be nasty, yet all he wanted from football was to be a success. He had tried to get on the board of Fulham for a long time, but was blocked because of his alleged dodgy background. For me, he was always fair and eventually very generous.

My signing was a huge moment for me and for QPR, and so it should have been. I'd dropped from the First Division with Fulham, and been playing with top internationals into the Third Division. My debut was at Peterborough and I spent the entire first half watching the ball being struck over my head. Long ball, bang, long ball bang, bang. "What the fuck am I doing here?" I thought. I feared I'd made a huge mistake. In that QPR side were the Morgan twins, Roger and Ian, Mark Lazarus, Les Allen, Frank Sibley, Jim Langley my old Fulham team mate, and Tony Hazell, as well as former England goalkeeper Ron Springett. Good players who deserved to play better football than I experienced in that first game at Peterborough.

In many ways, I was the Eric Cantona of QPR's future. The catalyst of change and the inspiration to make things happen, just as Cantona was at Manchester United following his surprise signing from Leeds. Sir. Alex Ferguson saw something in Cantona he liked and wanted, and Jim Gregory saw the same in me: the start of a new era.

Things at QPR changed quickly, and we began to play off the cuff, exciting football. We'd go away and win 7-0 and, so often, instructions from manager Alec Stock were forgotten or lost in the mood of the team once we started to play. Stock once told us going into an important top of the table game at Mansfield, to keep it tight in the first half. He ordered everyone behind the ball apart from me, who should be given licence to do my stuff. "I won't be unhappy with 0-0 at half time," he said. It was 4-1 to us at the interval, and I got a first-half hat trick! That was typical of Rangers and the way we played. Exciting and spontaneous, never boring or predictable. My kind of football.

I was also fortunate enough to play alongside someone like Les Allen. It was one of those partnerships you can't create, they just happen. We were born to play together, like Alan Shearer and Teddy Sherringham, or Gary Lineker and Peter Beardsley. Les knew the runs I would make, where I wanted the ball and I could read him too. It was telepathy and I was grateful to him. I lost count of the goals we scored and created as a partnership.

When you had a chairman like Gregory and a manager in the mould of Stock, unexpected things happened. They were totally opposite characters, one a tough local businessman who would trample over anyone to get what he wanted, the other an old-school manager who used unique man-management skills to bring out the best in his players. "Funny old game, Rodney," he would say after another breathtaking win as he skipped around the dressing room in his blazer and polished shoes, a hankie

My last game as an amateur footballer, playing for Alexander
Boys Clubs in September 1960. A few days later, I signed my first
professional contract with Fulham F.C..

All knocked out - Fulham captain Alan Slough looks to the bench after an elbow to my face knocked three of my teeth out.

Dumped on my ass again at Fulham.

At QPR during our first season in the First Division. With Frank McLintock of Arsenal.

Celebration having scored the winning goal against Cardiff in our promotion year, at Loftus Road.

Being shut down by Dave McKay (again) vs. Derby County.

Rodney Marsh for Prime Minister – Before the 1967 League Cup Final, QPR vs. West Brom.

Presented with my league winning medal at Loftus Road in 1967. QPR were the first 3rd Division club to win a league and cup double.

At my first England camp in 1971.
L-R Geoff Hurst, Martin Chivers, me, Francis Lee.

Quasimodo Summerbee - whilst at Manchester City just after Denis Law signed for us.

One of the proudest moments of my career,
as I lead out the City team, as captain.

Welcome to Maine
Road, 1972.

One of my first games in a City shirt with
Wyn 'The Leap" Davies.

In Bobby Moore's pub in Stretford.
R-L Bobby Moore, Malcolm MacDonald (Super Mac), George Best, Alan Ball, Frank Lampard (Snr), trivia question – name him, me.

From Elton, with love – with
Elton John and Ken Adam.

Come and get it Pelé, 1976.

Murderers Row, pre-season photo shoot at Tampa.
L-R, Stewart Scullion, Clyde Best, me, Derek
Smethurst.

2-1 down, expressing
my reaction to being
substituted in the 82nd
minute in the 1979
Soccer Bowl final – my
last game before retiring
from football.

Substituted after being pelted
with cups by the fans.

dropping out of his top pocket. Old-school was Alec. I'm not sure if he really knew how we got some of the results we did. He knew fuck all about tactics, although he understood and cared deeply. "Not a bad old life, old son, is it?" he would repeat over and over again.

He, like Gregory, had a one-off style of man- management. I once cut off a plaster cast on my leg following a metatarsal injury – yes, they existed long before David Beckham's injury ahead of the 2002 World Cup – because it was too tight, and I hobbled out of the treatment room. Stock went mad at me for taking the law into my own hands and defying the medical man, so he called me into his office. He said he was fining me two weeks wages. "It is the maximum I can do," he said, "I have to make a big example of you. The press will be told and this will create a lot of publicity." As I got up to leave, Alec moved closer and whispered "Don't worry son, I'll give it back to you in next season's contract, just don't tell anyone." He knew he had to fine me for disciplinary reasons, but he didn't really want to. It was sensational man-management and I chuckled to myself for hours afterwards. Stock got it right; that was the way to handle Rodney Marsh. He could have lost me as a player, and indeed as a person had he not made that gesture. "Don't tell anyone else," he reminded me, and it was his last comment before the door was opened and he put on his 'I'm in charge' face.

It was classic Stock. How I loved him and his methods. He did me in cold blood only once, over an article The News of the World newspaper wanted to run. It was two thirds of the way through a fantastic season for me and there was huge demand for me to play for England. Everyone was asking the same question, "How can England manager Alf Ramsey ignore this man?" I received a phone call from one of the News of the World reporters called Jim Thompson as I remember, who offered me £250 to do an article with the headline 'Sir Alf, I'm ready for England.' I was up for it, although I told Thompson I needed to clear it with the manager first. Alec wasn't keen when I spoke to him the next day. "Keep your head down, son," he said, "because Alf will think you're flash." I argued that £250 was a lot of money. "No," said Alec, "I don't want you to do the article, keep out of trouble, carry on with what you are doing and the rewards will come. Trust me."

That week, we played Tranmere Rovers in the League Cup and won 6-0. I got four goals in a brilliant team performance. Like all footballers, I dashed down to the newspaper shop the following morning to pick up the Sunday papers. Don't believe people in football who say they never read the papers, they all do. There were great headlines for me and then, when I picked up The News of the World, I couldn't believe what I read on their main spread. 'Sir Alf, Rodney is ready for England' it blazed. 'Exclusive by Alec Stock.' The old rogue had told me not to get involved and nicked the money himself. I laughed and we had a chuckle over it on Monday morning. "Funny old life, Rodney" he said. "Thanks Boss," I said, and put it down as just another learning curve.

It was important for me to be loved and wanted, and that is how I felt at QPR. The goals, praise, headlines and huge publicity for the club just kept on coming. Rangers and I were a partnership made in heaven. During a game at Bournemouth when we won 4-0, I stood on the ball for several seconds in an arrogant show of skill intended to send the message that I was better than my opponents. A defender lamped me from behind and I didn't care, I was the star and he wasn't going to stop me. That was the game when former Spurs manager Bill Nicholson turned up, saying he'd come to see Rodney Marsh play. He enjoyed my style of play and that was a huge compliment.

At that stage, I had no idea Rangers would be such a huge stepping stone for me. I was happy playing football my way. The sport has always been my passion and still is. Like at Fulham, I was happy to stay. Leaving did not enter my mind. Not at that moment, anyway.

It was relegation and a change of manager that eventually led me to seek my next career challenge. Rangers had gone from the Third Division to the First and I didn't want to play anywhere else. I'd missed the first eighteen matches of the season we went down with a metatarsal injury, and I knew it was time for another heart to heart with Mr Gregory. I told him I loved the club as much as he did, but I needed First Division football. "I'm twenty-six years old," I said, "I need to be playing with the best players." Typically, Jim understood and we shook on an agreement that if Rangers didn't bounce straight back with promotion, he would let me go. "You have been great for us Rodney," he said. "You have my word on that." You didn't need a contract with people like Gregory. If he said something, he meant it, as so many enemies found out.

Gordon Jago had taken over as manager from Alec Stock, and at his first meeting with the players I completely fucked up my relationship with him. The Loose Cannon struck again. He was an excellent coach but an FA man, an establishment man and not my cup of tea at all. I have always hated the FA and what they stand for but more on that later. Jago was all light and bubbly at that first meeting, and went through what he wanted, how we were going to play and what his plans were for the future. He said the slate had been wiped clean from the Stock era and that he was in charge now. At the end of his speech, I stood up and said that, on behalf of the players, we were all forty percent behind him! Me and my big mouth! To this day I have no idea why I said it. Terry Venables pissed himself laughing. Jago looked at me in disbelief, and was clearly devastated and hurt. It was definitely another Loose Cannon moment. There have been quite a few over the years. After that, Jago and I never got on and my exit was fast-tracked.

Newcastle came in with £195,000 for Roger Morgan and me, but Jim Gregory turned it down. Spurs increased it to £200,000 for the both of us and, again, Gregory refused. The next week Manchester City offered £200,000 for me alone and Gregory called me into his office. The season had not finished, although there was no chance of promotion, and Jim said that with £200,000 he could buy five or six new players. It was the end of a great working relationship. "Off you go, son," he said, and off I went. At that stage, I didn't know the club had turned down Newcastle and Spurs, but City and their flamboyant coach Malcolm Allison intrigued me.

City were top of the First Division and with players like Mike Summerbee and Francis Lee, they were playing my kind of football. They also had one of the best players in Europe, Colin Bell. I was excited, even though the press got hold of a story that it was only Allison who wanted me and not his partner, manager Joe Mercer. The prospect of me joining split the club, and created a wedge down the middle. It was not healthy, but Allison finally got his way and I was up for it. After another meeting with Jim Gregory, I was booked onto a train to Manchester and had to go home to Epsom to gather my things. By the time I was ready to drive to the station, there was a huge posse of journalists outside the house. I drove a Lotus Europa in those days, and I opened the garage door with the remote so I could roar away without them being able to catch me or know what I was up to. The master plan worked, apart from me driving straight into a tree! I just got out, my car and ego bruised, and said, "Okay boys, what do you want to talk about?"

I knew I would sign for City even before I met Allison. It felt like my kind of club, my platform. I had been at Rangers from 1966 to 1972 and scored one hundred and six goals for them. I have happy memories of my time at QPR, and they will always have a special place in my heart.

Manchester City was the ultimate step up for me, the biggest challenge. Everyone I had spoken to had nothing but praise for Allison and said that he was the best coach around. In so many ways he was the José Mourinho of the sixties. He knew he was good and was never afraid to tell you. Malcolm would spot things before or during a game and have the knowledge, brainpower, ideas and confidence to make his plan work. Yes, he was the first Special One.

Malcolm, throughout my City career, was flash, arrogant, confident and happy to talk about himself. He knew he was good and didn't mind boasting and was a great story-teller; it didn't matter whether it was true as long as it was a story. He talked about his London upbringing, how he only had one lung after contracting TB as a youngster and the underworld characters he had mixed with. I think it's fair to say that Malcolm wanted to be all things to all people. The champagne flowed, and so did the chat and the football. He was always a difficult character to break down, and very few were allowed to step into his inner sanctum. Perhaps this is why, in terms of football, he and I always saw eye to eye. In some ways we were similar.

Our relationship was the starting point of my career at Maine Road. A colourful five years that were not always harmonious, certainly controversial, and which ended in bitterness.

It had been goodbye to Queen's Park Rangers and hello to Manchester City. Apart from the emotional tie, I knew I had finished with Rangers. But that's the great thing about football and life, isn't it? You never know what's around the corner. Years later, in 1994, I received a phone call from a guy called Richard Thompson, who was then the young Chairman of QPR. He knew I had managed New York, Carolina Lightnin' and Tampa Bay Rowdies in the US, and had been Chief Executive of Tampa, and so he wanted to talk to me. Over the phone we chatted and he revealed he was having a problem with his manager, Gerry Francis. I'd played with Gerry as a youngster at Rangers and he was a fantastic talent, who I admired tremendously. He was also doing a fine job as manager so I was very curious to hear the story. Thompson said that it really touched a nerve with him when managers said things in the press to build an atmosphere and put pressure on the board. "I've heard you on television talking sense. What do you think I should do about what's going at the club?" he asked me. "I've done nothing wrong, yet the crowd are having a go at me," he added. "The manager is saying things about me in the press."

I only listened and was trying to understand his position when, out of the blue, he offered me a job. I told him the only position I would accept was Director of Football or in a role of Chief Executive. I would have nothing to do with team selection or anything to do with the football playing side. That was the exclusive job of the manager. I'd run the football administration side of the club from top to bottom, including the players' contracts and transfers, I told him. "But that's my job," he answered indignantly, and I quickly told him that clearly he wasn't doing his job properly. He didn't have control over anyone, including the manager. I said I would become the CEO, something like what Peter Kenyon has since done at Manchester United and Chelsea. Thompson agreed and we had a conference call with his father, David, to thrash out a deal. Extraordinary, really, but that is what they wanted, or so I thought.

Rangers were playing Liverpool at home the next day and they invited me as their guest. On the morning of the match, The Sun newspaper had a back page headline that screamed 'Rod's in to save Rangers.' It completely took me by surprise because only three people knew about the deal; me, Richard Thompson and his father, and I certainly hadn't told anyone. It had been leaked, and I have never been able to find out who by. Did Thompson and his father tell Francis? Was it leaked to a journalist and, perhaps more significantly, was the whole thing a set up with me being used as the pawn? Had I been fooled? Before the game, Francis quit and soon afterwards joined Spurs. That simply added to the mystery.

The next day Thompson rang me to withdraw their offer. He said, "We've decided that we don't need you, sorry." "Hold on a minute," I said, "we had a verbal financial agreement," but he answered quickly that there was no signed contract. You could have heard a pin drop when I told him that I always taped my business conversations. Richard asked me to wait while he called his father. I was ready to accept one month's compensation for agreeing a deal as QPR's Chief Executive, so they surprised me when they came back with an offer of three months. I signed a confidentiality clause and they personally paid me the money. They did it with a series of small cheques through their own private company and not through QPR's bank account.

When Richard Thompson reads this and discovers I DIDN'T actually tape that conversation he will no doubt call me a cheating bastard, but I can't help feeling that I was used as a lever for them to get rid of Francis. Richard had used me and I had to manipulate him.

Amazingly, two years later, Thompson called me again asking for advice. This time we met face to face at Brown's in London, shared a glass of wine or two and he explained that he had been offered shares in Leeds, and wondered what I thought was the best thing for the club. I told him that if I was involved, the first thing I would do would be to get the best possible manager and commit him to a four year contract. "Make sure it's a manager you feel can take you where you want to go," I said. "But who?" he asked. I told him to get an agreement and a letter of intent from George Graham, the man who had so much success at Arsenal but who had then been banned from the game for taking a bung.

"I don't fancy that," said Thompson and we left Brown's on amicable terms. A few days later, I learned that he took the shares and Leeds eventually announced that Graham would take over. It's probably what you call getting your own back, and this time I got nothing for my advice. Just like Alec Stock had fleeced me with the News of the World article years before, again I'd been done in cold blood. But, hey, the world goes round and everyone has their moments.

My only other offer of a manager's job in England came, amazingly, from Manchester City. Yes, chairman Peter Swales contacted me after Tony Book had left. Swales rang me in America to ask whether I would be interested in returning to Maine Road. He asked if I would pop in and see him the next time I was in Manchester.

I never did, because I couldn't have brought myself to work for Swales again. First he sacks me, and then he asks me back? The bloke was an impostor and I always disliked him intensely. He also did his hair like Bobby Charlton and I had a problem with that.

7

The Greatest Player Ever

On Friday November 25th, 2005, something strange happened to me. I woke up at nine o'clock in the morning with an overwhelming desire to see George Best in hospital. I knew it was something I had to do.

I called Phil Hughes, his agent and friend, and said I'd like to see George, but he explained that George was in a coma and that he'd have to make sure it was okay with Dickie, George's father, for me to pop over. Dickie said it was absolutely fine, so I went straight to the Cromwell Hospital in London. His son Calum was there, so too was former Manchester United team mate Denis Law, and Bobby Campbell, his Fulham manager. I had to wait while George had some tests, so I sat outside with Dickie, talking about Bestie and life until Phil said it was fine to go into the room.

George looked absolutely terrible. It was horrible to see him like that, unable to speak or recognise anyone, with tubes and pipes coming out of him. I sat looking at him, not knowing what to say or do. A voice inside my head had told me that I needed to be at his bedside that morning, so here I was, staring at the greatest player of all time as he lay in bed looking sad and pathetic. It was unreal.

Phil had his hands on my shoulders and I leant forward and whispered into his ear "George, you were the greatest player that ever lived." I was crying when I said it. He had once told me that all the stuff about the women, the drinking and the gambling meant nothing to him. The only thing that mattered to him was that people remembered him as the greatest player who ever played football. He said that to me one night when he and I were together, talking about life and the game. So, I said it to him as he was dying, and I truly meant it. Besty for a short time in the late sixties was the greatest in the world. Whether he could hear or understand what I said, or who said it, is another matter. It was, however, important to me. A big moment in my life.

It's no secret, especially to him, that for a long time he was destroying himself with the booze. He just didn't want to stop and, more significantly, couldn't. He liked drinking, but addiction is so much more than that. On the path to self-destruction people know it's all going wrong. They know what they are doing to themselves, and George was certainly no exception. Do addicts have the ability to stop? In so many cases, the answer is no. Whatever anyone says to them, or whoever tries to help, it doesn't matter. They carry on regardless. What goes on inside their minds, indeed, what George really thought of himself, we will never know. I suspect he fought long and hard with his mind, playing his love for football off against his overwhelming love of drinking.

We were in Tramps Night Club in London one night in 1976 after a fantastic performance for Fulham. A whole group of us had first visited the Duke of Wellington pub on the King's Road, where all the drinks had been on a man called Sir. Eric Miller, one of the 'money men' behind Fulham at the time who liked to mix with the players and be seen as 'Mr. Big.' By the early hours in Tramps, both George and I had had too much to drink and, with the tongues loose, I asked him if he had ever thought about going easy on the booze? His reaction startled me. "Don't you ever tell me what to fucking do Marshy!!!" he said, and his face was twisted with anger. I had touched a nerve and so I backed off. It was aggression caused by the drink, but we never approached the subject again. He'd snapped and I knew I had touched upon something that, deep down, he knew was wrong and couldn't do anything about. George, even at that stage in his life, was drinking himself to death. He was on the slippery slope with nothing to hold on to.

I stayed for fifteen minutes in his room at the Cromwell Hospital, said my goodbyes to Dickie and Phil, got in my car, turned on the radio, and twenty minutes later Talk Sport Radio announced live on the air that George Best was dead. How in the world did they find out so quickly? I'd only just left him. He must have died as I was walking out the hospital door. I was lost in my thoughts for the rest of the day. No, for the rest of my life.

Why had I woken that morning knowing I had to see George? Was it 'someone' telling me that I had one last chance to say goodbye? Who knows what tricks the mind plays? All I know is that something, or someone, called me to that hospital room.

For heavens' sake, where do you start with the George Best story? How do you explain what made him tick and why he died so young at just fifty-nine years of age? I'll try nonetheless.

The first time I met George was in my opening season at Manchester City in 1972. We had been invited to play in a charity match for under-privileged children.

We were both fit and at the peak of our careers. He was twenty-five and I, two years older at twenty-seven. It was just a bit of fun with the local bar owners and waiters, but for a great cause. Afterwards in the bar, someone introduced us and the stare George gave me didn't just go straight through me, it told me exactly what he was thinking. "Don't fuck with my patch, this is my territory," was what the look said. "I am king around here so just watch it." We hardly spoke and I got the message.

We later would go on to become good friends. We played for different clubs in America, were at Fulham together at the end of our careers in English football, did the hugely successful Best and Marsh Road Show in front of live audiences up and down the country, and drank, laughed and cried as one.

We roomed together at Fulham and I discovered first-hand just how big a personality George Best really was. Think of David Beckham and multiply the hysteria, publicity and feeling this Irishman generated by ten. He was special. The first football personality, the first pop star of the game and a product of the swinging sixties that changed so many people's lives. Good looking, with long hair and a smile that could melt a 1000 female hearts and always did. He was the Beatle of football. The word great is over-used in football. It never was for Best, it was an understatement.

Certainly, in the mid sixties he was the greatest player in the world. There was no one better, not Pelé, Cruyff, Eusebio, no one. He was untouchable against opponents who always tried to kick him to bits, in an era when there was no protection for the skilful players from referees, when we played on pitches that were often quagmires. It was not uncommon for George to beat five players in one of those wonderful runs that were his hallmark. His changes of direction were incredible and he had the ability to dummy opponents with the slightest twist of his hips. When he dropped his shoulder to go one way and then switched, the whole crowd went with him.

He just loved playing, football was his passion and he was a big student of the game. His knowledge was incredible. He knew the history of football and you could never catch him out on a question about the sport. The more I talk about Best the player, the more depressed I become. His life became a sad story that turned into a tragedy. Did he have to die? Of course not, but he just couldn't help himself. No one could help him. He just could not listen to advice.

At the end of his career, George ended up playing at a ridiculous level. In Manchester, he owned a wine bar called Oscars, and one day I popped in with Mike Horswell, a young player City had signed from Sunderland and someone I took under my wing. George was in the bar that lunchtime, sitting talking to a man I didn't recognise. After a couple of blackcurrant and lemonades, always my after-training drink, I approached George and he introduced me to the guy, who turned out to be the Chairman of non-league Dunstable. My thoughts were that here I was, captain of City and playing for England, and here was the greatest player that ever lived, being enticed by a non-league club. How the mighty had fallen and it just didn't seem right.

I don't remember the exact amounts but the conversation went something like this.

He'd offered George £2,000 a game. At that stage, I was on £500 a week, so it sounded a good deal to me. But Best said no because he didn't need the aggravation of getting fit again. Dunstable only got crowds of nine hundred for their home games and the Chairman said that Best would boost that figure to 9,000. "What if we give you £3,000 a game?" he said. Once more George said no, but he finally cracked when the figure got to £10,000 an appearance. George played five times for Dunstable.

That kind of money was amazing, and so typical of the people who just wanted a part of Best. He attracted all sorts, a cross section of the rich and famous, pop stars and actors, to the man in the pub with whom he would sit and chew the cud. That was his strength, he could mix with, and talk to anyone. That is why he was so loved. Best had no ego or image sitting on his shoulder. To some he was the greatest player of all time, while at this stage of his life, to others he was just another guy sipping his wine in the corner of the bar.

My last game of football was my Testimonial for Tampa Bay Rowdies in the US. It was October 1979 and I got two goals against Fort Lauderdale. After the game, the press came into our dressing room and asked me why I was retiring, if I was fit and playing so well? I explained that it was always better to quit when you knew it was time to go, and not when someone else made the decision for you. I was thirty-five years old and never played a proper football match again. I have never had any regrets, and never once thought I could and should have gone on playing for longer than I did. Besty carried on because of who he was, and for the simple reason that people kept throwing money at him.

Apart from the hundreds of girls that came into his life and bed and disappeared just as quickly, there were three main lovers in Best's extraordinary story. First wife Angie, who I didn't like and never got on with. It was mutual. I think she disliked me intensely too. Mary Shatila, who together with Phil Hughes rescued George from despair when his life was a mess and put him back on his feet, then Alex, his wife when he died who could stand toe to toe with George when it came to drinking.

None of my business, but I always felt Angie wasn't good for George, that she never really had his best interests at heart. We once had a spat in Tramps nightclub,

London when she threw a glass of champagne over me. It got silly and I threw one back. It had started when I told her to leave George alone after we had just experienced a poor game and she wouldn't let go of him, moaning and complaining about something. I told her to stop whinging and to give him space, and the next thing I know champagne was dripping down my face. "Who are you to tell me what to do!" she screamed. It was quite an explosive situation, with George walking out, and club-owner Johnny Gold rushing over to make peace. It calmed down and I took Angie home in taxi. It was always "George this," and "George that," with her and "I am this," and "I want that." I think she loved the reflected glory, and on that night I'd had enough and told her. I just never felt Angie had George's interests as her number one priority. But hey, they were married and me and Besty were only friends.

In the early nineties it's fair to say George was in a state. He had enormous tax bills to pay, he was virtually bankrupt, and he was in danger of losing his property. He was penniless, but got lucky when Phil Hughes, an old friend of his and a mate from the London club scene, introduced him to Mary. Phil worshiped George, became his manager and Mary and Phil started to run his life for him. Together they were a powerful team and they gave him a second professional lease of life. Mary, a Lebanese girl, and George soon became a couple. She looked after him in so many ways and George often told me, "She's good for me," and everyone felt happy for him. I had a lot of time for Mary.

She ran his business from The Phene Arms Pub in London, just off Oakley Street. There was a public phone that sat on the bar and it became the HQ of George Best Enterprises, run by Mary. The phone rang non-stop with requests to talk to Mary or George, asking could they do this or that, was it possible for him to talk to some businessmen or be at functions across the country? "How much would you charge for that?" and "would this figure be okay for a fee?" You could even hear Mary negotiating when you went for a pee. George just sat in the corner of the bar, drinking heavily, of course, doing crosswords, he loved his Mirror crossword, and talking to the locals. They were lovely times, he was happy and his career was on the up again, despite his drinking.

The drinking was a problem it seemed, for everyone but him. One day in the pub, I noticed seven drinks lined up for him, large wine glasses filled to the brim with his favourite tipple, Sancerre. I said to the Irish barman, Pat, "why not just take the money and top his glass up when he needs it?" "Because," he said "Everyone likes to see the drink poured for him. They like to be seen to be buying George Best a drink." It was a Catch Twenty-Two situation. George was working again and earning good money, but he was also drinking as much as ever.

His career, with the ups and downs, the highs and lows, the decline and sadness of George Best, is a topic of conversation everyone enjoys and likes to contribute to. That will never end. Everyone loved his company because he was special, from Prime Minister John Major, to pop stars like Rod Stewart, or the man in the pub having a pint. The fact he was the greatest footballer that God ever made simply added to the attraction. We are talking mega, superstar here.

I went through a big chunk of my career with him. We went from being rivals at City and United in Manchester to being players in the US and at Fulham. We were drinking partners, buddies on the Road Show that became a smash hit, but then we all had to watch his decline thanks to the bottle he couldn't and wouldn't put down. What did his drinking hide? Who knows? I don't believe he was unhappy, and George certainly knew what he was doing to himself. All the stories people tell you about his drinking are probably true, and I will try and explain just how he lived his life. I can't call it a fight with the bottle because he enjoyed drinking so much. It was another of his passions and he was brilliant at it.

One day, we were in The Ritz Hotel having afternoon tea. George told me that he'd had a pellet fitted in his stomach to stop him drinking so much, and that he was also on pills. Then he moved closer and said, "'But, Marshy, I've discovered that if I mix water with the alcohol in smaller amounts the pellet doesn't work so well." George had found a way to cheat the help someone had given him. He just couldn't stop himself. I smiled.

A lady once approached me and asked me about George. This was not uncommon, although she seemed more interested in his well being than going to bed with him, which was strange. She explained she was a Duchess or Lady or something, I paid little attention, but she said that she knew him from Manchester, had heard about Best's drinking problem and would like to help him. She said she would like to get him to a rehab centre and that she was prepared to pay for everything. Why? I have no idea and she never explained, but that is the effect George had on people. They felt close to him and wanted to help him if they could.

She seemed genuine so I eventually set up a meeting between them at The Carlton Towers Hotel in London and told George an attractive lady wanted to meet him. He had that look of "not another one," although I said she wasn't a bimbo and that she had an interesting story to tell. I hadn't told him she wanted to try and help him stop drinking. At that stage, at the age of forty-eight, he still had twenty year olds chasing after him, so me telling him a lady wanted to meet him was not a novelty or an attraction. She was a good-looking lady with a posh accent, and as soon as George sat down I could see him concentrating more on her tits than on what she was saying.

That is, until she started talking about drinking. His favourite wine was on the table, and he was sipping as she asked him about his habit. She said she had followed his career, and asked him what he thought about going into rehab to get some help. "Why do you drink so much, George?" she finally asked. Bestie took another sip, looked at her and said, "Because I like it. In fact, I love it. That was the last we saw of the Duchess. Couldn't make it up, could you?

Over the years, he tried to stop drinking more for those close to him than for himself. He'd have a few days when he would appear to be drinking less, then bang; it was back on the hammer. He was a world-class player and a world-class drinker. Boy, was he good at it, and he would drink anything he could lay his hands on; white wine, his favourite, and lots of champagne and brandy.

When Mary and Phil formed the Best and Marsh Road Show our lives became a fantasy. The public up and down the country couldn't get enough of it, and so it went on for a couple of years. George drank and drank his way through the shows, and how we completed some gigs I will never know. Occasionally some we simply didn't, as he went missing and just didn't turn up. Once in Oxford at a football club sportsman's dinner, I had to stand up and explain that George wasn't coming but they had me instead. It all kicked off. "Fuck off Rodney, we want George!" they screamed, and soon I was being pelted with rubbish. "But I've got some good stories to tell you," I explained. "Fuck off, fuck off!" they chanted, and so I did. I don't know why, but being slagged off for Besty never bothered me.

I don't believe he had any regrets. If you break it down to the common denominator between us, he didn't care what people thought of him or what they said and we had that in common. He enjoyed drinking and carried on with it regardless of what anyone said or what the consequences were.

Once, we did two Road Shows in the Manchester area in one day. The first was lunchtime at the Piccadilly with an audience of one thousand four hundred. It was amazing that everywhere we went, the fans came and all shows were a sell out. The attraction of George Best was limitless. This was a massive gig and George, who hadn't had a drink that morning, was on magnificent form. He was sober and he spoke for thirty minutes. He told outstanding stories, was funny, lucid, opinionated, bright and got a standing ovation. George opened up that day and the audience loved him. Afterwards, he said, "Shall we have a bottle of champagne?" and my heart just dropped. I persuaded him to have a glass instead to see how we got on. Mary was there, and a glass turned into two, and then a bottle. At five in the afternoon the organisers for the evening bash turned up, saw the champagne on our table and asked George if he would like another. I refused, but George said yes and they brought him a bottle of the best. I knew there would be trouble ahead.

Three bottles later, with George probably consuming the majority of the bottles on his own, he was still okay, although I was worried. In the limo taking us to the Mere Country Club in Cheshire, where local entrepreneur Max Brown had hired us to do a Blue & Red dinner. There was champagne laid on for us and I spent the short journey shaking my head at the event organiser. George drank. It was a black tie, £100 a ticket function, packed with 'faces' like Sir Matt Busby's son Sandy and other such VIP's. When we arrived, the MC, former referee Neil Midgley, greeted us with some more of the sponsors and organisers. "What can we get you to drink?" was their first question when we got inside. I said "no more to drink before we go on," but they ignored me and George asked for a large brandy, which he downed in one. The table we were sat at was heaving with wine. More trouble lay ahead, and now I was really worried, especially when I saw George do his little trick of twisting his fingers in front of his face. I'd seen him do it hundreds of times, the eyes go and the devil lies in waiting. He was still trying to focus when Midgley stood up to make the first welcome speech. "Gentlemen," he said, "This is a great day for City and United, and we are proud to welcome two greats from their history." Midgley was then interrupted by a thud as George fell forward, head first into his bowl of tomato soup. His face, beard and suit were covered. It was hysterical, and we had to usher him out quickly to clean him up. We cried laughing later.

Through the wine and brandy, Best said to me "Marshy, I really don't want to go back in there." We persuaded him to return and I said to Neil "Do a couple of questions and that will have to be it." As we sat down with George looking decidedly worse for wear, a sponsor said "George would you like another brandy?" I couldn't believe the stupidity, and said "Are you fucking mad?!" Someone in the audience shouted "Piss artist!" and from that moment onwards there was chaos. Someone threw a punch, probably a United fan to a City supporter, and fighting broke out across the room. There I was, holding George up and watching grown men in black ties throwing punches. Not our greatest or proudest moment.

I got hold of George under the arms, dragged him out and put him in the limo with Mary. I went back inside and tried to talk to the crowd. I told them that we would donate our fee to charity and that I was sorry. "Piss Off!" was the call back from them, and so I did. In the car travelling back to our hotel, George was spread-eagled across the back seat with his head in my lap. After a couple of minutes, one eye opened and he looked up at me and said, "Marshy, did you get the readies?" I laughed out loud. He was completely oblivious to what had gone on. That was George; great player, great drinker and completely unpredictable.

It was such a mixture with him, a cocktail of charisma, the man everyone wanted to touch and meet, and the drinker who quickly slipped away from that public persona. People forgave him because of who he was and what he stood for, because he was the greatest player on the planet.

There was a conveyer belt of women who just wanted 'him.' In bars they would come up and literally offer themselves to him on a plate. Sometimes he would chat to them, on other occasions he would not show any interest and blank them, and at other times he'd encourage them. He was selective and could afford to be. He knew all the bars in London and had favourite watering holes all over the country. "Seen George?" was the ask, and the answer was invariably "He was in earlier and has gone onto . . . take your pick." Puzzi's was a favourite of his, although it's gone now. Why did women still find him attractive when he was older and on his way to being destroyed by booze? Perhaps because the legend that is George Best will never, ever die.

Everyone wanted to be George Best when he broke onto the scene. I watched him as a seventeen year old dazzle football crowds and the world in general. Here was a superstar in every sense, and he never lost that appeal. He could do everything and anything with the ball and regularly did. People who didn't see him play live will never know how good he was. Being with him on the same pitch, albeit for me in the later stages of his career, was a privilege.

I was once rung by Denis Signy the organiser of The Football Writers Awards and asked if George and I would come to a dinner in his honour. "You probably are the only person who can guarantee George will show up," they said. They said he'd turned them down the previous four years. I was a bit offended but I managed to persuade Besty to go. It was the offer of a Chinese meal afterwards that finally convinced him it was a good idea. That was the night I went into the VIP area to order a drink, there was Alan Shearer, Johnny Haynes, Dave MacKay and loads more. Former Liverpool superstar player and manager, Kenny Dalglish, spotted me, he came over and with a dead pan straight face said "Hey Rodney, what are you doing here in the Legends bar?" I never knew whether he was being serious or taking the piss. I just said I was George's driver, which was certainly how I felt sometimes.

I felt a little bit responsible for him and saw his deterioration unfold before my eyes. When I was in America, I read that he had collapsed and contacted Phil Hughes. "I'm coming over in three weeks," I said, "and I'd like to see him straight away." Phil explained that he wasn't good, had lost a lot of weight, was in pain and was on some kind of support. I hardly recognised him when I walked into the hospital. He was a shadow of the George I knew. His face was yellow and he looked as though he'd gone ten rounds with Mike Tyson. His eyes were black and shrunken, and he'd lost fifty pounds. I was so shocked and dumbstruck. I asked him if he could get out of bed, and he and I, Phil and Alex shuffled down the corridor for a cup of tea, him in a hospital gown looking like a fragile little man, and me in a complete state of shock.

When I left him I had tears in my eyes. That is a big thing for me to admit, because I have not often cried in my life, but amazingly, the sight of Besty and the realization he was probably nearing the end brought tears to my eyes and a lump in my throat.

This thing about showing emotion, especially saying "I love you," started at home and has haunted me throughout my life. I just find saying it to anyone really difficult. Only the people I love are aware of this. They understand because they know my life story and what I have been through. How I was treated, physically and mentally, in my early years.

There is a big difference between crying and emotion, isn't there? When my children Joanna and Jonathan were born, I was emotional with happiness and that is not crying as I know it. Tears can often come when you least expect it. Jean once relayed a story to me that made me cry. I was driving along in America, and she told me over the phone that our son Jonathan had been looking out of the window at our house in Teddington, Middlesex, and had seen a neighbour and his son cleaning their car. "Dad and I used to do that, didn't we Mum?" he said, and when she told me I stopped the car and sobbed. You can't bring those moments back, can you? I had been in the US for six months and it just caught me. Some things I can brush off easily, while others stick with me. That haunted me and the fact that I'm telling the story means it still does.

I think of George often, of the times we had together, the Road Shows, the nights out, the drinking and laughter, the sadness at the sight of seeing him drown his life. He and Mary had started to row, and you sensed their relationship was coming to an end. Mary and I had become professionally close, and it was she who got me my first gig on Sky television, with one of their former presenters Paul Dempsey, and Sue Barker, now of BBC fame. Mary and I got on well, although she too was a big drinker and that led to huge conflict between George and her. She wouldn't give in over matters and neither would he. It sometimes got nasty, and I took many late night calls from Mary complaining that she had no idea where George was.

The boys from the Chelsea fire station on London's King's Road were brilliant to him at that stage in his life. If they found him struggling home, or in a drunken state anywhere in London, they used to take him back to the station and put him into one of their little overnight beds. It was like his own private hotel, since it happened a lot at four in the morning. George would happily sleep the rest of the night away, and most of the next morning.

One night, at two in the morning, the front doorbell of my flat in Wimbledon rang. I stumbled to the intercom service, and it was a distraught Mary. "He's kicked me out, Rod, I've got nowhere to go and I got a taxi here because I didn't know what to do." This was all I needed. "Go home Mary, it'll be ok," I said and she started to cry. Eventually, I went downstairs and let her in. "I'll make you some black coffee, you can sleep on the sofa and get a taxi in the morning," I told her. She was wobbling all over the place because she'd been drinking heavily, and I couldn't get her to sit down. "Wait there," I told her, "Stay in the living room and I'll get you some coffee." I hadn't even put the kettle on when I heard a huge smash and the sound of glass breaking. Mary had fallen through the glass coffee table and there was blood everywhere, all over her, on the carpet and down the wall. Her arm and foot were cut. "How did I get myself involved in this mess?" I thought, "I was asleep a few minutes ago and now look." The cuts weren't that bad and I bandaged her up, got some towels and water, mopped up, calmed her down, made her drink some black coffee and eventually got her on the sofa where she slept until the morning. She was devastated when she woke up, embarrassed and unhappy. She left in a taxi to go and find George.

Mary was a character who lived on the edge. After one successful Road Show gig in the North, we were returning home on the train the next morning and Mary hadn't yet paid George and I for our appearance. Together we were owed £9,000, and on more than two occasions the previous night, I'd asked her for the money. "Later Rod," she said, and changed the subject. On the train, I pushed her for it and she admitted that she didn't have it. "Where is it then?" I demanded and she whispered, embarrassed, that she'd used it to pay off a debt. I never asked what the debt was about but I got the picture. I was angry but she was good at her job and I cut her some slack on this one. To her credit, a few days later she gave me a cheque and nothing else was said.

Once Mary had disappeared from the scene, George's business deals were taken over by Phil Hughes, and then Alex also got involved. I never thought Alex and Besty were right for each other; they seemed to be like oil and vinegar, although they were the perfect match when it came to drinking. They drank buckets between them, and their relationship was always volatile. George told me that one night she threw a glass in his face after a row had turned nasty and he had a deep cut over his eye. I was doing Gillette Soccer Saturday on Sky with him at that stage, and he had to appear on television with stitches in the wound. On another occasion, George got into a row with Alex at her parents' house and her brother, apparently threw him over a balcony.

He was taken to hospital with cuts and bruises. I'm not qualified to judge any one's relationship, but Alex always said that she deeply loved Besty, I believe her, but as always with George and his ladies, it was a volatile relationship.

Alex had previously been going out with the former Spurs and Liverpool player, John Scales, who was a handsome bloke. It was amazing that George still felt he could chat up the girls and, sure enough, he pulled Alex in Tramps nightclub. She dumped Scales, and they became an item and later married.

It was a privilege to be playing in the same side as Best and Moore at Fulham. Happy days. George had been in California before he joined Fulham, and if there was a more handsome man on this planet at that time I've never seen him. The first day he walked in, tanned in a light blue suit, looking so groomed, with a chain around his neck that the pop group 'Yes' had given him. He looked like a movie star. Really, that's what he was. Like Beckham today but with this fantastic Irish brogue that tripped off his tongue. He had been playing for LA Aztecs while I'd done one year in Tampa, and it was Ken Adam who had spoken to Fulham manager Bobby Campbell and asked if he fancied Best and Marsh to join Moore in his team? As soon as Campbell put the plan to the board, especially Miller, it was a done deal. Miller loved notoriety.

In fact, I did a Beckham with Tampa loaning me to Fulham for the season. George was on loan too while Moore was already there, having played in the FA Cup Final against his old club West Ham the previous year. I worshipped Moore and I loved George. We felt like the three musketeers, and we had one season together. It was romantic and lovely to go back to the club where my career had started. George had lost a couple of yards of pace by then, although he was still brilliant on the ball, and Bobby too was coming to the end, but I just revelled in being in the same team as them.

It felt great to be back at Craven Cottage, and for the first twelve games we couldn't do anything wrong. We played superb football and the crowd loved it. The publicity was great for the club. Then the rain and the winter came. The pitches cut up, the tackling got ridiculous as defenders saw us as trophies, and the fantasy football we had played wasn't always possible. In one match at Wolves, we were 5-0 down when goalkeeper Jerry Peyton cleared the ball and it dropped down in a puddle between George and I on the halfway line. We looked at each other all covered in mud and he said "Marshy, what the fuck are we doing here?" That was the match after which I came out with my now, infamous quote, "Football in England is a grey game, played on grey days by grey people" and I meant it. This was not how I wanted to play the game.

George and I were targets for those big alehouse defenders with not even a third of our ability. I was a target more than George because they had more respect for him. I was kicked in every game, and there were lumps coming off me on Saturday evenings. There was one player who did me badly, Colin Waldron of Southampton I believe his name was, and he went straight through the back of me and left me with a terrible ankle injury. "Why am I doing this?" I asked myself as I was carried off. It could only be for the money.

That was in February, and I spoke to manager Bobby Campbell about going back to Tampa. He told me to stick it out until the end of the season because at Fulham they had a system where you only got your signing on bonus if you saw out a full season. I told him to stick it, because being kicked by lesser players who saw George and I as a prize was not my idea of fun.

Campbell was a good coach although not a great manager. Bobby was everything Alec Stock wasn't. Put the two of them together and you would have had an outstanding manager. Campbell was good on the training ground and he communicated well as a coach. He was teetotal and this led to a hilarious story Bobby Moore told me of the night before a cup-tie. By this time I had gone back to America and apparently Bobby Campbell decided to spend the night at a London hotel and travel by coach early on the morning of the game. There was only one problem with that plan; they couldn't find George Best on Friday night. He'd gone missing.

Picture the scene: Bobby Campbell, Bobby Moore, physio Ron Woolnough and Chairman Ernie Clay, sitting in the lobby of the hotel at ten o'clock at night. All the players are in their rooms apart from one, George Best. "Where could he be, Bobby?" Campbell asked Moore. "He might have gone to a little wine bar just off Berkley Square," said Bobby, and so they all got into Clay's Rolls Royce and headed off into the night to find the missing George. Campbell spent the entire journey looking out of the window and muttering to himself, "George, what are you doing? I'm going to have to fine you."

The barman at the wine bar said he was in earlier, and that he might have gone to Puzzi's another favourite of his. Back in the car the Fulham contingent got, and headed off to Puzzi's. Campbell was still agitated and talking to himself, saying, "You're fined two weeks wages George…no I can't do that." It was the same story at Puzzi's. No George and they were told to look at Tramps. Back in the roller and off to Tramps. Campbell was now talking loudly to himself. "Bestie, you are on the transfer list and no longer a part of this club." By the time they got to Tramps, Bobby was in a state. "I am the manager of Fulham Football Club," he announced to the doorman, "and I am here to get George Best." "He's downstairs," came the reply, and sure enough, there was George, sitting at the end of the bar sipping his drink and talking to anyone he fancied. Bobby strode up to him, his face like thunder, with a speech rehearsed and said loudly "George, let's have a bottle of champagne." Two hours later, they got back into Clay's Rolls and Bobby was pissed. He couldn't drink. One drink with George and he was out cold. Priceless. And that, my friends, is the effect George had on people. He got away with anything because of who he was.

I want to put something straight here, and that is that people have always said George and I were very close. Indeed, great friends. We weren't. We played together for years, went out a lot, and had years of great times. We shared highs and lows, and his deterioration as a person because of the booze will live with me forever, but we were never close. We were buddies, that's all. I never once really opened up my life to George and he didn't to me.

George transcended all parts of life, from the bus driver in the corner of the pub, to pop-stars and Prime Ministers. They all wanted the same conversation about football; "What about him?" "That goal was offside," "No it wasn't." It didn't matter who you were, you were all the same to George Best.

Malcolm Wagner once told me that Rod Stewart once turned up at the Slack Alice nightclub in Manchester, which George part-owned. He asked around if George Best was in, and was told that he'd be coming along later. Stewart waited at the bar, sipping his drink and looking conspicuous. But he'd made up his mind that he wanted to see George and tonight was the night. When George arrived and went over to meet Stewart for the first time, Rod, who was one of the biggest names in the pop world couldn't speak; such was the magnetism of Best. Stewart apparently was over-awed. That evening ended, I understand with George having to pull Rod to one side and tell him to buy a round of drinks. There were a few in the group as the drinks flowed, and Stewart hadn't once put his hand in his pocket. My lasting memories of George? The wonderful player who mesmerised opponents and the public. The playboy out there on the pitch, dancing his way through games and winning them on his own. There are not enough videos around to do him justice. Then, I remember him as everyone's friend, skipping into the bar and ordering Dom Perignon all round. That is why people loved him; he was never untouchable to the public, not like so many so-called superstars today.

Finally, the broken man I saw on that morning in hospital just minutes before he died. Different images, yet always the same George Best.

I went to his Memorial Service at Stormont in Ireland, and I made sure I got there early. I was sitting alone in my pew when a security man came up to me, introduced himself and asked me to go with him. I followed him through dark corridors and had no idea where he was taking me. It was quite intimidating, and at first I thought there'd been a bomb scare and he was leading me to safety. Finally, we came to a large oak door, which creaked as it was pushed open, and there inside, as I remember, was Manchester United manager Sir. Alex Ferguson, along with Chief Executive David Gill, Ole Gunnar Solskjaer, now a youth team coach at Old Trafford, and former manager Wilf McGuinness. It was the Old Trafford inner sanctum. The boot room, if you like. "Come in, Rodney, have a cup of tea. I saw you sitting there on your own," Fergie said. I appreciate Ferguson doing that for me, it was a nice gesture and I always shake his hand when I see him around these days.

There was only one thing to talk about and that was the life and times of George Best. It is a never-ending story because there will never be another like him. He was a one off, a priceless player and person.

He was a world-class talent who drank himself to death. His is, in so many ways, a sad story. I, for one, will never forget him.

8

Manchester City - It's All My Fault

My arrival at Manchester City caused so many splits between the players, the fans and the directors that I blame myself for the club's fall from grace. I didn't mean to do it, I was just a player. I had no idea it was happening at the time, but when you look back at the history of the club, I think you'd have to conclude that I was the iceberg to Man City's Titanic, and that they're only just starting to recover, all these years later.

While I was playing for Queens Park Rangers I'd seen how well Man City were doing. I thought they were one of THE best teams going, not just at the highest level of English football but all over Europe. The fact they'd won the Cup Winners Cup and they had international players all over the pitch, like Wyn Davies of Wales, Mike Summerbee, Colin Bell, Franny Lee and Willie Donachie. I knew at the time that they'd won six trophies in five years, including the Charity Shield, so they were absolutely at the pinnacle of the game.

I thought so highly of City that's it's probably the only club I would have joined. I would never have gone to Manchester United because they already had Bestie, Denis Law and Bobby Charlton. I turned down Tottenham and Newcastle. Both had offered the same transfer fee as City, which was around £200,000, a lot of money at that time. One of my QPR team mates, Roger Morgan, ended up signing for Spurs as I signed for Manchester City.

We had such a great team at QPR, which meant that a lot of managers were looking at our players, including people like Gerry Francis who went on to become England captain. I was so happy at QPR and had a fantastic seven seasons there. The crowd loved me and I'd have felt I was deserting Rangers to go to another London club like Arsenal or Spurs.

My only motivation for leaving was that I felt I had to play at a higher level. QPR were easily beating teams like Leicester for example, who included world-class players like Gordon Banks; in fact, we stuffed four past him. I wanted to be part of top football and I had an agreement with the chairman, Jim Gregory, that if we didn't get promoted back to the First Division that season, he'd let me go. He honoured that agreement.

I knew a lot about City, I knew all the players, some of them personally. Mike Summerbee was my first contact when I played for England. Bell, Lee and Summerbee were all in the squad and I went to my first England party with Mike in 1971, which was the year before I joined City.

England had played Switzerland, and in those days we used to have a lock-in. Many of the players would go to a bar with a lock in and we'd be there until 5 o'clock in the morning and we'd do all sorts. We'd be drinking and gambling, listening to the music, playing cards and having a great time. Sometimes a couple of strippers would turn up and put on a show and all that sort of nonsense. It was all private, and the media boys would be there as well, though they knew the score and that what happened at the parties stayed within those four walls.

Bobby Moore was our leader and as England captain he kept everything together. Bobby Moore was great, a gentleman. He was the senior man, and I was a young player who'd only just got in the team.

As far as the move to Manchester City is concerned, I remember someone calling me, a go-between, because a direct approach wasn't allowed. I think it was a City director called Chris Muir. He asked me, "If Manchester City were to approach you about a move to Maine Road, would you be interested? We're not going to approach you if you're going to say no." We'd call that tapping up these days.

The City manager Joe Mercer couldn't have called me himself, so this was the back door approach, ahead of a formal request. I told him that I would be very interested because I had a gentleman's agreement that I could leave at the end of the season. Mr Muir pushed it further and wondered, "Well, what about now?" I told him it would be up to the QPR Chairman to decide, because my agreement with him only kicked in at the end of the season, but I told him I would be happy to make the move if he agreed.

Malcolm Allison, Joe Mercer's coach, later called me to tell me that a formal approach was being made, also discussing the role he envisioned for me, and what part I'd play in the team. He told me what I already knew, that they were a great team. He was selling the club to me though he didn't really need to; I already knew I'd fit into it brilliantly. So when the QPR Chairman called me I was happy to sign, as per our agreement.

I knew of Malcolm but I didn't actually know him personally. I found out later that he had actually tried to sign me three other times for City. He had a scout, Arthur Shaw, who'd reported back two or three times that I was playing brilliantly for QPR, but he'd never been able to do the deal, until then.

Jim Gregory acted with great dignity and great professionalism by letting me go to City, as he'd promised. £200,000 was a fortune at the time, (1972) about the equivalent of around £40 million today. It was hard leaving QPR, but I knew that I had about four or five years of my career left and I wanted it to be at the top level.

Malcolm met me at the airport. It was just pandemonium. Malcolm, being very showbiz-y, had called a few friends, and they'd called their friends, and there were loads of people, masses of media and everything. Malcolm gave a short press conference and then took me for something to eat.

My contract as I remember was something like £200 a week basic, based on the transfer fee, appearance money of another £100, and then a win bonus and a crowd bonus. After the first few games the lads were all over me, because the average crowd had been about 32,000 before I'd arrived, and then suddenly it was around 53,000, which was a massive, massive increase. There were 20,000 more people watching the games, and the rest of the players were also on a crowd bonus, so they loved it.

I unashamedly take the credit for that. What else could it have been down to, apart from my arrival? They'd won the title a couple of years earlier and still only averaged 33,000. They'd won the FA Cup too, but the average crowd had stayed the same, so it was entirely down to me! That was part of what Malcolm had said to me. He'd said, "We're a great football team but we're not a showbiz team and we can't get any more people to come to the games."

I put Manchester City in a different perspective and the fact that things happened so quickly was a testament to how big the whole thing was, because at the same time Manchester United had signed Ian Storey-Moore, which received no great recognition. The publicity City had got when they signed me was enormous. I was a bit of a marquee signing at the time, a bit like Robinho's arrival at City when the new rich owners came in.

City put me up at the best hotel in town, which proved to be a problem for me. I was eating the wrong foods in the hotel and snacking, instead of having a proper diet. I was also carrying a groin strain that I'd got at QPR about three weeks earlier, which had forced me to miss a couple of games, so I wasn't fit. I'll hold my hands up on that.

At the end of that first few months at City, during the summer, my family - Jean and my kids Joanna and Jonathan, who were four and two - moved up, but for that first three months they stayed in London and I was in Manchester; alone.

Mike Summerbee helped me a lot in those early days, advising me on how to buy a house and other things that I needed to do; which were the best schools, etc. Mike and Franny were brilliant to me. Franny took me out fishing and we did other different things together, stuff I'd never done before.

We went to Westhoughton, by the side of a little stream that runs through the area. I remember getting up at 4am on the morning he took me fishing. We had these little miniature bottles of brandy and sat on the bank, freezing cold, catching nothing, but just chatting away without any cares. I loved listening to him talking. It was really good and we had a great time.

There we were, at the height of our fame, sat in our wellies, fishing. Franny was an England International, he'd just played in the World Cup finals, and I'd just joined City for the biggest transfer fee in their history. Yet there we were on the banks of the river, fishing. International Playboys, fishing. We didn't catch anything, though that was the plan, but it always seemed to be a bad day and we'd inevitably get soaking wet. I always had a smashing time and I was really happy in Manchester.

I remember a lot about my debut against Chelsea. I knew I wasn't 100% fit and Malcolm had very cleverly left my debut for a home game. I'd trained for two weeks before I played, during which I'd thrown up a couple of times, because I couldn't compete with people like Alan Oakes, Mike Doyle, Willie Donachie and Belly. Their fitness was so superior to mine. They were all very, very fit.

Malcolm had picked a home game where he knew we'd be favourites. There were over fifty thousand fans there and the atmosphere was sensational. As soon as I walked out of the tunnel, I was mobbed by reporters from TV, radio, newspapers, and photographers - everyone. It was very adrenaline sapping. The rest of the players were warming up and I was just posing for pictures and chatting to people.

Then came what I regard as the most significant moment of my time at City. A small section of the Kippax Stand crowd, which was opposite where the players came out, started singing a song. It was to the tune of "Son of My Father" by Chicory Tip, which was a big hit at that time. It was only a few of them at first, singing, "Oh Rodney, Rodney, Rodney, Rodney, Rodney, Rodney, Rodney Marsh".

Within two or three minutes the whole stadium was singing the same song. During my time in Manchester, at every game, they sang that song. It had never been sung to me by the QPR fans or anyone else, it was unique to the City fans, and was sung to me by them on my debut. It must have simply been a few wags in the crowd who thought of it, but it meant a lot to me.

Speaking more generally though, part of the problem I had at City, was that I had such self-confidence. My attitude to football was, and this will sound terribly cocky, that I was THE player and that the other players were my extras. It was like I was the headline act in a play in a theatre, or in a movie. I always looked at myself in that way, even if I was playing for England.

I was never over-awed by anybody and I think it was because of that attitude that I would play in an arrogant manner, although that meant I intimidated and upset some of my opponents and even my own team mates.

It's part of the reason I believe that Mike Doyle hated me. To my face Mike would always tell me I was brilliant and be grateful for the money he'd made on the crowd bonus and for being part of a team that was winning games. At the same time he was stabbing me in the back. I never really got to the bottom of it all, but I suspect that was the reason. Maybe one day Mike Doyle will reveal why he hated me. I could always feel it and sense it, but I could never change it.

When I walked into the City dressing room for the first time, I felt like I was there to make them a better team, though I never actually said that.

I know there was a bit of resentment towards me. I think Glyn Pardoe was one of those that felt that way, as did Tony Book, but Tony Towers, Summerbee and Lee were different.

I'm not sure how Colin Bell felt. He is, in my opinion, an enigma as both a player and a person. Still to this day I've never felt like I know him. I always thought there was something deeper in Colin that he's never allowed to come out and I've got no idea what that might be. I still don't know how Colin Bell felt or feels about me, even now.

There were a certain number of players that were for Joe Mercer, and a certain number who were for Malcolm. Joe Mercer didn't want me in the squad, but Malcolm Allison did - I found that out later. The Board of Directors were split too, with some backing Malcolm's judgement and others on Joe's side.

When City signed me I put a wedge through the whole football club, from the boardroom to the management and from the players to the fans; but I was unaware of it at the time. I was a footballer who just loved playing the game. I had no knowledge of all the politics between the Alexander's and Peter Swales and all those kinds of people.

Later in life, I've come to realise that I'd caused, unwittingly, a division through the football club. Even today some people say I was great, others say I fucked the club up. People who've never seen me play tell me that that's what their parents have told them, that I still divide people.

The first time I became aware of the resentment some players had towards me was when one of them said, "Watch out for Mike Doyle, he keeps calling you behind your back." I come from a place in the East End of London, where if you've got a problem with somebody, they tell you to your face and it's either sorted out or not, as the case may be, but at least you know where you stand.

When I came up North, I'd been led to believe that Northerners, generally speaking, were the type who would also be straight to your face. The overwhelming majority of them are that way, so it surprised me to find this a little different.

People have told me recently that he hates me more now than he ever did before, because of my success on Sky Sports; I was told that in October 2008, at a golf tournament in Mere. Hate is a strong word.

I don't think I'm a person that has made any difference in this world, although I might have had an effect on Manchester City. We've all seen what's happened to City since 1972, which shows I did make a huge difference.

I accept the blame for losing the First Division title in 1972. That season was a nightmare for me. I really do accept the blame for that. Over the years, people have tried to slice it and dice it. Mike Summerbee once said, and what a great quote, "Rodney was the right player at the wrong time," and I agree with that.

It was my fault because I completely upset the balance. I can remember a few games we played towards the end of that season, like Derby County at home. We absolutely slaughtered them and I had a great game, personally. As a team we were passing the ball and moving; it was brilliant. We won 2-0 but it could have been 10-0. We absolutely played them off the park, but speaking generally, I'd upset the balance of the team.

Wyn Davies was rarely involved with the first team, and after I got there he only played now and again. Before I'd arrived, City had developed a pattern of play where any time they were under pressure they could launch it to Wyn, he would get it and knock it down, keep possession and hold it up, whereas I was never a "hold up" type of player, I was a ball player.

I've heard some people suggest I was a ball holder, but that wasn't true. I was a ball player in the old sense of the expression. Give me the ball and I'd try and knock it off first time, if I could. I created plenty of goals for Colin Bell, many of them tap-ins from five yards out. They were all first time passes or flicks. I always saw myself as being a ball player.

Colin Bell criticised me in his book for overplaying, and I accept that. At times I did, and I know that it slowed down the momentum of attacks, but I only did that now and again. The majority of the time I didn't. I'd only hold onto the ball when I felt it was appropriate.

I remember playing a game at Maine Road against Middlesbrough in September

1975, at a time when they were flying under their manager Jack Charlton, but we beat them 4-0 and I scored two. We absolutely murdered them. During that game I was juggling and flicking the ball and just enjoying playing football. I did indulge myself from time to time, but I still think Colin's wrong in his overall assessment, respectfully wrong, because there were times when I played the ball incisively, and early and I used to enjoy that as much as anything else. That Middlesbrough game was one of the best I ever had for City.

I remember my first Old Trafford derby, where we won 3-1. I came on as a substitute and scored shortly after Mike Doyle had been dragged off by Malcolm Allison. Doyle was absolutely fuming when he was brought off. I scored more or less straight away. I think that was another major part of the reason Doyle hated me. After that game he said, "You never win anything with players like Rodney Marsh." He said that on TV and I thought at the time, that's something you keep within your own camp, you don't go on TV saying things like that. If you've got a problem like that, say it to the person involved.

He was 100% right though, if we'd won the League Cup Final in 1974, it would have been different. Other clubs won things with me in the team though: QPR, three years earlier, became the only team to win a double as a Third Division team; the title and the League Cup.

That will probably never happen again, so you can win things with Rodney Marsh, it was City that couldn't win things with Rodney Marsh. Doyle was right though, so I respect his comments!

My first full season at City, the year after we missed out on the title, was terribly disappointing. I think there was an undercurrent in the team that was suffering a hangover from the previous season. I think there was a hangover from the previous Chairman, Eric Alexander, Peter Swales, Malcolm and Joe Mercer. Then there was Mike Doyle's little group of people that was against me, which I didn't fully understand, and all that residue carried over into the next season.

From City's point of view it was a disaster. Even though we finished half way up the League Table, that wasn't acceptable. There were loads of games where I scored and the team won but it just wasn't enough.

I wasn't really aware of all that stuff at the time, but I can see it now, with the benefit of hindsight. I was as fit as ever. We'd gone to Sweden in pre-season and I was on fire when I came back, as were the rest of the team. I hadn't seen any of it coming. I wasn't thinking about the Mike Doyle thing or anything like that, I just wanted to play football. That's all I ever wanted to do.

When I look at Wayne Rooney today, I see myself. I don't mean as a player, comparing him and me but purely for the love of football. You can see it on his face he just loves to play and that's what I did. I was never into the politics.

My family had moved North by the beginning of that season. I was out of the hotel and in my own house, I was settled and happy, and so were they. During the mid-part of the summer I'd trained, by myself, at Cheadle. I used to do 220's on my own because I knew I had to be fit for pre-season, and I really enjoyed it all. I did the same thing, later in my career at Tampa Bay in 1979. I was doing 2000 sit ups a day when I was in the States because I was trying to get fit for the start of my final season. I wanted to play well.

Joe Corrigan, who was always one of the last to leave training at City, will tell you how hard I trained. He'll confirm that I was always the last to leave training. Mike Summerbee and me would hit volleys and shots at Joe and he would make saves, almost on a daily basis. It was never my job to track back, during games, like they seem to have to do these days. I never liked to do it and I was never good at it. The only time I did, I gave away a goal at Wembley in the League Cup Final in 1974. I tracked back and stuck out my foot and the ball went straight from a cross into the middle of the goal into the reach of John Richards, and he scored the goal that won the game. I didn't like doing that and I thought there were other players who did it much better than me anyway.

You can't compare eras, the 70's to the 90's or whatever. There are players that are good at what they do, whenever they play. For example, in my team, Mike Doyle was a terrific footballer, regardless of our clash of personalities and the fact that he hated me. If I'm being honest, he was a very good footballer. He had a good brain, a good understanding of the game, but he was never going to score loads of goals a season, because he wasn't good enough to do that. If he had been, he'd have been a centre forward.

I could not do the things he could do defensively but I could make and score goals. I couldn't chase back and get the ball off the opposition, because I'd give away stupid fouls. My abilities were best displayed in the final third. I used to get kicked to pieces and get elbowed and punched and fouled but I played at the sharp end of the football pitch.

With today's training, psychology and diets etc, I would walk into any Manchester City team. Could a Rodney Marsh type player, in the way I used to play, get in the modern side? Yes. If I did, they'd have to build the team around me, because I wouldn't fit into the system that they tend to play. Having said that, Tevez is a little bit of a floater, like I was, and I think City have been playing around Tevez, allowing him to be that player, so yeah, I think I could do that.

The split of Joe Mercer and Malcolm Allison was rooted in their difference of opinion over me, without a shadow of a doubt. There were two distinct factions among the board of directors. Mr Alexander, who was a lovely man, Ian Niven and Chris Muir were on Malcolm's side.

Peter Swales seemed to just want to knife someone in the back and I was never sure which side he was on. His own, probably.

Malcolm was, without a doubt, the best coach I ever worked with and I've worked with some great ones, but he was the best. Later he lost his way. He fell in love with the theory of the game rather than the game itself, and he was trying to do things for the sake of doing them, rather than working on a game based on the players.

Here's a perfect example, which I saw for myself. He went to the USA in the mid 1980's. I was there with Tampa Bay Rowdies, and was on the panel that interviewed him for the position of coach of the national side. During the interview, he said he would only pick players that were over six feet tall, because of the need for height at dead ball situations. He wanted all his players to be powerful, strong and big. The USA had tremendous athletes.

We asked him, "What if there was a fantastic player who was only 5'8?" and his answer was, "I wouldn't have him." Malcolm had fallen in love with the theory of football not the reality. Anyone with a brain would have said, "If it's Maradona, you'd have him." I think Malcolm lost his way - in football and in life. At City, when I first joined, he was at the peak of his powers.

There are managers I've seen and worked for that don't have one tenth of Malcolm's ability. Two of his great strengths were recognition and correction. Recognising what's going on in a game and having the ability to correct it. Most managers that I've ever known would come in at half time, throw a cup around and shout and jump up and down, saying stuff like, "You're not marking him, what happened for the corner?" Malcolm would come in and say, "Willie, (Donachie) you're too tight on the winger, I want you to drop off and Tony Towers, you drop back in the gap." He'd give specific help that would actually make a difference.

He'd say things like, "Their centre forward is moving you around too much Tommy, (Booth) we're going to make a change there." Malcolm was best at that sort of correction and advice. People today tell me that Mourinho is just like that, so perhaps Malcolm was the Mourinho of his day.

Personally, I never had an ego clash with Malcolm. He was one of the few people I knew who lived in his own cocoon. He wouldn't take any notice of anyone. He would listen to what others had to say, but he wouldn't act on it. He would just do his own thing all the time, though he was never rude.

He gave me some great advice. He was the first person who spoke to me about passing at goal. I'd never done that before. We'd go out training and he'd have me passing the ball at the corner instead of slashing at it or trying to power it. We also worked together on my heading, something else I'd never worked on before.

What Malcolm didn't go through with me, which later in life might have proved to be a great help, was my movement. I was a player who played on instinct, with natural ability, but I think I could have benefitted from being coached to move a little bit better. I'm talking about my movement when we were in possession. I used to just put my hands in the air, and rely on intuition when the ball was knocked up to me. Other players would make a run and then check and stop to make time and space for themselves but I never used to do that.

What people don't know is that Malcolm would sometimes call me into his office to tell me what he was going to be doing, tactically, and why and what my role was in that system etc. He would ask for my input before he implemented things sometimes.

I've previously mentioned how Malcolm talked to me when he started to consider leaving City and to drop down two divisions. Crystal Palace were in the Third Division and City were a top First Division team, but he told me the reason he was going down there was to be closer to Serena Williams, his mistress. He knew he'd brought me to City, in a massive deal, and he wanted to know if I had a problem with him moving down to Crystal Palace. I told him that he had to do what he had to do, for himself. He took that on board, and it was as simple as that.

I did go out with Serena and Malcolm on many occasions, whenever the team travelled to London. We'd meet up and have dinner together and a bottle of champagne. If anybody says there was a different reason he left, they don't know the truth. There might have been problems behind the scenes, in the boardroom etc, but I can only tell you what he told me and how I reacted.

We were never really friends in the truest sense, but I think that's probably what Malcolm would've liked us to have been. Malcolm loved football players and absolutely idolised Colin Bell. In our conversations, he would mention things about "Nijinsky" and all that stuff, and of course that nickname stuck. He loved footballers and he loved us all, the team.

I remember Joe Mercer as a gentleman. We had very little to talk to each other about, but he was a gentleman in every sense of the word. I'd say he made no impact on me whatsoever as a player or a person. He was too nice, as a man, to ever express any resentment towards me.

I was captain at City for two seasons. When I became skipper, I began to get more feedback from all the other players. That's when I began to hear about the big split I'd caused between Malcolm and Joe, but Joe had never said anything about that to me. As far as I'm aware, he never said a bad word about me.

I can't remember the specifics of the split between Joe and Malcolm, but Joe was the manager and Malcolm was the coach. In my second year at City Joe left and Malcolm took over both roles.

Joe's departure made no difference whatsoever to me and I don't mean that callously. There's always been another side to me that you don't see. The way I grew up prepared me for all the rotten, shit aspects of life, so almost nothing really bothers me. Whether Joe Mercer lost his job or even if it had been Malcolm, or the Chairman of the Directors, it wouldn't have fazed me at all.

Whether Joe Mercer moved on in his life or Malcolm moved on to Crystal Palace, when his time came, I didn't care. I realise those comments might shock and hurt.

I'm big enough and ugly enough to hold my hands up. It was Rodney Marsh that upset everything at City. Things before that had been going so well. I would be stupid to say they weren't.

If City had started winning trophies again, within five or ten years, everything would have been put to rest, but the fact that we've not even been close for so long, suggests it's been down to me.

There has always been one thing I have cared desperately about, still do and always have done, and that is my respect for the way the City fans treated me. I wanted to go out in every game with the aim of entertaining them and to win, and I never lost that or my respect for those fans. I still have a huge affection for the City fans. Man City is always the first result I look for.

If the fans hadn't reacted to me in that way, I wouldn't have given a shit about that either, which is sad to say. But the fact they did means they have my eternal gratitude because they treated me sensationally.

I've never had a better relationship with fans than at City. It was so personal. It was a personal relationship with 50,000 people, if that's possible.

I remember games where we'd be winning and I'd put my foot on the ball and look up at the Kippax Stand and they'd all cheer, even though all I'd done was look up at them. I felt like their conductor. The fans warmed to me, and me to them. It was a special time that couldn't have been replicated anywhere else.

It was never that personal anywhere else. At Tampa Bay Rowdies I had a fantastic relationship with the fans, and at QPR too, but it was more team-related. At

QPR, I was part of the team that won the Championship and the double. I believe I was the first Third Division player capped by England, but it was all team-orientated. At City, it was personal and I sensed that. People still write to me today, inviting me to events and saying nice things, all these years later. Maybe it was so special because it couldn't be repeated anywhere else. I still get choked up when I hear, "Oh Rodney, Rodney...."

After Malcolm and Joe left City, there was Johnny Hart, Ron Saunders and Tony Book as managers in quick succession - and by the way, I take absolutely no blame for that quick turnover. All those different managers saw me as a different player. The players felt that, during Johnny Hart's time in charge, I should be left out. Ken Barnes, who was involved with the reserves and youth team, at that time, told me that.

Their opinions had no effect on me, and I just wanted to play. I was a footballer and that was my job. I got on great with Ken because he'd always tell it as he saw it. He was never frightened of telling me I'd been useless, if I had been. On other days he'd tell me I'd been fantastic. With Ken a spade was a spade. One day he told me, "The lads want you out of the team, they've told me." I just thought, "What will be, will be." It was no skin off my nose; I'd just keep playing, whenever I was asked.

My opinion of Johnny Hart was only negative. As a man he was nice, but I found him to be quite a weak person. That's not good, bad or indifferent. I'm not criticising him, that's just what he was. I never signed up for Johnny Hart, but he'd suddenly been thrust upon me as my manager. I gave it no thought whatsoever, because I couldn't really see him going on and being manager, long term. I relate to, and admire, strong people.

Johnny Hart then had a health problem and Ron Saunders came in. The whole time of Hart, and then Ron Saunders, was incredibly insipid. It was as though everyone was going through the motions. The football club was just in limbo. It had suffered this catastrophic hitting of the iceberg by signing Rodney Marsh, and the club was now limping along on one engine out of six, going nowhere.

Saunders was all over the place. I didn't think he knew how to manage big players, and City had several. By that time, we'd signed Denis Law, so we had Marsh, Summerbee, Lee, Colin Bell and Denis Law – all big players, and he just didn't know how to handle us. Despite that, we still got to the League Cup Final against Wolves, but Tony Book took over before the end of the season.

In my opinion, signing Denis Law was an incredible mistake for the club, but I didn't care. I didn't express my views at the time, but I knew Denis Law was finished long ago by the time he came to City for his second spell. I was fighting fit. Denis was at the other extreme, and he had an injury.

Denis Law was my idol growing up, but when we signed him I thought, "Why are we signing a crippled old man?" All this, after the club had hit the Rodney Marsh iceberg!

During my second full season, Colin Bell almost single-handedly ran the club, as a player and with his performances. He was absolutely brilliant. I can remember it vividly. Without Colin, that season would have been a disaster. Without him we could have been in the bottom four or five. The respect I have had throughout my life for Colin came from that season.

I didn't play in the last game of that season, when Denis Law scored the goal at Old Trafford against United. I remember the game very clearly though, because I was the one that told Tony Book to take him off. I was sat next to Tony, in my civvies, because I couldn't play due to a groin injury.

I could see that scoring that goal had badly affected Denis Law. He was devastated. His face was drawn and I knew that was the end of him. When people write up history and look for defining moments, I think they'll say it changed his life.

Denis Law became a bitter, resentful man. When I was young, I used to sleep in a number ten Manchester United jersey, even though I didn't support the team, but my family got me this number ten jersey and I'd sleep in it, like pyjamas. I idolised Denis Law. In the end, I looked at him as just being a bitter man and I think part of that was his back heel against United, the team he'd played for, for so many years. He, in essence, got them relegated; even though we know that was not absolutely the case, to everybody else it looked that way.

I thought that changed his life, only he will know for sure. I'm only guessing. He did become a grumpy old man though. He obviously thought he should never have done that. When he left United, he should have gone to Preston or Burnley or somewhere like that, but not City, where he'd then had to score such a significant goal. I always thought that it was a life altering experience for Denis.

He won't talk about it, and he would never play football again. He never even played charity games. Whenever he was asked about that goal, and he's still the same, he'd just blank whoever asked him.

He became edgy and obviously it was a devastating thing to happen to him, but he's got to live his life with that. I didn't see Denis Law again until 1994, and by then he had become a bit of a miserable bastard. The change in his personality was staggering. He was great when I first knew him, but by then his face looked like thunder and he seemed soulless, he didn't even laugh. I didn't want to be around him, and he probably didn't want to be around me either.

He was never the happiest person, but by scoring against United that day, he must have felt that he'd let his old fans down. He was like Judas, spent all his life with a team and then went back and scored the goal that relegated them, his team. You couldn't get a bigger Judas, and I think he knew that. The fact that he'll never talk about it probably indicates that I'm right.

We had a great run in the League Cup that season - all the way to the final. I scored three or four goals too, which was nice. We completely outplayed Wolves in the final for the whole game but lost 2-1. We played them off the park. I didn't go and collect my runners-up tankard that day, but it wasn't through being emotional, it was the frustration of not winning. I called the Football Association on the Monday asking if I could have my tankard and they told me that wasn't going to happen, in no uncertain terms. I'd refused to go up the steps for it. I actually respect the Football Association for their decision.

I didn't care what other people thought, at that time. This is part of the problem I've had over the years, people read too much into the things I say and do. People ask me what I was thinking, at that time. I didn't care enough about anything to give it a second thought, that's the reason I've made so many mistakes in my life. That tankard could be worth a couple of grand on Ebay these days to a City punter, and I just walked out and left it!

I was devastated by the fact we'd lost. I thought it was my fault, because I gave away the winning goal and I was upset because I couldn't prove Mike Doyle wrong. That's just it. It is what it is. Would I do things differently if I could go back in time? I'd have to give that a lot of thought. Most things I've done, I wouldn't change.

When I came out of the jungle, after "I'm a Celebrity, Get Me Out of Here," I did an interview. I got involved in a shouting match with a couple of people and I was asked that question, about the regrets in my life. Lynne Franks was one of those I'd had problems with. In that interview I said, "I can't regret anything in my life, and I wouldn't change things because if I did I wouldn't be Rodney Marsh, I'd be somebody else."

I do look at myself from the outside sometimes, that's why sometimes I refer to myself as Rodney Marsh, in the third person. Sometimes it's like I'm debating things with myself. I'm glad I'm the only Rodney Marsh in this world, because it would definitely be a strange world if everyone was like me!

It was a big day for me when Barney Daniels joined City. Francis Lee left and Tony Book simply said to the players one day, "I'm bringing in Barney Daniels." I shook my head. Franny Lee, a world-class player, replaced by Barney Daniels from Telford.

"If we get a free kick anywhere within 35 yards of the goal, Barney Daniels will be taking them," Book told us. I can remember thinking to myself that the football club was going nowhere. He did take a few free kicks, and most of them ended up in row z. He was a lovely boy and a smashing bloke, but he couldn't play football. At least to Manchester City standards.

Here he was, wearing the number nine for Manchester City Football Club. I couldn't help thinking, "Summerbee, Bell, Wyn Davies, Francis Lee, Rodney Marsh, Dennis Tueart and all these players, and now we've got Barney Daniels. Is this the future?"

It turned out, that from that point, the club went down and down and down. Franny had gone to Derby but was still a good player. Whoever made that decision got it completely wrong. It was an amazing ricket, because it was one, if not two years too soon. Derby won the league that season with Franny in their team. There was that famous piece of commentary from Barry Davies, when Franny scored against us at Maine Road at Christmas, when he said, "Just look at his face, look at his face."

The deterioration of City was obvious; it was there for everyone to see. We'd lost the greatest coach ever, there'd been a change of direction by the board of directors, three managers in one season, Barney Daniels was now our centre forward and Franny Lee, a world-class player, had gone to Derby County. You couldn't make this stuff up.

I've always said that Peter Swales was the worst thing that ever happened to Manchester City Football Club, ever. He'd jumped into the void that was created by the split in the board over my arrival. It was all the back dealings and behind the scenes crap that I hated. I can remember all sorts of deals going on at the time. We signed about half a dozen players that were never going to be good enough for City.

Even after I left, they were still signing players that were useless. We signed Steve Daley from Wolves and paid five times more than he was worth. The club was just going nowhere. I always thought Peter Swales was the person behind that, and still do.

He was involved in team selection and the recruiting of players. You could see by the type of people he hired that he didn't want strong characters in the club. It was only when it started to go wrong that he tried working with the fans, but by then it was too late. I don't know what my former team mates would say if you asked them now, but it was obvious to me that it had all gone wrong.

I've seen it happen at other top clubs like Leeds United and Derby County. I think Peter Swales was the catalyst that made everything implode, and even to this day the club is still trying to battle back.

As the club began to deteriorate, they seemed to be trying to get back to where they were so much so that they even brought Malcolm Allison back. They brought John Bond in too, but it was all nonsense.

Despite everything I could see going on around me, I still loved playing for City, and I loved all the interaction with the fans. I loved performing. I remember a game against Newcastle at Maine Road, where I scored a fantastic goal. I bent it and it skidded off the turf into the far corner. Willie McFaul was the goalkeeper and I nutmegged Jimmy Smith five times during the game. In the end he was chasing me around the pitch trying to kick me.

Every time I nutmegged him, the fans were going ballistic. I just loved being there. It was like I was their entertainer, they'd come to see me play and I loved that, I respected it and I loved it. I absolutely didn't want to leave.

It was funny really, because after four years at City, and just a fortnight after such a great performance at Arsenal, I was gone.

When they sacked me it was nothing to do with football. By that time, I'd turned people's opinions about me around. We'd scored loads of goals and were winning games, but my departure was because of my bust up with Chairman Peter Swales and manager Tony Book.

That was one of the key moments in my life. In my professional career I've always said that things didn't bother me, but that did, in a big way.

We'd had a series of fantastic games where we'd scored loads and loads of goals. I'd just scored the winning goal at Highbury against Arsenal in a fantastic 3-2 win, which had been a great game too, and I was captain.

The game that proved to be my last was at Maine Road against Burnley. We should have beaten them, since we completely played them off the park, but we drew 0-0. Ian MacFarlane, the assistant manager, and Tony Book, were jumping up and down throughout the match; they were furious because we weren't scoring.

After the game, we went back into the dressing room and Ian MacFarlane went absolutely ballistic at all the players. Dennis Tueart said, "Ian, calm down, calm down.

We're playing great and we haven't got beat." MacFarlane flew across the dressing room and threw a punch at Tueart, hitting him hard in the throat. Everyone was completely in shock. It was something so unexpected that it was incomprehensible. How this story hasn't come out over the years I have no idea. How it's not been repeated by Doyle, Oakes, or anyone else really surprises me. Maybe they were afraid, I don't know.

I went to Tony Book and asked what he was going to do about the incident, which several players had just seen, and he became very sheepish. MacFarlane walked out and very quickly other people started to find out what had happened. I thought Book was going to sack MacFarlane on the spot.

Can you imagine Alex Ferguson or Matt Busby, or whoever, reacting like that? They'd have sacked the coach on the spot. Can you imagine something like that happening in today's football, a coach hitting a player? They'd be out the door in a second.

On the Monday, Peter Swales called me and said, "Rodney, I understand you were very, very upset about the incident on Saturday, would you come in and talk about it? You're the captain and I want to hear your opinion about it." I told him that the coach hit a player in front of everyone, and that the manager should do something about it. I said you can't have that sort of behaviour in football.

I told Peter Swales that, as manager, Book should have done something that night, straight away. MacFarlane was a 6 ft 4, 17 stone Scotsman against Dennis Tueart. I said that I believed the incident was out of order.

Swales then asked me how I thought the team was playing. I said, "We just beat Arsenal 3-2 last week, so clearly we're playing well, but that's a separate issue." He then asked, "What's your opinion of Tony Book and Ian MacFarlane?" I'll never ever forget this, because I said to him, "Do you really want to know?" He said yes, be honest, so I told him that they were both fucking useless.

He was clearly shell-shocked, so I left his office and went back into the dressing room. Within ten minutes Book called me upstairs into in his office. He told me he'd just been speaking to the Chairman and asked if I had a problem with him.

I told him that I didn't actually have a problem with him, as such. I explained that Peter Swales had asked me what I thought about him and Ian MacFarlane. I told Book exactly how I'd replied to the question, word for word.

Book came back with, "How can I have you as my captain, if you have that opinion of me?" I told him that I believed in telling the truth. I went on to tell him how I felt about the way the team had been playing, that I felt there had been some marvellous performances, including my own. Dennis Tueart was playing great, as was Joe Royle up front, and Asa Hartford and Colin Bell were great in midfield.

Book's response was, "How can I go forward, knowing what you've said?" Of course that wasn't my problem; I was a footballer, simple as that.

He thought about it for about ten more minutes and then he said, clearly, I had no respect for him and I told him he was right. Two totally opposite people talking like a couple of strangers, not like manager and captain. "I'm going to transfer you." He asked me not to try and talk him out of his decision and I said I wouldn't, and said, "OK!" That's how my time at City came to an end. It was a terrible way for it to finish, but that's life.

As far as City were concerned, I'd seen myself being at the club forever and I wasn't going to change my personality and suddenly become a diplomat. I will toe the line as long as it's not hurting me, or the people around me. If you ask me a straight question, I'll give you a straight answer. I'd had reservations about Ian MacFarlane a year earlier, but I hadn't said anything, because he hadn't punched anybody at that stage.

I remember us playing Middlesbrough away, where we lost 3-0. I think Mike Summerbee was the captain that day. We were in the hotel, having a team meeting, and Tony Book would always defer to MacFarlane, probably just because he shouted. Book read out the team. MacFarlane said, "Lads, this is very important to me, this game. I was here with Jack Charlton and they sacked me. For me to go back to Middlesbrough is very, very," and then he burst into tears, "because I was so upset when they got rid of me".

He was sobbing and all the players were looking at each other thinking, "What the hell's going on here?" He was bawling his eyes out in a team meeting, trying to talk about how he got the sack from Middlesbrough. I looked at Summerbee and he was as stunned as I was.

I didn't say anything that day because it didn't seem relevant, and no one in authority had asked me. I had felt like going in and seeing Peter Swales there and then and saying, "Do you realise we've got this lunatic who's our coach?" but I didn't. I later found out he was on anti-depressants . So you see, there have been times where I would toe the line. But be sure of this: if you ask me a question, you'd better be sure you want the answer.

There have been millions of times when I've been incredibly positive and praised people, truthfully, like saying that Colin Bell is the greatest and most underrated player of all time. It's true, in my opinion. It can be negative or positive, I'll simply tell you what I feel.

What disappointed me the most about the incident that led to me leaving City was that Dennis Tueart never stood up for me. I stood up for him, but he never stood up for me, never said anything to anybody, and I got the sack.

Willie Donachie organised a drinks session for me to mark my departure. "You've been part of our lives," he said, "so we'll go to Slack Alice, George Best's club." The majority of the players turned up. I was sitting there with Joe Royle and Willie Donachie and we were having a laugh and a good time. I've always had the mentality of, "I don't give a shit." Something happens, it upsets you, and it did upset me, but then you move on.

We'd had a few drinks and the people who didn't like me at the club hadn't turned up, and that was fine too. Suddenly Dennis Tueart walked in, sober as a judge. He looked at me, held out his hand and said, "Rodney, I just want you to know that I don't think they treated you right." I looked him in the eye and just said, "Fuck off!" straight to his face, and he just walked away.

I never really got the chance to say goodbye to the fans because of the way it all ended. I didn't even get on the pitch again. I never played at Maine Road again, even in opposition. I went to America after that and then to Fulham, who were in a lower division. I had no idea, that day against Burnley, that it would be my last for City and at Maine Road.

About seven years after I left, I was back in Manchester while I was with the Tampa Bay Rowdies. We played three games in the North, at Leeds, Scarborough and Hull City. I stayed one night in Manchester and went to a little fish restaurant in Hale. I was with a few friends and we were laughing and joking and suddenly, in walked Peter Swales and sat down.

We looked at each other and I walked over to him and held out my hand. He shook it and said, "Rodney, you wouldn't believe the number of letters I got when I let you go. We got 7,000 letters of complaint." He didn't say anything else but at least he told me that.

Once I moved to Tampa Bay Rowdies, I put City behind me as much as I could emotionally, but I did say to myself, "What am I doing here?" It was clear to me that I was far better than all the other players. I'd make a 20 yard pass and a guy was running backwards instead of forwards. It made me look bad. I thought, "What have I done?" I suddenly realised though, that while it had not been a great footballing decision, it was the best thing I'd ever done for my family, moving to the States.

As I look back now, one thing I will always fondly remember is my first few minutes on the pitch for City. I scored some great goals and I was part of some great wins, and I scored some goals against United, in particular that one at Old Trafford.

My happiest times as a player were at City, though nationally and internationally most people seem to remember me more from QPR or Fulham. I don't know what it was about the dynamic of this cockney boy coming up North, but I just hit it off with the fans. I loved it. I said at one point that when I retired, I'd come back and live in Manchester, but life didn't work out that way. I got on great with the people of Manchester.

I feel as if my name should be up with the City greats around the stadium. The reason I'm not is because it's no longer a people's club. It's executive-run, and every decision is made by the board. I'm sure that if the names written around the stadium were decided by the people, then things would be different. One of the biggest things that offended me in recent years was when I was in America and someone sent me a link, on the Internet, to City's greatest players of all time. I was number eight.

Robinho was number five. I wanted to write in and say, "What the fuck do you think you're doing? You put me behind Robinho?" I take that as a personal insult. He didn't want to be there, he only came for the money, and his attitude was scandalous. Yes, I would absolutely agree that he is a fantastic talent, a brilliant, brilliant talent, but his attitude was absolutely awful and I've only seen him play a dozen times. He was number five and I was number eight. Who did that poll? But at least I was in the top ten!

As I get older, I've come to the point where I can see both sides. I couldn't when I was younger. As I've said before in this book, when I left England, I made a well-reported statement that football is a grey game, played on grey days by grey people. I absolutely meant that.

Today it's not like that, because there's so much going on and it's fantastic - I really love it. In those days though, at least it was for the supporters, and you'd argue about the game in the pub. Back then it was the people's game for the people, but not anymore.

I'll bet that the majority of modern football clubs don't give a flying toss about the fans. Are you telling me that people like the Glazer family actually care about the supporters, or that that the Liverpool owners care about the scousers? They don't even know the history of the football club. The people's game is no longer the people's game, and that's sad. If they asked, via the programme or a hand out, tell us your top twenty players throughout the history of Manchester City Football Club, and don't just write it down, think about it and go back and talk to your dad or your granddad and come back and tell us the top twenty players, I bet you it would be very different from the names around the stadium.

I think it's important now that I tell you what I thought about all the players I played with at City. Some will be upset, while others will be thrilled. There are plenty of City fans, the younger ones in particular, who never saw us play, so now they can hear it from a former player; a former captain.

Joe Corrigan, big and brave and manufactured, worked on his game as much as any player I've ever known in football. We would stay out after training almost every day, Joe and me, and sometimes Mike Summerbee. The reason Joe made rickets in the early days of his career was because sometimes he didn't adjust his feet quickly enough to the flight of the ball, but on a straight basis he could catch the ball and make saves. Ultimately Joe developed into one of the best goalkeepers City have ever had, but my guess is that he is probably even better as a goalkeeping coach than as a player

Tony Book was the most economical player who played within himself, and very few people got past him. He never passed the ball more than about 10 yards, played within his limitations, and is somebody I'd have in my team every time. He was capable of quick, quick recovery.

Willie Donachie should have been a left side midfield player. He should never have been a defender, because he was too good to be a defender. He could pass the ball and had two good feet. He could tackle, cross the ball and should have played further up the park.

As for Tommy Booth, if it wasn't for Bobby Moore and Jack Charlton, and later Roy McFarland, I'd have seen Tommy as a regular for England. Both attacking and defending, he was a fantastic header of the ball and a brilliant player, a brilliant footballer.

Alan Oakes was one of the most underrated players ever. He was a fantastic passer, and had a great engine that would easily get him up and down the pitch. He was a good leader and I've got a lot of respect for him.

Mike Doyle was a terrific player, I always liked him as a player. He could win the ball in a tackle, he was a good header, he could pass the ball all over short distances and get the occasional goal. He was a good captain.

Mike Summerbee was the best crosser of a ball I ever played with, ever. I would put him in the Beckham category. He scored goals and was a brave lad with great character. I'd have him in my team every time.

Colin Bell, well you know what I think about him. He was one of the greatest footballers ever. Nobody, to this day, gives Colin Bell the credit he deserves, for being as good as he was. He could do everything. If you saw him in training, on a daily basis, he could jump higher and further and could run faster and longer. He could head the ball better, and shoot with both feet. He was just an absolute world-class footballer and athlete. How, over the years, people never include him when they pick world teams, I just don't know.

Franny Lee was the cleverest, thinking player I ever played with. He knew how to dive to get free kicks, because people were pulling at him and kicking him, elbowing him, and all that, and he certainly made them pay for their indiscretions when the occasion rose. Franny was a top, top-drawer player. Summerbee, Bell, Lee and me, what a forward line!

Dennis Tueart, well, Joe Royle nicknamed him "Richard the Lionheart," because when it came to fifty-fifty tackles he always slowed up before the challenge. He would be very skilful, very direct but very lightweight. He had a lot of good skill, but I'd never pick Dennis Tueart to be a player in my team. I would go for Asa Hartford, even though they played in different positions. If I only had the choice of Dennis Tueart as my left sided player, and this isn't personal, I would play without a left sided player.

Joe Royle was the last of the great headers of a ball, and he could jump and hold in the air. He was better on the ground than everybody gave him credit for. He could score goals with both feet and had a head like a shoebox. He's been a friend, too, over the years.

Tony Towers I liked a lot as a person, but he got nowhere near to fulfilling his potential, much like Derek Jefferies, and I put that down to attitude.

Asa Hartford was a terrific little player. I'd have him in my team, or in my squad.

Peter Barnes was my kit boy. I always liked Peter; he had excellent skill and played for England. He was a bit lightweight, but had real natural ability.

In the case of Glyn Pardoe, I never played with him much, but I can remember that he never bought a round of drinks! We went on an end of season tour to Greece and all the lads went out for a beer one night in this Taverna place. There were seven or eight of us, and Glyn was one of the group. Summerbee bought a round, then I did, then it was Franny's turn. We had a few drinks and then it came to Glyn's round, so he said, "I've got to be going now." My reply was, "You're not walking out without buying a drink are you?" He simply said, "It's time to go now." "Buy a round!" I shouted and he went, "No, no, no, I've got to get going." Everybody laughed their bollocks off, it was hysterical. I give him the award for the tightest player. Great days.

People think that when I played, we were always out in nightclubs. The truth is that like today's footballers, on certain days of the week, after we'd come back from a game or we'd played at home, it was serious party time. In those days, most players did drink, not in moderation, in excess, but loads of players were like that. We'd talk about the game and would laugh and joke and some players would end up in a late-night drinker or casino. The time always seemed to go by very quickly.

I just heard a quote from Frank Lampard junior, in which he said that the difference between today's footballers and footballers when his dad, and Harry Redknapp, who's his godfather, were playing, was that in those days they'd do what they did with no fear that people would have mobile phones and all that stuff, and that's how it was. He is right.

My experience of Manchester was absolutely fantastic. I loved it, even when I got thrown out of pubs for doing things like wearing flip flops in the Admiral Rodney in Prestbury. They threw me out one day, because I was wearing flip flops, a pair of jeans and a t-shirt. "No bare feet in here!" It was all good fun.

I don't think anybody was ever squeaky clean, that would be a misrepresentation of what went on, but my sense tells me that today's footballers have got it harder than we did. You get away with less today than in the 1970s. Look at the WAGs today; Posh Spice says she went out to try and pull Ryan Giggs, but Beckham was the only one she could get. He was her second choice. I might be naïve but I don't think there were women around doing that in those days.

We went on this end of season tour when Mike was captain. I got to the airport and I bought a bottle of vodka for the trip, duty free. Franny bought a bottle of brandy and Summerbee bought a bottle of Jack Daniels. We'd planned to have it in the hotel rooms, like a cocktail before dinner or whenever.

We were on the plane going over, Malcolm was the coach. Franny and Mike were sitting together in the back and they'd had a few drinks on the plane and I'd had a few too. We got on the coach at the other end, with our duty free for the journey to the hotel. Franny and Mike were on the Jack Daniels at the back. Feeling no pain, we got to this magnificent Greek hotel, marble outside, and it was beautiful.

Waiting to meet us, stood outside, was the hotel's general manager, a couple of chambermaids with bunches of flowers, and all the staff lined up either side. We all got off and Franny was smoking a cigar and Mike, the captain, walked up to the general manager and said, "It's very nice to see you." The girls moved forward and Mike tripped and fell and hit his head on the bottom of the step. Franny leant over, blew cigar smoke in his face and went, "Are you alright, pal?" It was boiling hot and that incident always sticks in my mind. This was Manchester City Football Club.

We beat Panathanaikos, and we played absolutely brilliantly. After the game there were two long banquet tables, one with all the City players drinking wine and beer and the other for the Greek team all drinking cokes and water. Our travelling director stood up, "We were very fortunate tonight, we played very well, and you just got us on a bad day. And thanks for your hospitality." He spoke very well.

The great Hungarian player Puskas was their coach, he got up and said, "Tonight is very embarrassing. My team, we cannot play, but worse still, we cannot drink!" Brilliant!

9

Go West Young Man

The Rocket Man flew me to America on his private jet plane and gave me a new life in football. What a star. I can never thank Elton John enough for what he did in 1975.

As I mentioned previously, it was a really bad time in my life when Elton and his manager intervened.

I had really got down on myself. I had lost all respect for Swales and Book at Manchester City and I didn't know what was going to happen until I received an incredible phone call out of the blue from Elton John's manager. He said Elton had been reading about my problems in the newspapers, where the situation had made big headlines, and he asked if I would like to get away for a couple weeks. Through a personal friend of mine Ken Adam, who later managed both George Best's and my affairs, they flew me to the USA.

"Come to Los Angeles and have a look at the Aztecs, the team Elton's investing in," he said. They arranged a private plane, picked up all the expenses in Los Angeles, and gave me VIP treatment at an Elton John concert in Dodgers Stadium. It was one of the most amazing periods of my life. I went to all the parties, champagne all the way. I got to meet all different types of people: I met Cary Grant, Ray Cooper, Charles O'Reilly. Elton John told me years later during an interview, that because he was so high, he did a 12-minute version of Rocket Man and in the end he was just making the words up. There were more than 55,000 people going ballistic and he didn't know how to end the song. That Elton John concert was the most fantastic entertainment I have ever experienced. He's wonderful, a genius.

They said they were going to try to sign George Best for the Aztecs, which eventually happened, and that they would love for me to play in Los Angeles too. It was an enticing prospect, but while I was staying at the Beverley Wilshire hotel I had a phone call from Tampa Bay, from their general manager Beau Clare Rogers

87

IV. As I mentioned earlier, that phone call changed my life forever.

"Hi Rodney," he said. "On your way back from L.A. we would love you to come down and take a look at Tampa Bay. We'll send you a first class ticket for you and your agent."

"Where's Tampa Bay?" I said. I didn't have a clue, I'd never heard of it.

He told me, and so we were off to sunny Florida. And the moment I stepped off the plane in Tampa I just knew I wanted to live there. I absolutely fell in love with it before I even knew where it was. It was like a spiritual thing. It was meant to be.

There were hundreds of Rowdies fans who had been rounded up to come and meet me at the airport, together with around fifty local media guys and girls. Dick Crippen from NBC's Channel 8 interviewed me live from the airport. You already know, that's where the famous quote came from.

Dick said, "Rodney, you're known as the Clown Prince of Soccer. We understand you are the white Pelé?"

Pelé had signed for the New York Cosmos the season before, and was the biggest name in world football and my reply was, "No, that's not quite true. Pelé is the black Rodney Marsh." Pelé didn't like that too much and that's how the titanic rivalry between the Tampa Bay Rowdies and the New York Cosmos was born.

Eddie Firmani, the head coach of the Rowdies, picked me up at the airport and the formalities were over quickly. I had a great contract that included a villa, a car, and medical insurance. It felt like paradise. I returned to England to take care of my personal affairs and wrap up my dealings with Manchester City and arrived back in Tampa full time in February 1976. I moved my family over, but that was a mistake. Every time I read about Posh and Becks it brings back the same memories I had; a case of déjà vu. The kids were still young and in school, and it just wasn't working out, so they went back to London and Jean put them into a school there.

My move to America was almost identical to David Beckham's move to LA Galaxy, but 30 years earlier. How was I received by the game in America? I can't be the judge of that, I'm just Rodney Marsh and I never apologise for that. I am what I am. I'm the same person now that I was 30 years ago. I make my own mistakes and I've made loads and loads, but I always do it my way. Sometimes I'm wrong, but I don't apologize for it. You either take it or leave it. I do think the players at Tampa Bay were all happy because we won so many games.

My greatest memory of the early days in the USA is the "Pelé who?" game in Tampa Stadium. It was the first televised live regular season game on ABC and tens of thousands of provocative signs saying, "Pelé who?" were plastered round the stadium. Pelé was, and remains, the biggest name in world football, and the wonderful

Brazilian player at that time was the star of the New York Cosmos team. They were the side to beat and our Tampa stadium had been sold out for weeks before the match. On the day, we absolutely destroyed them and I had a brilliant game myself. We beat them 3-1 and it could've been 10-1. We were just outstanding that day. I firmly believe that the "Pelé who?" game was the game that put the North American Soccer League on the map. It certainly put Tampa Bay into the limelight.

Then we had the return game in Yankee Stadium, and Pelé kicked lumps out of me because of what I did to them in Tampa Bay. I had taken the piss back in the first game, sitting on the ball and telling Pelé to come and get it. Now, at his home ground, Pelé sized me up and kicked me. As I lay there, he tapped me on the head as if to say, "Don't you mess with me son."

The referee was Gordon Hill, an Englishman, and I said to him, "What the fuck was that?"

Gordon said, "What do you want me to do, send him off? In front of 40,000 New Yorkers who've only come to see him play."

"Yeah, I suppose you're right," I said. I could see his point.

The Rowdies was a great name for the team, and I fitted in easily to the mayhem. We had some fine players, like our goalkeeper Paul"cage"Hammond, who was much better than anybody ever gave him credit for. He was decent on crosses, and he was a fantastic stopper of shots either with his hands or his feet. I don't know how, but I got stuck with Paul as my 'roomy' on a road trip. I think we were out in Los Angeles, I went to bed around 11pm and Paul went out and had a few drinks. When he staggered back into the hotel, he went up to the clerk and told him he had a game the next day and needed a wake-up call and he better make it for 7:30am.

The clerk replied, "But sir, it's 20 minutes to 8 right now!"

Mike Connell and Stewart Jump were defenders during that period and I thought they were top class. Mike could actually use the ball very well. In the middle of the park we had Tommy Smith from Liverpool, who had just arrived from winning the European Cup and scoring the winning goal. And of course you had me and Derek Smethurst up front. On top of that, later on the team added Steve Wegerle on the wing. I still maintain Steve was the fastest player over 25 yards that I ever saw. Overall, we had a fantastic team and in the crucial areas of the field, the spine of the team, we were brilliant.

Off the field, the chemistry was even better and we went everywhere together. The second day I was in Tampa, as I remember two British Rowdies being released from being held overnight in jail, after being taken in for being drunk and causing a fracas. They were real Rowdies.

It was a bunch of wild, crazy guys who could play some very attractive football. But if we were losing, I could be as nasty as any player, and I was, the proof being that I was sent off four or five times.

I was fond of Derek Smethurst, the striker, who when we first met used to drink vodka and Coke whenever we went out, which was a lot. Of course, that was before he became religious. We'd go to all the pubs: Robbicantes, Boneshakers, Victoria Station, and the Proud Lion Pub, and those were the places the boys would go and earn their reputations. You could always find the Rowdies in the pubs.

Come Saturday, though, it was all business. The team always gave 100 percent and it showed in the number of games we won and goals we scored. It was wild. We were the team. The Tampa Bay Buccaneers were losing, the Rowdies were winning. We were attracting 40-50,000 to Tampa Stadium and were highly successful on the field and at the box office.

I'll never forget that first season in 1976. We were the darlings of the Tampa Bay area. It was a wild time and everybody loved the Rowdies. We should have won the league because we were so good, but we were beaten 1-0 in the play-off by Toronto, who had the great Portuguese superstar Eusebio playing for them. We played them off the park in the Tampa Bay Stadium, and we should have won by five or six goals. I remember it so vividly.

I thought Firmani was a terrific coach for the side. What he did was very good, not so much on the technical side, but on the man-management side. There was only one problem really; the fact that he just didn't like me. He wasn't alone by the way. In actual fact, no coach ever liked me.

I think people have always had a problem with my instability. I wasn't a stable personality when I played. I get things in my head sometimes and I'm very single-minded. It was the way I played, on the edge. I've lived my entire life on the edge and I always get myself in trouble. You would think with my unstable personality, I would be inconsistent on the field, but eight out of every ten games I would be very good. But then for two games I would go missing and not show up. I was never your run of the mill athlete. I was very highly strung.

It seemed that I was a particular problem for Firmani. Back home in England between the 1976 and 77 seasons I got a phone call from Beau Rogers saying that Firmani didn't want me back at the club. I couldn't understand why after such a fantastic first season, when I'd played some of the best soccer of my career. Anyway, the club wanted me back and we started the new season well, winning seven of the opening ten matches. It was terrific, but obviously not for Firmani because he took the first opportunity to leave, and left us in the lurch by joining the Cosmos. I was very disappointed in Eddie Firmani when he left like that. He should've waited until the end of the season. That was a strange one.

The club put Lenny Glover in charge for a couple of games until they could bring back John Boyle, the Rowdies captain from 1975. But by that time, it had all gone to pot; it had all gone to the dogs. We did well just to reach the play-offs, where fate ensured we had to face the Cosmos in the Giants Stadium in New York. It was Pelé's final season, we were up against the coach who'd deserted us, and we were terrible. We played very poorly and lost 3-0.

I've spoken to Eddie Firmani only once since in 30 years.

If that defeat was a big disappointment, it was still great to play a part in showing to the world how good the NASL was. It was a time that vindicated the idea that soccer could be popular and high quality. Look at the people I was playing against: Pelé, Franz Beckenbauer, Eusebio and Carlos Alberto. Finally, the world started looking and said, 'Christ almighty, it's for real'. And some of the games were magnificent. The 5-4 game we lost to the Cosmos in New York when Pelé scored a hat-trick was one of the finest games I played in my life. Talk about getting your money's worth. Nine goals, they hit the crossbar twice, we hit it once. It was just fantastic soccer. If George Best was the greatest ever player for a couple of seasons, Pelé was a god; over the long haul, Pelé was and is the greatest player to ever play the game. Pelé played in four World Cup Finals.

We played major touring teams well. There was Manchester United in Tampa Stadium in front of a full house, and we beat United 2-1. We, the Rowdies, gave credibility to American soccer in the 1970s by beating so many teams in Tampa Stadium. I remember Moscow Dynamo were another.

It was sport and it was soccer, but it was also an event. Going to a Rowdies game was going to an extravaganza; it wasn't just about going to watch soccer. It was promoted as a big event and it was a big event. We were the talk of the town. 'Soccer is a kick in the grass' was the Rowdies song, and it was about branding that image and then bringing over a lot of young single Brits to play who were drunk and fighting and chasing all the local women.

We had that Rowdies image, but on the flip side, we were always there for the kids with the camps and the clinics. All the kids wanted to be Rowdies. I must say a lot of the credit must go to Farrukh Quraishi, a young player from Slough. He was always in the community, going out to all the youth teams and arranging for the Rowdies players to be everywhere: shopping malls, parking lots, doing demonstrations.

Soccer in Tampa owes Farrukh a great deal of gratitude for how he developed youth soccer. The Rowdies and soccer in Tampa Bay wouldn't have been so successful without Farrukh.

Another new coach arrived for the 1978 season, Gordon Jago, a man I'd known at Queens Park Rangers. I recommended him along with Alf Ramsey and Malcolm Allison, and Gordon was the one they could land. He was a good coach with terrific organisation and we swiftly erased 1977 from our memory banks. It all clicked straight away under Jago and in the early days he was very clever because he left the players alone. He stayed out of the way, and we would work out our own free kicks and corner kicks and all that. We were so successful; we scored fantastic goals from corners and free kicks. Jago primarily worked on the defence and Steve Wegerle and I worked on the attack. It went well, I was scoring goals for fun and we reached the Conference Championship against the Fort Lauderdale Strikers.

That was 'The Game': a second leg at home that went to a sudden death shoot-out in the pouring rain, with the winners getting to the Soccer Bowl. It was absolutely amazing. We played two brilliant matches, the first away in Fort Lauderdale and then at home in Tampa.

There was double extra-time, then into a mini game, and it was still level at 3-3 with five minutes to go when Ron Newman, the Strikers coach, made the biggest mistake in NASL history by taking off George Best who then couldn't take part in the shoot-out. Best walked off the field and threw his rain-soaked shirt straight in Ron Newman's face. George Best, still one of the greatest players in the world, was on the bench for the shoot-out. It ended up that I took the fifth and final kick. If I scored, we went through. The rain was coming down in torrents and not one person had left Tampa Stadium. The entire 47,000 were still glued to their seats. I was lucky enough to score the winning shoot-out goal and the whole stadium went absolutely wild. The fans stormed the pitch and took the nets off the goals. They strangled me, took my shorts off, stole my shirt, tore off my gold chain from around my neck, and I ended up walking off the field nearly naked! Everyone was on the pitch, it was just pandemonium. It was the most surreal, exciting moment of my life in America.

What nobody realised at the time was that I had suffered a serious injury during that game. Their left back, a guy called Maurice Whittle, came in high with his studs 'topped me up' and caught me on the calf. The studs actually went into the muscle and I got an infection from it. We were due to play the Soccer Bowl final against the New York Cosmos five days later and I couldn't train because it was so swollen. They gave me antibiotics and that kind of stuff, but nothing worked. The night before the final, John Kauzlarich, the team doctor, came to my room at about ten. I lay there with my leg elevated, and as soon as he looked at it, he went, "Fucking hell man, you can't play with that." Literally, I couldn't even pull my sock up over my calf it was so swollen, and it was agony.

We rang Gordon Jago from my room and told him there was no way I could play, and I was amazed by his response. "Don't tell anybody," he replied. "It will affect the attitude, so don't tell anybody."

I argued that they were going to find out eventually, but he said we would announce it before the game. So I told him, 'Okay', and I limped down to the stadium. He only told the team an hour before the kick off that "Rodney's not fit", but he knew the night before. The thing was, the club was so secretive that it caused all sorts of ugly rumours, like that I'd been out partying all night before the game. As if that was possible. I was never going to play; I couldn't walk, let alone kick a ball. I don't know why Gordon and the club never told the truth. When I got the Tampa Bay Athlete of the Year award later that year, in front of an audience of about 1,000 people, I thought about telling the real story then. But I decided I didn't want to hurt the club or the players, so the fans never knew the truth.

If Jago had done it right and announced it the night before to the players, they would have had the opportunity to mentally prepare for me not being in the line-up, especially because I was captain as well. It's like losing your quarterback the hour before the Super Bowl. The players saw my leg and said, "You can't play with that," but it was never announced. I thought that was a ridiculous mistake by Jago. We lost 3-1 to the Cosmos by the way.

Looking back, that was maybe the end of the great days of the NASL. What happened was that they didn't replace the world-class players like Pelé and Eusebio. The second phase of the NASL, and I always call it the second phase, was a failure. In that phase they started to bring in other players and were paying too much money for ordinary players. We signed a player called Mirandinha, who was coming back from a broken leg. He was going to be our next great player, but he was a disaster, a complete waste of money. But it wasn't just the Rowdies who were struggling, it was the entire league. The superstars dwindled away. The players who came across in the first couple years I was in America were all quality international players. The standard of play and entertainment value was incredibly high, maybe one of the best in the world.

Another big mistake I think the NASL made was the abolition of the 35-yard line for offside. Even Franz Beckenbauer said it was the greatest thing to happen to soccer.

There was one player who did arrive in the second phase that I thought was fantastic. It was Oscar Fabbiani from Chile, and I even started learning to speak Spanish so that I could talk to him on the pitch. I learned all the Spanish soccer phrases like 'Solo', the word they use for the situation when a player has time to turn or hold the ball. I didn't mind one bit sharing the limelight with Oscar in the 1979 season when we reached the Soccer Bowl final once again.

If Mirandinha was a nightmare, Fabbiani was the perfect signing. He was an out-and-out predator, a fantastic goal scorer. I had a lot of respect for his talent as a player. That season together, he and I slaughtered teams. Believe it or not, I had a couple of open goals that I knocked square for him to tap in. It was a conscious thing because Giorgio Chinaglia of the Cosmos was the leading goal scorer, and Fabbiani was ahead of me at the time. It was the right thing to do. I've got to tell the truth, I was great at both: at scoring and at what the Americans call 'assists.' I could have been a 100 percent 'assist' player like Steve Wegerle or a 100 percent goal-scorer like Derek Smethurst. I was the combination of both, and I did both of those things as well as anybody.

We reached the play-offs and faced San Diego, who were a fantastic team. The problem for them was that we were even better. The match went to a mini-game and I scored the winning goal. It was such a high, but little did I know that it was my penultimate game for the Rowdies. The last one was the 1979 Soccer Bowl. It ended early, and in true Rodney Marsh style, it ended angrily.

There were eight minutes left of the game, and we were 2-1 down against the Vancouver Whitecaps in a tight match. Then I saw the number 10 being held up by the official on the sideline. Now it's all electronic, but in those days it was a card. I was so angry at the decision. I was the captain, it was the final, and the player that coach Gordon Jago was bringing on was a little Yugoslavian called John Grnja, who hadn't had a good season at all. I was so angry I just flipped, and I have a fantastic photograph at home of me giving Jago a mouthful and arguing that it was a stupid decision.

Eventually I was taken off and Gordon Jago came up to me and said, "Rodney, I just wanted you to know that I thought we needed a little bit of pace up front."

"Gordon, fuck off," was my response. "I've known you all this time and suddenly, in the last eight minutes of my career, you realise I'm too fucking slow?"

Vern Lundquist, the ABC sports-caster on the sidelines was standing right next to me, struggling to cover the microphone. I believe it went out live on national TV.

The decision was madness to me. Why would you want your shoot-out specialist on the bench just in case the match ended in a draw?

And that was the end of it: the end of our relationship, the end of our season, the end of my career.

Jago was actually a very good coach, but he was more the organizing type than the guy who goes in and motivates the team. He was more of an administrative coach; he was brilliant with the travel arrangements for example.

It takes all sorts at a football club. I had been persuaded to join the Rowdies by Beau Rogers, then the general manager, and I thought he was terrific. He had an incredible understanding of what it takes for entertainment to be a part of sport. I inherently understood that, because that's what my role was, to entertain as a sportsman, as a player. That's where the "Clown Prince" came from. He picked up on that and promoted that image. I never liked that name because I was very serious when I played. All the things I did were a little bit outrageous, but always done when we were ahead in the game.

Another man I liked very much was the owner of the Rowdies, George Strawbridge, who was the owner of Campbell's Soups. I thought George was a first-class, quality man. He was hands-off management in style, but he used to come down to games and brought the team up to Philadelphia for end of the year get-togethers.

By the end at the Rowdies, the place was being dominated by Gordon Jago and the new general manager Chas Serednesky. And by the time the 1979 Soccer Bowl came around, the pair of them obviously felt I had become bigger than the club. I've been told that since by Dale Wellhoffer, the Company Rowdies Secretary and PA to Chas. I knew it then really, because Farrukh Quraishi, the guy who was so good with youth development, told me that Jago had said I was becoming too powerful and that they were going to try and find a way of dumping me.

They knew they couldn't just transfer me because the fans and media would've run them out of town. So Chas called me on the phone, and said that rather than negotiating a new deal because my contract had ended, why not have the first testimonial game in American sports history? That was the offer he made to get rid of me. I would get all the proceeds if I agreed to retire, and he insisted that the club thought I was coming to the end of my career.

I asked him how much cash he thought it would be, and he thought around 15,000 people would show up for a friendly game. He guessed around $85,000, minus expenses. Well, that was more than a year's salary for me. I went home and thought about it, and my thinking was, if Serednesky and Jago wanted to get rid of me that badly, even though I loved the fans, I wouldn't enjoy myself if I carried on playing for the club. So I accepted the offer. As it was, 22,000 people showed up. It wasn't a bad deal at all. However by the time they had deducted all the expenses, which seemed huge, it wasn't nearly as much as I thought it would be.

Then there was a testimonial dinner that earned more bucks. I saw none of that money. There were so many people at the dinner, it was a nightmare. But that dinner is where I told the legendary story about Gordon Jago when he was a young player at Charlton. No one ever knew if it was true, but apparently he was a full-back and never much good; he was just an ordinary, average player. He got into the Charlton team and they played in the quarter-finals of the FA Cup, which for Charlton was massive because they weren't a top-tier team. They were playing against Chelsea, I think, and it was 0-0, and in the last minute Chelsea got a corner. Gordon Jago is on the line and heads go up for the cross as it comes in, and it's headed towards the goal and Gordon is on the line. He tries to shut his legs and the ball actually dribbles between his legs and goes into the goal and they lose 1-0. After the game everyone has their heads down in the dressing room, devastated by the loss, and the manager is walking around and can't think of anything to say.

Gordon holds up his hand and says: "I'm sorry boss. That was completely down to me. That was my fault. I should've kept my legs shut."

The manager says, "Not you Gordon, your mother."

I told that story the night of the dinner and he didn't like that too much. I didn't speak with Jago for probably 10 years after that. I don't even think he came to the testimonial game.

People have always asked me if I made a mistake retiring too early. And the answer is definite: No.

I felt it was time to stop. I could have gone to other NASL clubs, to Philadelphia, who tried very hard to talk me into a contract. I could've gone to San Diego, who had been trying to sign me for two years. The manager called me numerous times for two years. But Fort Lauderdale was never an option, never. They hated me. They hated me more than Gordon and Chas.

So the question was, "What next?" It was October 1979 and I got a letter from the INS, which said that they had been advised that my contract with the Rowdies was up and had not been extended. Therefore, it said, your visa runs out October 31 – and you have to leave the country by that date.

In other words, it was obvious to me, and I have always thought that Chas had ratted on me to the immigration service. He could've waited until I got my affairs organised, but he didn't, so I never forgave him for that.

My Green Card application had been sitting on the club attorney's desk for years. He was the immigration attorney the Rowdies hired, who, I was told later, had boasted to friends that he had 'shelved' my Green Card application. On top of all this, my mother back in England was dying.

I had to leave the country and I did. I'll never forget one of the last nights I was in Tampa. It was all so overwhelmingly messy because I had to sell the house, and the condo on the beach that I'd bought as well. I remember sitting outside crying by my pool, with a bottle of champagne. I was on my own, rat-arsed drunk, and I was sobbing by my pool at midnight.

It was devastating. I didn't have time to get organised.

I made all the arrangements to go back to England, I gave away furniture and all that, and then I got a phone call the week before I was due to go back. It was from my dad, to tell me my mum had died. Once again I was devastated.

I changed all the plans, flew back the next day, went back and buried my mum, and then returned to Tampa to move the family. It was such a traumatic time, and I got no help whatsoever from Chas or Gordon. I didn't ask for any because that's not me. I'm not the sort of person who goes around asking for help, I figured I had to sort it myself.

I treat it all as parts of the heartache of life. The highs of living are enhanced because of the lows and depressions you go through.

10

Mooro - A National Treasure

It remains a national disgrace that the English Football Association dumped Bobby Moore like an out of date tin of soup when his fantastic career ended after one hundred and six caps. They discarded him without feeling, with no regard for what he had given them or had contributed to the game. This iconic national treasure was allowed to disappear into thin air. What were they thinking? The treatment of Moore, and of Sir Alf Ramsey for that matter, is something that should haunt an organisation with a history of shooting itself in the foot.

We must be the only country in the world to have no respect for the Captain or Manager of our only ever World Cup winning team, the team of 1966 who brought home the only trophy England has ever won. Just imagine how the current FA would have lauded David Beckham over us had England been successful in 2002 or 2006. It is so ironic that Beckham is now being used as the face and image for so much of what the FA want to achieve in the future; he is an ambassador for the World Cup bid. Beckham has nothing on Moore as far as presence is concerned.

Bobby was such an inspiring person, and it is impossible not to think of him as someone who meant everything to everybody. Schoolboys wanted to be Bobby Moore, and he was a people's champion. The media loved him and so did the players around him. He was unflappable in every circumstance, and when he looked you in the eye and shook your hand he made you feel special. Before my England debut, as I was pulling on the white shirt with the Three Lions for the first time, he came over and put his hand on my shoulder. "Good luck Son," he said and my heart jumped. It sounds corny but that's how I reacted. It was special to play for my country, and for Moore to say that made it even more perfect. That was just the impact he had. He was an untouchable figure in so many ways. He didn't have a huge personality away from playing; Bobby was a quiet man and was never the greatest talker or inspiring mouthpiece, but he had something special. He was born with that sprinkle of stardust.

He didn't scream at team mates on the pitch or in the dressing room; he was someone who led by example. Without question, he was England's greatest ever captain.

He was similar to Germany's Franz Beckenbauer in many ways. Both had so much time on the ball, and created space for themselves using their uncanny ability to judge situations. I played against Beckenbauer many times and I couldn't get near him. When I played with Moore, he was always a step ahead of anything the rest of the team would be attempting. We were always told to close down Beckenbauer as quickly as we could, yet he manipulated games his way without anyone knowing how. He had a touch like velvet, while Moore had this wonderful way of receiving the ball, looking up and finding a team mate even when under pressure. He played the game in slow motion, and you must remember those lovely little dinked passes he made out of defence. He was the master of his craft and is missed by everyone who knew him. I remember, hard man Frank McLintock sobbing uncontrollably when Bobby's death was announced.

I respect David Beckham and think he has been brilliant for English football but I definitely have a problem with the way he is treated by the FA compared to Bobby Moore. They are almost subservient to him, and there are people inside the organisation who behave like fans in his company. As a player Beckham is good, not great. As a captain, again, he is only good, not great. He would not be in my top ten England players, let alone captains. This is not to put David down merely to put Mooro in perspective and it's only my opinion, so you may see it differently.

Moore played all of his England career as a kingpin of the team, and most of his caps were as Captain, not someone who slipped on for the last fifteen minutes just to win another cap. I get the impression that Beckham is still trying to hold on to his International career to beat Peter Shilton's England 125 cap record, which devalues what playing for England means. Beckham might look good when he comes on, and of course he still appeals to the masses in this era of celebrity, yet how is making a couple of crosses or taking a few free-kicks worth another cap? For me he should have done the honourable thing a long time ago and called time on his England career. He should have thought, "I've had my day, and now it's time for a younger player to come through." You would never place Beckham within the same bracket as Moore, yet he's won more caps! I believe he has reached one hundred and fifteen caps for England more because of Beckham the brand, than of Beckham the player.

Not many people knew the real Bobby Moore, and perhaps that is why he and I got on well. Interesting, isn't it, that I managed to befriend people like Bobby Moore and George Best, men who most struggled to break down and understand? With Moore, I could have been looking in a mirror. Moore had a barrier up around him, just like me, and we were never close, yet we were friends. He kept people at arm's length, and that was part of the image of the man. People would ask me, "What's he really like?" but it was impossible to answer because no one knew the real Bobby Moore.

He did take me by surprise after one England game at Wembley. In the dressing room, he came over and said that he and a few friends were having a get-together in the East End if I fancied a night out. "We've taken over a place in Stratford if you fancy it?" he said. "Great," I said, and off we went, Bobby, me and Mike Summerbee. By the time we left Wembley it was after eleven at night, and Moore explained that we were a little late and that we should "make an impact entrance for the boys." Mike and I looked at each other, because this was not the Moore we knew. "I know," he said, "let's take our trousers off and walk through the entrance of the bar with them neatly folded over our arm, like a waiter serving drinks. Keep our shoes and socks on but go in carrying our trousers," he added. I looked at him as if he had three heads.

Sure enough, Mooro led the three of us upstairs to the private the bar, and just said "All is well?" to everyone as if this was the norm. It stunned me, and probably brought me closer to him. This showed a different side to Moore the England captain; this was the character and personality of the man shining through. I have used that phrase "All is well?" millions of times since. Another of his favourite sayings was "Ten out of ten," and again it has been used in his honour. "All is well?" sums up Bobby Moore perfectly. The class of the man, he was revered everywhere he went. In the street, people would nudge each other and say "That's Bobby Moore!" as if he was made of glass and untouchable. In so many ways he was.

His career glittered with West Ham and England, and it was a privilege to play alongside him when I went back to Fulham for a second spell. After our playing careers ended we went out separate ways, me to America and Bobby trying his hand at management in England with Southend. To see him having to flounder around trying to make a living was sickening. Where he should have been was at the forefront of the FA, as their face and their image. But instead, he and Alf were made to walk the plank and drown. The FA didn't lift a finger, and shame on them for discarding them so cruelly.

In 1983 when I was Chief Executive of Carolina Lightnin', I received a phone-call out of the blue from Ken Adam, who had arranged mine and George Best's loan to Fulham and was part of the London football scene in the seventies. Ken told me he needed a favour because Mooro was in trouble. His contract with Eastern Airlines, who sponsored his playing career in Hong Kong, was not being renewed and Bobby needed to work. "He hasn't got a lot of money,'" said Ken, "and now no job. Can you help?" I immediately told Ken to get him over to the States, and that I would give Bobby a six month contract as a coach for the team. Isn't that what friends are for, helping each other out in times of need? My deal, I thought, would help get him back on his feet and I included a club apartment, a car and some insurance cover for his family in his contract.

It was hard to stomach, trying to imagine someone with as much aura and reputation as Moore scratching around for a living in the USA.

Moore's arrival, as you can imagine, caused quite a stir at Carolina. We did a deal with the local property developer, who was happy to have his name linked to one of England's great institutions. As soon as the word spread, the local people came out in their hundreds to welcome him. The ex-pats came out of the woodwork, showering gifts on him, and the local newspapers and magazines all took out advertisements linked to his name. "We love you Bobby!" became the local catch phrase. It was good to be working with him again.

For the first few weeks I took a back seat, as Bobby got to know the players and stamped his own style on the team. The only thing I found strange was that not once did he come to my office. He carried out his work at the training ground then went back to his temporary home. Strange, because he was on his own, since his wife Tina and children Roberto and Dean were back home in the UK. After a month of no real communication, I invited Bobby to lunch and he said that he couldn't fit me in at the moment. "What about a drink after training then?" I added, and again he made an excuse. It was a mystery because this was not the Bobby Moore I'd known as a player. I was his boss, and for some reason he was avoiding me. This went on for a few more weeks, and even when I pushed him for a meeting to talk about playing matters away from the team, he found some way of not getting it together. "Of course, Rod, no problem, let's do it next week." But the days went by without him coming anywhere near me, and it really became a worrying mystery.

I am the last person to talk about relationships and have had my own well-documented troubles over the years, but I sensed something was wrong.

Eventually, his wife Tina arrived to visit, which provided another opportunity to try and get Bobby out, albeit socially. At last we all went for dinner, and Bobby chatted comfortably and easily. It was all happy families. I wondered what had been the problem for the last few weeks, and there were still some questions left for him to answer. A few days later, it all became clear, and this is how: I threw a big party for family and friends, and at the back of our house there was a huge deck that ran the width of the property. There were lots of people there, contacts and many others linked with the club. Bobby was sipping beer at one end of the deck and Tina, at the opposite end, appeared to be enjoying herself as she mixed and talked. Suddenly, all hell broke loose and as all the other guests fell silent, Tina and Bobby were seen screaming and ranting at each other.

This was not Bobby's style at all. Here was a very private man under attack from his wife, who was brandishing what looked like a phone bill in her hand. The language was fierce, especially from Tina, and Jean and I did our best to separate them and resume calm. Bobby tried to move away from his wife but she followed him, throwing abuse and accusations.

The next day, he came into my office and I asked what the story was. Bobby sat down looking sad and worried, and admitted he'd been having an affair with a lady called Stephanie, and that she had been over in the States with him (hence his strange behaviour in not mixing with anyone after training or in the evenings; he wanted to keep her a secret.) He then told me that Tina had found out after finding the phone bill from his villa.

Stephanie was a BA air stewardess, and Bobby's phone bills tracked her trips after she'd left him and gone back to England to work. Tina found out and boom, the bomb went off right there in our garden. Bobby had been torn between doing the right thing for his marriage and being true to himself. Here was the former captain of England, a huge figure to so many people, in bits as he attempted to sort out his private life.

Tina stayed for two more weeks and ran rampant with the credit cards. The whole situation was difficult for me because I'd known Tina and Bobby for twenty years and had often been to their home in Chigwell, Essex. I'd played hide-and-seek with their kids when they were growing up, and here I was in the middle of their broken marriage.

At that stage I had not met Stephanie, but I suspected Bobby had made up his mind where his life was going. Sure enough, he and Tina were soon to divorce. My image of Moore had always been of someone who was in complete control, but yet again, here we have an example of not knowing what goes on underneath the public surface. How he hated that row with Tina, the mess of his broken marriage, and the fact it all became public knowledge.

What happened to all the money Bobby earned throughout his career? Why did he have to come and work in the US just to make ends meet? It's a sad story in so many ways, the fall of England's greatest Captain. I know of five business ventures that went tits up, and there were probably more. He never took to management. What he was tailor-made for was being an ambassador, the man in the smart suit meeting and greeting, polishing the image of the FA at functions and meetings. There is not a football person across the world that doesn't respect Bobby Moore, and those same people don't give a shit about the FA. Yet our men in suits who control the game just didn't get it. They were all lost in their ivory tower of self-indulgence. They didn't mind flying around the world at someone else's expense, but they just couldn't see beyond the end of their noses that Bobby Moore would have helped them, just as David Beckham will help the current FA.

How sad it was to see Bobby shortly before he died, working for Capital Radio as a pundit alongside their presenter Jonathan Pearce (now of the BBC), scraping a living and clinging onto the sport he loved. Bobby died on February 24, 1993. He was just fifty-one years old. Fifty-one? What a waste, what a tragedy.

Watching him deteriorate physically, seeing him still sitting in the stand at games and working for Capital Radio, he was not the Bobby Moore I knew and loved. It was not the lasting image I wanted of him. He was the best captain of all, and that is the memory I will keep. He was born to be a skipper and it came so naturally to him. You just couldn't imagine Moore not walking out first ahead of his team. I captained every team I played for, apart from England, and no doubt that will surprise you. Marsh the Captain: doesn't sound right, does it? You're right, I should never have been captain, but I seemed to get the nod for political reasons. I was always going to have my say, be creative, constructive and critical. But Captain Moore, now that sounds good, safe and right.

Being skipper of Fulham, QPR, Manchester City, and while playing in America certainly didn't change me. I didn't think, "Now that I'm captain, I have to be different." I have always played as I wanted to, by my own rules. I had to be different. I told the manager and the team when I was made captain that if they followed me fine, and if they didn't want to that was also fine by me. I would conduct myself in a certain way, and if that was good enough for them, okay. There was no middle ground. I took the responsibility of taking penalties, scoring goals, creating chances for others. That is all I wanted to be judged on, even as captain.

In my opinion football is not a popularity contest, and the older I get the more obvious that becomes to me. I have never worried what people think; I didn't when I was playing, I didn't when I was captain and I don't now. That feeling has grown stronger over the last ten years. When people try to be popular for the sake of it, by saying the right things and trying to climb ladders by acting a certain way, it's bollocks, complete and utter bollocks. Be yourself and let others decide; if they don't like it, bollocks to them.

Moore didn't have to try to be good or to win friends. It came naturally to him.

I once asked him, "If England got a penalty in the last minute of a World Cup final, who would you want to take it? If your life depended on that penalty, who would you want to see step forward and take the responsibility?" He hardly hesitated before answering "Me," and that was so typical of him. He liked his destiny in his own hands, to be in control.

Bobby Moore's image will live on forever. He will be remembered as a wonderful player, as one of the best defenders who ever lived, as England's greatest captain, and as a person we all looked up to. Class, pure class, was Mooro. "All is well?" I can hear him saying it now, see him standing in the England dressing room, hardly breaking a sweat after another immaculate performance. I can see him getting nods of approval from people in the street as he strode along, his blond head held high. All is well, Bobby. It always will be.

11

England Hell

By the time you read this, I do so hope that England are NOT World Champions. I never thought I'd say such a thing, because there is no one more passionate and patriotic towards England than me. I played nine times for my country and, like all fans, I want them to be successful at all tournaments they qualify for. Yet this time, heading to South Africa in June, I felt different. Different because I have never accepted Fabio Capello as England manager.

An Italian in charge of our national team is totally alien to me. I felt betrayed when he was given the job. I wasn't happy with Sven Goran Eriksson, although I accepted that when the FA saw what other countries were doing, they tried their luck with a Swede. But an Italian? What next, a manager from Germany?

That is not being racist; it is purely a proud Englishman talking from the heart. Would Italy appoint an Englishman to manage their national side? Not a chance.

I wrote an open letter to the FA as soon as Capello was appointed, protesting that they had made a huge mistake. I was ready to hand back all my England caps to confirm how strongly I felt. I told The FA it was a disgrace that this country could not find an Englishman to manage the national team. I didn't get a proper reply, only a general comment from the Press Officer, Adrian Bevington, which said that the FA didn't respond to individual cases or to the thoughts of former England players. Funny, then, that the following day my views were all over the internet, and consequently in the newspapers. So I wrote a blog, stating that I was prepared to send back my nine caps – eight actually, because I'd already given my first one to Queen's Park Rangers Chairman Jim Gregory as a thank you for his support and help – and it was only after three or four people had said "What are you thinking? A lifetime achievement gone, over a principle. You're being stupid." It made me feel like a naughty schoolboy. They were right, of course, and I eventually saw sense and withdrew the plan to send back my caps. However, I still feel just as strongly over the appointment of Capello.

The FA offends me, and my dislike of them is deeply ingrained. As an institution, they have always been, and remain out of touch with the real people. Football should be the people's game, but it no longer is. I love all forms of football and still play five-a-side matches in the US. Football has been my livelihood and so I care about issues and situations that affect the man in the street. The FA lost me completely when they allowed Manchester United to drop out of the FA Cup to go and play in the World Championships because it would be good for public relations. That was the biggest betrayal in the history of the game, made by people with no real passion for the sport. I have always loved the FA Cup, and it was an ambition of mine to play in one at Wembley. It never happened and now, when I see the competition devalued and tampered with, it makes me weep. Semi-finals at Wembley? Are you sure? Growing up, FA Cup Saturday was a magic moment of the year, and now what? It is just another game, another competition. It has been overtaken by the money-mad.

That's the trouble when you appoint commercial people to the roles of Chief Executive or Chairman. Do they really understand football? Do they care? When Adam Crozier arrived from the advertising world of Saatchi and Saatchi, he became a leader with no background in the game. That is a scandal. Was it not Crozier who once said that Peter Taylor and Steve McClaren were the future of English football? That doesn't appear to have worked. Ian Watmore resigned as Chief Executive earlier in 2010 because he became frustrated at being unable to push what he wanted to achieve through the FA. Out of principle, he walked out, and good luck to him. I'd probably last ten minutes working for the FA, until the first person said, "You can't do that."

Of course there are commercial deals to be done, although they should never be to the detriment of the supporters. The continual changing of the shirt for home and away games is a joke. The Chairman, Lord David Triesman, seemed a sound enough bloke. I've met him and heard his views, yet he still stands for something I can't get my head around, the fact that the FA and the supporter are so far apart. I always go back to the fan. To myself as a kid, growing up when football was for the working man on a Saturday afternoon. That spirit has been eroded now, gone in a commercial whirlpool of greed and money. Roy Keane was right when he said a few years ago that football was becoming a sport for the prawn sandwich brigade. It has become more important for football to keep the sponsors and commercial people happy than the fans, and I think that's wrong. How many seats are left vacant for the first ten minutes of the second half at big matches, as the sponsors and their guests fill their faces while the supporter queues for a pee?

The FA Cup now feels like an add-on to the season. I used to like the semi-finals

On the Jasper Carrott show in 1979.

With Jean and Ken Adam, who helped us
move to Tampa for the first time.

Pre-seaon in 1978, with Gordon Jago on the
bench, trying out young players.

No idea what Dave Bassett is doing with those three legends!
L-R Jeff Stelling, George Best, me, Frank McLintock, Dave Bassett.

Interviewing Mike Tyson whilst at Talk Sport.

With Christopher Biggins, winner of Celebrity Get Me Out of Here, and other contestants from series seven, 2007.
L-R John Burton Race, Anna Ryder Richardson, Cerys Matthews, me, Christopher Biggins, Jason J. Brown, Katie Hopkins, Gemma Atkinson, Lynne Franks.

With my fellow chefs on the award winning show, Celebrity Come Dine with Me, Jan 2009.
L-R: Abi Titmuss, Lesley Joseph, Paul Ross, Linda Lusardi, me.

Playing tennis with the brilliant Tim Henmann, who is one of the most under-rated tennis stars of all time.

First tee at Wentworth.

Fun at Stanford Hall.

With my son Jonathan, owner of The Marsh Group, who had just finished building the house in South Tampa.

Rod with daughter Joanna at the Firefighters Awards where Rod was a speaker. Jo runs EMG Sports, my management company.

Interviewing USA Coach Bob Bradley in Tampa, who was preparing to leave for the World Cup in 2010.

With Ian Cheeseman of BBC Radio Manchester at the City of Manchester Stadium November 2009, helping to promote Ian's book.

With my grandson, Addison.

at Villa Park and Hillsborough, but now we get them at Wembley because the FA needs the money. The Wembley pitch has become a joke because it's used for too many functions, (again for the money) rather than being protected for what it should be, the best surface in the world. Ten times in four years the pitch has been re-laid and that is absurd. When you build a national stadium, the starting point is the pitch. Like the FA Cup, the pitch feels like an add-on. Ticket prices too are going sky high, and are becoming out of reach for the ordinary working man who wants to take his kids to the game. If we are not careful we will lose a new generation of supporters because of greed.

The other problem this country has is the erosion of real feeling for the England team. English football is now geared towards the club game rather than the national team. How many people in England really care if England win or not? When the World Cup comes around, everyone gets passionate and packs off to the pub for a knees-up, but what about for the rest of the year? Do we honestly believe Sir Alex Ferguson, Arsene Wenger, Rafael Benitez and Carlo Ancelotti, our four top managers, none of whom are English, care about the England team? Harry Redknapp is England through and through, yet he would still put Tottenham first. Like most other supporters, club football is all-important to him. The old question, "What would you prefer, for your team to win promotion, or for England to win the World Cup?" always depresses me because the answer always lies with club football. It was never like that when I was growing up or when I joined Fulham at the start of my career. England was the ultimate, the pinnacle of everything that football stood for. The honour of playing for your country was the dream. Watching England was huge back then, and I just feel like that special feeling is no longer with us. Too many things have overtaken the national side; club football is so big, and the commercial world is so much more significant than it was. I believe that having an Englishman in charge would make a difference.

When I was picked for England for the first time, in November 1971, I felt it was confirmation that I had arrived as a top player. I still look back on that moment today with pride and feel the same way, even though the England team has been devalued. In those days you felt you had made it. Today, the barometer for players is the Champions League. Top stars think more of playing for that prize than they do of playing for their country.

I had played for the England under-23 team consistently before my full call up, and I heard from my club manager, QPR's Gordon Jago, that I had been selected for the England team. That's how it happened in those days. The pride I felt enveloped me and it still does when I think back.

I'd been knocking on the door for some time, and there had been huge pressure from media for me to be selected by England manager Sir Alf Ramsey. One of the highlights of my career came the season after the World Cup, when a young England team beat the '66 winners 5-0 at Highbury. I got two goals; Alan Clarke got a couple and John Sissons the fifth. I had it off that day and beat three players in two yards before tucking it into the corner. The clamour for me to be selected started, but I still had to wait until 1971 for my first cap.

It came against Switzerland on November 10, 1971 at Wembley, when I was twenty-seven years and twenty-nine days old. The team that night was Peter Shilton, Paul Madeley, Larry Lloyd, Bobby Moore, Terry Cooper, Peter Storey, Mike Summerbee, Alan Ball, Geoff Hurst, Francis Lee and Emlyn Hughes. I, ironically, came on for Lee, who was soon to become a team mate at Manchester City. I came on for the last eight minutes, and waited for some words of wisdom from Sir Alf Ramsey, the man who won the World Cup for England. Instead, all he said to me before I trotted on was "Rodney, run yourself into the ground." "Is that it?" I thought, and we drew 1-1.

A strange little man was Alf. I was very much the rebel when I arrived in the England squad, but I had complete respect for Ramsey the football man. If you win the World Cup you are the best, never mind what people say about home advantage and lucky breaks. If you win it, you win it, and have still got to achieve against all odds. I didn't have so much respect for Ramsey the person.

On one occasion when we played Scotland at Hampden Park, our headquarters were out in Troon, where they have played the British Open golf tournament. The games between England and Scotland were massive occasions in those days, with a Hampden crowd of 130,000. There must have been 200 newspaper reporters waiting for us in Troon when we got to our hotel, and they were kept back behind a roped off area. As we walked from the coach to the main entrance, I spotted a craggy old Scot in his mac, tape recorder in hand. As Ramsey approached, the man leant forward and said to the World Cup winning manager. "Welcome to Scotland, Alf". Ramsey, in his best elocution-honed voice answered, "Fuck Orrff." Why did he do that and what was the point? It was outrageous even by my standards. We knew Alf hated the Scots, and it was out of order, but then again I'm no judge and shouldn't be.

The first time I met him was at England's Bank of England training HQ in London. "Welcome to the England squad," he said in his clipped voice. It was obvious that he'd taken voice lessons. Pathetic really, what was he thinking? That he had to speak all posh because he was something special. "Remember your roots, Alf," I always thought whenever he spoke to us.

In the dressing room he was completely expressionless. Throughout my career I have been with character managers like Malcolm Allison, Dave Sexton and Alec Stock, and in comparison this man was like a mouse, standing there with a clipboard. Mind you, you couldn't fault his communication skills, and no team he sent out was unaware of what to do. You could never say afterwards, "Alf, I didn't know what you wanted," because he was meticulous with detail and his tactics were good.

In that Switzerland game he kept going on about one of their players who was a free-kick expert. In training, Alf asked our goalkeeper Peter Shilton how many players he wanted to stand in the defensive wall if Switzerland got a free kick 40 yards out? Shilton smiled and said, "From 40 yards out, I don't want anyone." "Okay," Ramsey said, "30 yards out?" "Perhaps two," Shilton said. Alf replied, "You are familiar with this player, aren't you?" "Not from 40 yards I'm not!" Shilton replied, half laughing. Sure enough, Switzerland got a free kick and Shilton was all over the place as it bent three yards and flew into the net. Ramsey didn't speak to Shilton after the game, and although he didn't criticise him in front of the rest of the team, I don't think Shilton played in the next match. That was typical Ramsey. He demanded loyalty and if you didn't respect that you were out. He felt Shilton had let him down by not listening and following his instructions.

Not once did Ramsey ask me to be myself on the pitch, or to do my own thing. Everyone knew I was an unpredictable player who played off the cuff and was the master of the unexpected, yet he tried to change me. It was a mistake, and the day he asked me to play like Geoff Hurst I knew I was never going to be a Ramsey man. In training one day, he had Martin Chivers as his main striker and said to me that he wanted to see runs like Hurst made. "Spin off your marker," he said, "get to the far post, feint and get to the near post." What I wanted to hear was the England manager admitting that he'd picked me for my strengths, and telling me to play like a Loose Cannon, but it never came from him.

I'll admit that I never played for England in the same way I did for my clubs, and that is down to me, but I'll also say that Ramsey never allowed me to express myself. I once had a conversation about it with Malcolm Allison, and admitted that I didn't really want to carry on playing for England because it just wasn't working out. He told me to keep my head down and carry on. England had played one game with me on my own up front, Mike Channon deep, and two wingers. I didn't enjoy it at all, and that match was a complete waste of time for me.

I played with some outstanding players in my nine caps, including men like Norman Hunter, Colin Todd, Kevin Keegan, Malcolm MacDonald, Joe Royle and Emlyn Hughes. Keegan was standoffish at first and it was only later that I got to know him better. His personality developed with his international career. When you look at these players, plus all the established names like Gordon Banks, Bobby Moore, Alan Ball and Colin Bell, then think of players who have got caps since, it makes you wonder. Can someone please tell me how characters like Carlton Palmer, Geoff Thomas and Andy Sinton got so many caps between them? Talk about devaluing the national team and what it stands for! Once, during a Road Show with George Best, a member of the audience asked Best who he thought was the better player, Carlton Palmer or Thomas? George came back straight away and said, "Arnold Palmer is a better player than Geoff Thomas."

Talking of England and controversy the John Terry situation is such an interesting debate, and a great topic. What it did was put into perspective the huge impact the media has on our game. Terry might have been a prat, but what he did is nothing that hasn't happened in the past, and certainly nothing people haven't sorted out on their own before. Yet once the media gets hold of something like this, the pressure mounts on those in charge. I would argue that the media can have a negative effect on situations like this because people are not given the time to put things right when they go wrong. You need breathing space, yet in the space of 48 hours England coach Capello, Chelsea manager Carlo Ancelotti, Bridge, Terry, wives, girlfriends and anyone else involved were hounded. The media drove the story on because they wanted a quick outcome. Of course Terry should not have been stripped of his captaincy. Football is different to personal life. Terry shagged someone else's former girlfriend and the mother of his son. So? Deal with it, get over it and move on. Had Terry been a salesman, it would not have been an issue.

My only goal for England came at Ninian Park in Cardiff against Wales, on May 20, 1972. We won 3-0, and I'll never forget the goal because it was exactly what I have always been about. Mike Summerbee went down the right and crossed, Malcolm MacDonald nodded it down perfectly into my path and, on the volley, I screamed my shot past Welsh goalkeeper Gary Sprake. It didn't, however, mean more to me than other goals I have scored, but it was for England and no one can take it from me.

I had some fun at half-time with Malcolm MacDonald, who was playing on my left and complaining that I was not feeding him the ball when I had it in tight or difficult situations. "I've been unmarked so many times, but you keep ignoring my calls," Malcolm said. "Sorry," I replied, "but I'm deaf in my left ear and haven't heard a word from you!"

Never one to conform, once on a tour abroad with England, we were invited to a big do at the local Embassy. Ramsey rang Bobby Moore during the afternoon, and told him to make sure that I was dressed properly and that I was wearing a bow tie like all the other England players and officials. "No problem, Bob," I said on the phone and sure enough, when Mooro arrived at the function, I was standing at the end of the bar dressed smartly in dinner jacket and bow tie. "Ten out of ten," Moore said, and all was well. It was until I moved, and Alf noticed I was wearing no socks and flip-flops. I had total respect for Moore, but I did it just to wind Alf up. Why? It's me, isn't it, forever the Loose Cannon. "You never said what to wear on my feet," I joked with Bobby afterwards.

I hated being told what to do, especially by people I didn't respect. At City, Tony Book introduced a new players rulebook. Can you imagine how I felt about that? I'm a very positive person, yet this was so negative. "You must not do this, make sure you do that," it was a list of boring, boring instructions. One of them was that all players had to wear a tie to team functions. On one visit to London for a game, we stayed at The Europa Hotel, and shortly before we were due to go down to dinner Book rang and spoke to my roommate, Willie Donachie. "He was just making sure you were wearing a tie," Willie said after he had come off the phone. I said that a meal was not a team function, and that I didn't have a tie with me. So, I went to the area in the room where all the complimentary tea bags and biscuits were, took the lead out of the kettle, tied it around my neck with the ends in my shirt pockets and marched down to dinner. Book looked at me in disgust, especially when I told him it was the new fashion. He had no comeback. "Everyone's wearing them these days," I said, and he stormed off fuming. Willie, God bless him, just about held onto his laughter in front of the manager.

In those City days I used to drive around in a custom built Mini, beautiful it was, chocolate brown with a soft top. On the doors was written 'Smile,' and Tony Book thought it was a coded message. I was just trying to tell him not to dwell on the negatives and to be positive. It was a car that the famous actor Tony Curtis tried to buy from me.

My last game for England was against Wales at Wembley on January 21, 1973, when I was twenty-eight years, one hundred and two days old and it was another Loose Cannon moment. I self-destructed yet again. Before the match in the team meeting, Alf Ramsey was going on about work rate, about winning our own individual battles, saying that if we didn't work hard enough there would be consequences. "I have told you all before," he said, "if you don't work hard then you can't, indeed, will not play for England." All this was delivered in his false posh accent. He then looked at me and said, "Rodney, I will be watching you in particular, and if you don't work hard then I will pull you off at half-time." It was then that I delivered the line that ended my England career.

"Christ, Alf," I said, "At City we normally get a cup of tea and an orange!" As I recall Peter Storey pissed himself, and you could have cut the atmosphere with a knife. I knew that was it for me with England, and it was.

I was disappointed with the whole England thing. It fell flat for me and always felt fragmented. There was not the camaraderie and atmosphere that I wanted and had been led to believe existed. There were cliques, with some players always sniping at others behind their backs. When it was all over, I felt well out of it and that makes me sad.

No one, of course, can take away the memories. I have played for England and that sounds good. I'd love to have helped win the World Cup for my country, and often wonder if I will ever see a repeat of 1966 in my lifetime. The image of Bobby Moore holding the most famous trophy in football aloft.

Fabio Capello is a fantastic manager with a club pedigree to match most but I hope I didn't see England win it in South Africa because, out of all the things that have happened to the England team over the years, even though I have many friends from Italy and love pizza, I can't accept an Italian as the national manager. It's not right, it just doesn't feel right. I don't want them to win because of Fabio Capello, and this is a true Englishman talking. Maybe I'm just an old dinosaur.

12

Rowdies USA

I was like a barge going down a river without a rudder when my playing career ended at the Tampa Bay Rowdies in 1979. I was bouncing off one bank and then another. I had absolutely no idea what was going to happen next. I had money, because I'd had a fantastic contract with the Rowdies and then the proceeds from the testimonial game. I was fine for money, but I'd lost my purpose. That time at midnight when I was pissed on champagne, sitting by the pool of the Condo just about summed it up. Tampa Bay had stolen my heart, but I didn't know how to stay there.

The first thing was to remain in America, but for that to happen I needed a visa, and to get that I needed a job. A former Rowdie helped get me one. It was Adrian Alston, who played for Australia in the 1974 World Cup and who was then coach of the St Pete Thunderbolts, a new club playing in the Southern Soccer League in Florida. The club gave me a six-week contract as general manager, and there was some hopeful talk from them that I might become the owner. But I did it just to get a visa and have time to tie up the all the loose ends in Tampa. It was just the first small bump in the riverbank.

I bounced off that one and ended up next in New York. Not with the Cosmos, but with United. That's New York United of the ASL. How I joined them was an absolute joke. I had a call asking me if I would like to come and coach a semi-pro team in New York on a salary of $100,000 a year. I think the highest I ever earned as a player, at any level, was $75,000.

Within 48 hours I got a first-class round trip ticket in the post from a travel agent. I got off the plane and there was a limousine waiting for me. I got in the back of the limo and the guy got out his wallet and counted out $500 saying, "Here's your per diem, while you're here." I still thought it was a joke; that it was going to be some sort of Monty Python sketch or something ending up in Candid Camera. Then he told me it was $100,000 a year, but we only pay you for the season, so I would get $25,000 for the job because it was a three-month season.

I took it anyway. It was better money than I was earning at the time. Eventually, I met all the owners in a little Italian restaurant. As the majority owner was talking he was eating, as though he was rushed and really didn't have time for the conversation. I couldn't take my eyes off one of the group's hands. On his little finger, the nail was about half an inch longer than his other nails and it was painted gold. A voice in my head was telling me, "This is not for you!". I stayed and worked there for the summer, coaching the team. I was there for a few months and played about a dozen games. The team was going well and I enjoyed the coaching side of it, but I'd had enough of New York. I'd hit the riverbank again.

The escape route came from another phone call out of the blue. "Rodney Marsh, this is Bob Benson from Charlotte, North Carolina. I've been told you're not enjoying New York," he said.

We chatted, and he told me he was starting a brand new franchise the following season in Charlotte. I told him I knew nothing about him or the team - the Carolina Lightnin'. So, days later, yet again, a first-class ticket arrived in the mail.

I got off the plane in Charlotte, and there was a limo waiting for me. Bob Benson was in the back, and he was the perfect business gentleman. One of the nicest, most proper businessmen I have ever met in my life. He took me around the town and we did the deal driving along in the car. I signed a four-year contract as general manager and coach. I had four wonderful years in Charlotte. We won the championship in the first year, with 22,000 people at the championship game.

Charlotte was a saviour for me - not professionally, but personally. I was 36 years old then, and it gave me renewed energy, renewed purpose in life. It didn't hurt that I had a $1,000 bar tab at the Radisson Hotel!

There are so many stories from my time in Charlotte that you might think I'm making them up. But they happened. It was crazy at times. In one game we played a team from Dallas in the middle of the summer, and our biggest crowds were around 7,000. So, I said to the owner, "At the Rowdies, we always had a Fourth of July game on Independence Day, and we would get a band to come and 50,000 people would fill Tampa Stadium."

I told him I'd like to do that. I wanted to get a band, I wanted to get fireworks; I wanted to get the media on board. The owner told me if the operation was 'deficit neutral' I could go ahead. I went out with Ed Young, our assistant general manager, and got the local media rep for a radio station and offered a joint promotion. We worked out a deal and their TV partner was involved as well. I looked down the list of band names they had given me and was asked who my first choice was.

I couldn't believe it when I saw the Beach Boys. He said it was $145,000 for the Beach Boys. I went back to Bob and said, "I can get the Beach Boys for $145,000."

"Jesus Christ, how much?" he said. We did the deal, though. Our media partners guaranteed that 10,000 tickets would be bought at $10 each and on the day we played the match first, beating Dallas 3-1 in a magnificent game. 18,000 people turned up to watch. Then it was the Beach Boys, and we had a 15 feet high stage wheeled out on hydraulics. The band ran on the stage and started performing, and everybody was going nuts.

Dennis Wilson was playing piano and the piano fell off the stage, taking him with it. You cannot make this up. He fell down with the piano on top of him. It was mad. He must have been out of it, because he got up, they hoisted the piano back on the stage, and he started playing again. There was a 20-minute delay, but they finished the show. I tell that story and nobody believes me, but it is 100 percent the gospel truth. You can't make things like that up. We had a fantastic night, a great promotion and we made money.

So, of course, I wanted to top that. About two months later, near the end of the season, I told the owner I wanted to do a promotion that nobody else has ever done. We had a meeting of all my staff and we discussed giving away a sports car, or paying off someone's mortgage. But that had all been done before.

Then somebody said, "Why don't we give away an aeroplane. Nobody has given away an aeroplane." I agreed, and so we went for it. We did a deal with Piper to get a plane half price with their name attached to the promotion. The biggest radio and TV stations joined in, and so did Iveys, the biggest department store in Charlotte. And then we had to figure out the best way for someone to win it. There were some very creative people on the staff and we decided we would draw six people out of the stands via tickets. They would stand next to one of the goals and we'd wheel out the plane to the halfway line. The idea was that the person who could throw a Frisbee closest to the bottom of the propeller would win the plane.

On the night we played the game, and it was another fantastic match, they wheeled out the plane and it looked marvellous. It was painted in the Lightning's colours, and it was lovely. We had the game live on television, we drew the six names out of the crowd and they were given their Frisbees. The first contestant was an old woman of about 70. She threw the Frisbee all of 12 feet and the whole crowd started booing. So, the next person is another woman, and she threw it twice as far and the crowd started to boo even louder. The fourth person comes up, and it's a young kid, maybe 18 years old. He was obviously a Frisbee player because he runs up and flicks it like a pro. Remember, it's 55 yards to the halfway line, yet with perfect flight the kid lands his Frisbee five feet from the bottom of the propeller. Everybody in the stadium erupted and the place went absolutely crazy.

Channel 13 was the television station covering the game. They started announcing somebody had won the plane at half time. The announcer, on live TV, rushed up to the young man, put the microphone in his face and asked what he was thinking.

And the kid said, "I don't want it."

The announcer repeated that he had just won a plane worth $150,000, and the kid repeated, "I don't want it. I couldn't afford the tax. Give it to somebody else."

All the sponsors are there with the look of, 'Are you fucking kidding me?' on their faces. Anything that can go wrong will go wrong.

One pleasant memory of my time in Charlotte was the six months that Bobby Moore spent coaching the team. Bobby was keen for a job because his contract to play for a Hong Kong club wasn't being renewed. As I said earlier, I respect Bobby so much, and I offered him a six-month contract, a car, and an apartment. He was absolutely first class in every way. He conducted himself with enormous dignity and pride, even though he was coaching at a level that was 100 times below his own playing career.

I have to admit that not every English player who came over to America in those years had the same attitude. Some looked at it as a joke, and I always remember Peter Osgood in that way. We, the Rowdies, were in the middle of a road trip when I saw Osgood and he told me that he thought football in America was a joke. I just ignored him because I was with a team that was going somewhere and I think he was with the Philadelphia Fury at the time. There were players who came over here and treated it as an almighty piss-up, but there were others who respected themselves and the game. Franz Beckenbauer, for instance, was a consummate professional. And so was Bobby Moore.

I had four fantastic seasons in Charlotte and it was a wonderful time. In the last year we reached the semi-finals of the ASL Championship, but were then knocked out. I was really disappointed by that, but the next day my life hit the riverbank again. And this time I was travelling back to Tampa, where I'd left my heart the whole time.

The day after the semi-final, I received a call from by Dick Corbett. He said that he, Stella Thayer and Bob Blanchard were going to take over the Rowdies, that they were buying the club from George Strawbridge, lock stock and barrel. Dick said the first person he wanted to speak to was me, because the Rowdies were a mess. He confided that the player contracts were a mess, their budget so completely out of whack with the rest of the league. I was head coach and general manager of the

Carolina Lightnin', so I understood exactly what he was talking about.

My contract with Charlotte had just run out and I was about to negotiate a new deal. It was fortunate timing. And my first thought was, 'Here we go again'. Dick said he'd meet me in New York. He flew me up to New York, I stayed in his Central Park apartment and the next day, I met Stella Thayer and Dick for lunch. We talked about what my role in the club would be and we shook hands on the deal that day. Within a few weeks I was back in Tampa.

I always found Dick Corbett to be incredibly direct, which I love. That's why I have the reputation I do. I can't stand bullshit. I've got no time for bullshit. I really warmed to Dick Corbett. We used to joke that he's actually an alien, not from earth.

When I'd left Tampa, I said at my testimonial that I'd absolutely loved being part of the Rowdies, but that it was time to move on. I also told the fans that day that I would be back. I just didn't think it would be so quick.

So, the script at the press conference for my return was set up by Ted Moore, the marketing guy. "I told you I'd be back," was the message I had to give. It was all choreographed and I didn't agree with it, but that's what they wanted. They thought it would get the most bang for their bucks. And it did. The amount of publicity the Rowdies got when I returned was staggering.

The trouble was, there was a cancer infecting the club. Even before I returned many of the old guys had been fired like Al Miller and Francisco Marcos. Ted Moore resigned pretty much as soon as I got there because he just didn't like me personally. And the old general manager that I'd had some run-ins with, Chas Serendesky, had also gone. I didn't think Chas would've stayed when they hired me anyway; he would've been beside himself because it looked, in the end, as if I had won and they had lost - which was true.

The place was a complete mess. The only thing I can compare it to is when you buy a house and and you find out the roof is leaking and the pipes are leaking and the carpet needs replacing, the pool doesn't work and the all the electric needs replacing? The house is a complete mess. In the inventory of the transfer of the company there was only 50 percent of the stuff listed on the inventory list. So much had gone missing and God knows where all that stuff went.

It was a mess. And it was also a joke. In just a few years the Rowdies had gone from the very peak of American soccer to being a complete joke. It was embarrassing. I couldn't believe that some of the players had agreements which included providing tickets for pets to fly back to a player's home country. Who in the world signed that fucking contract? That was just the tip of the iceberg; there were so many things wrong. They had soured so many relationships with the community. I found out very quickly that the Rowdies had really, really, taken a dive.

The fans loved the Rowdies because they were just rowdy players and rowdy people. I thought that was what made the franchise. I know it upsets people in England but there were no better fans anywhere in the world than Rowdies supporters. The Fannies, as they were known, were totally loyal and dedicated to the team. The Fannies would do anything for the players, within reason - and maybe not within reason in some cases.

They lost sight of that in the Marcos-Miller era. It didn't work and they kept going with it until they drove it into the ground. When I came back, the club was in pieces.

The thing that provided us with even more problems, though, was the North American Soccer League itself. I don't think Howard Samuels, the chairman of the NASL, had a clue about sport or about soccer, and he was the chairman of the league. I would go to the meetings and there was no community effort for the league. It was more a case of, 'What's the best thing for me?'

I think Lee Stern of Chicago was the worst of the owners, with Joe Robbie from Fort Lauderdale a close second. Robbie's attitude was that the last person at the table was the winner. I remember him saying that one day, and I thought, 'What a great fucking attitude that is. How do you run a league like that?' Lee objected to everything that wasn't in the best interest of Chicago. Lee was huge on the indoor game and said he would only play outdoors if everybody else played indoors. The NASL bosses forced the Rowdies into playing a full indoor season, and we just weren't prepared for that.

And that was a problem for American soccer. The highs were so fantastic in the early seasons that the next few years, when the level of play dropped, fans were asking what was going on. Soccer in the United States became a cheap imitation of the 1970s. The media latched onto that and they also questioned the league forcing teams to have seven Americans on the pitch, which was a mistake. To this day I still think it was a mistake. They did it way too early. So, in the end, it all collapsed.

The 1983-4 indoor season was an absolute disaster, not least because I think the mind of our Brazilian striker, Tatu, had been soured by Marcos and the previous regime. I found it very hard to communicate with Tatu because Marcos had already convinced him to get away as soon as he could. So in the end, I had to sell him to the Dallas Sidekicks during the next summer outdoor season. We still had some sensational players. Roy Wegerle was fabulous in his rookie year, and we beat the Cosmos and Chicago. But the whole thing was falling apart. I can remember going to the Meadowlands to play the Cosmos indoor and there must have been 200 people there. Nobody in New York cared about indoor soccer. They would get 70,000 for outdoor matches with Pelé and Beckenbauer. They didn't care about indoor soccer. Chicago would get 14,000 and sell out the arena. But the point is that Lee Stern was doing what was right for Chicago, to the detriment of every other team.

I have to admit that I hated indoor football, and I still do. We won some fantastic games but when we won, I didn't say, 'It's all good'. I made it clear that I didn't want to play the indoor season. Even when we were beating people, in the press conferences afterwards I would still be saying that we were wasting our time and that we should be getting ready for the outdoor season.

The expectation was incredibly high for that 1984 season, both for me and for the players, but I didn't realise how deep the Tatu cancer was. I had always respected Tatu as a player, watching him from afar and when I returned to Tampa. He was a fantastic little player, much better indoors than outdoors, but still fantastic. The trouble was that our relationship was irrevocably soured and I can only assume Marcos was to blame. There was one exceptional match against Chicago, where Tatu scored a brilliant goal. As I'm standing there cheering, he ran over and gave me the finger. We won 3-2 and I let him calm down afterwards before calling him into the coach's room.

"What was all that about Tatu?" I asked him.

"What do you mean?" he said.

I told him not to give me any nonsense, and he said he was just telling me he scored the first goal.

"Yeah, but you used the wrong finger," I said.

I never liked bullshit, but I was always willing to admit my mistakes when I made them. And I did make a howler in the first game of that season when we played Minnesota at home. We were winning 1-0, we were playing fantastic and we could easily have been three or four goals up. With 10 minutes to go, I thought I would put on a fresh player. I sent on Roy Wegerle and took off Steve Wegerle. It was like for like as players, so we didn't change anything. Roy gave the ball away just outside our box, they scored, and then Minnesota won the shoot-out.

So it went from a really great start to the season to losing our home opener. I always felt that was a big downer, even though we had some great results after that.

I had asked Mike Connell to be my assistant coach for that season. I wanted him to be player/assistant coach because I felt I needed somebody I could bounce things off. I thought Mike would be the best person for that job. But he said no. He just wanted to be a player and captain on the pitch.

Instead, I brought in Malcolm Allison, who was one of the greatest coaches in the world, and who I knew from my days at Manchester City. He was a big character, a big man, and he came to the Rowdies from Sporting Lisbon in Portugal. Malcolm wouldn't tolerate the lack of professionalism shown by some of the players, whereas I had been in America for a long time, and I understood the way the game was played in the USA. Malcolm wanted total professionalism all the time. Well, at least on the training field. After training was another situation entirely.

Malcolm had been around for a few weeks, and he loved to drink. One night I was lying in bed and the phone rang at 3:30 in the morning. I picked up the phone and a voice asked, "It that Rodney Marsh, Rodney Marsh, with the Rowdies?"

It was the Hillsborough Sheriff's department. The Sheriff said they had one of our coaches in the cell. He was incoherent, but they did get the name 'Rodney Marsh' out of him. Malcolm had been arrested for driving at 8mph, going the wrong way over the Howard Frankland Bridge. He was English, so he drove on the wrong side of the road. I told the cop to let him sleep it off and I'd be there in the morning. We got him bailed out, but Malcolm never actually appeared for his arraignment. He ended up going back to England before the end of the season.

During Malcolm's time at the Rowdies we had some great wins, and I think it's important to mention that. It wasn't all doom and gloom on the pitch. In Connell, Refik Kozic, Greg Thompson, Roy and Steve Wegerle, we had a good team.

But a big problem occurred when, in my opinion, Mike Connell and Refik Kozic, our two central defenders, did not give 100% effort in two consecutive matches we played on the road, away to San Jose and Toronto. They embarrassed themselves, and my view is that our collapse that season centred on those games.

I believe Connell and Kozic didn't try because they wouldn't accept Malcolm Allison's coaching methods, because they wanted to make a statement. They allowed those San Jose and Toronto to attack at will by not marking, by pushing up to the halfway line. Malcolm had this drill where we pushed up to the midway line to condense the pitch and play the offside trap. They had never done that before and they didn't want to do it.

So, fundamentally, they just let players run free on goal once they got past the halfway line, and we conceded nine goals in San Jose and nine goals in Toronto. It was a huge embarrassment.

Later in the season, after Malcolm had left us, we thrashed San Jose and went up to Toronto and lost 1-0. Everybody knew what they had done, and I spoke to both of them. I told them what I thought.

I called Mike, my captain, in personally. I wanted to say to him that I knew what he'd done, and what I thought of him. He denied it and said it was just one of those things. I said, no, it was just two of those things.

I didn't go public with it, but two weeks later, there was a knock on my door. It was Refik Kozic, saying he wanted a word. He said he'd been talking to his family and been thinking about the last couple of weeks, and that he was really sorry for what he'd done. Refik said that I was completely right, and that he was ashamed that he'd let me down, the team down, and the fans down.

I held out my hand and said, "Refik, at least you're honest." I thought he was a real man for doing that. That put an end to it. But the attitude of the team had collapsed so far because of those two games, and we couldn't rebound to get into the play-offs.

It turned out to be the last season of the NASL. I could see it was collapsing fast, and at the end-of-season meeting, the plug was pulled. It was obvious there were only three or four strong teams left, like the Cosmos, Fort Lauderdale and the Rowdies. A couple of other clubs wanted to continue, but they didn't have the money. There was almost nobody left to play, and it would have been an embarrassment to have a league of just a few teams. I thought that was stating the obvious.

Why did it collapse? I think it all goes back to the biggest mistake they made: expanding too quickly, and over-expanding. It's all right to grow over a long period of time, building markets, but they did it in one season, going straight up to 32 teams. It was all too much.

The consequence for the club was obvious. The owners had made the decision. I had to fold it. It was sadly my responsibility to fold the Tampa Bay Rowdies as a North American Soccer League entity. It was a very traumatic time in my life. How did I keep going? Well, I took a 100 percent pay cut. I told the owners I would build up deferred income until such time as we got money from playing again. I think I went 18 months without pay. Cornelia Corbett wrote me a promissory note. They valued the club at $1 million and I had a promissory note for $240,000 for the amount of salary I lost. So I owned 24 percent of the club.

We continued doing Camp Kikinthagrass, which brought in quite a bit of revenue. We still had players we could use for that. Camp Kikinthagrass actually kept the Rowdies name alive for a couple of years. Roy Wegerle worked with us on the camps for a while but eventually I got him a move to Chelsea. I also did a deal with one of my old clubs, QPR, to come and train for six weeks in Tampa and we put on a series of matches against the Rowdies. QPR paid the players' salaries and we continued the battle to keep the Rowdies name alive in Tampa.

Another idea was to bring back the Fourth of July game to Tampa Stadium with a match against an NASL All-Stars team. Pelé was supposed to kick out the first ball.

He cancelled at the last minute and we ended up having to sue him for breach of contract. We had paid him a substantial fee in advance just to take the kick-off and then stand on the sidelines. When I heard he wasn't going to turn up I knew I was going to get crucified. I contacted his lawyer, who just told me Pelé wasn't feeling too well. He knew we had to sue Pelé, and the lawyer didn't argue. They just settled before I took it further.

The trouble was it hurt us with the media and the public. The attitude was that it was the Rowdies fucking up again.

It was a hopeless time. From being a great team playing fantastic football, we had become beggars at the banquet, finding competition wherever we could. The only viable league to play in at the time was the AISA indoor tournament. I still hated indoor soccer, but I was Chief Executive and I had to do what was best for the organisation. The Board of Directors then was just Cornelia, and she said we had to play, so we did.

I brought in an excellent coach called Wim Suurbier, who had played for Holland in the 1974 World Cup with their famous Total Football side. He created a good little team and I played occasional five-a-sides in training with lads like Steve Wegerle, who had come out of retirement. One day Wim said he was short of players through injury and was going to put me on stand-by. I was 41 years old -- too old -- so I asked Wim why he didn't put himself forward. He said he was even older, so they registered me to play in case of an emergency. Of course, on the Friday, two more players got injured and I actually had to play. I scored two goals and made a couple of assists and was named Player of the Week - the oldest ever Player of the Week. I didn't complain too much about that.

Unfortunately, soccer at that time in America was just limping along; it was on life support, waiting for someone to pull the plug. We entered the American Soccer League from 1988 to 1992 because Cornelia wanted to keep the Rowdies name going. She had dignity and pride and she was the best owner I ever worked for. Every year we would have the same conversation. I would say to her that it wasn't going to work, but she disagreed. She didn't want to quit. She didn't want to end the Rowdies name. Every year I would give in and say let's play, and then by the end of the season, it just didn't make sense. We were getting about 4,000 people to games in Tampa Stadium and it just didn't make sense, even with some quality players coming over. We had Mark Lawrenson, Ricky Hill, Peter Barnes, Peter Ward. We had a lot of top players come through, but the whole soccer situation in the States was on life support. The sport was just dying. It just needed somebody to pull the plug. And I think I was the one who finally pulled the plug in 1994.

At least I was right in the end - even though it was a terrible wrench.

Football in America had given me so much, and it came home to me when a film producer called John Battsek came to interview me for a film he was doing called "Once in a Lifetime" about the New York Cosmos and the days of Pelé and Franz Beckenbauer. He said I was the only person outside the Cosmos that he wanted in the film, because of the upset and aggravation I had caused the team and its fans. He said the film could not be done properly without me. Thirty years after I was a player, they were coming to me for quotes about the Cosmos.

That was one of the biggest compliments anybody could pay me.

13

Shut Up Marshy

When you are a Loose Cannon sometimes there are things you can't control. Many times I have asked myself, "Why did you say that?" and I have never really known the answer. At Fulham, Queen's Park Rangers, Manchester City and with England, I have forced my exit with a comment, joke or sarcastic remark. I can't regret any of it, even if the reasons for me saying such things have never been entirely clear to me. Not everyone shares my sense of humour. In my media career I have always been someone to say what he feels and if people don't like me, so what? If they don't like what I say, who cares? But often, people did like what I said and my controversial, straight-talking image was an attraction for television and radio when I quit playing. I became a pundit and loved every minute, before it eventually ended in tears.

The public, I believe, want to know the truth, not to listen to waffle from former footballers protecting their profession, sitting in a television studio waiting and hoping for a job back in the game. I'm sure some pundits only accept the job as an advert for themselves. Take the money and smile. I have never been like that, and everything I've done and said has stemmed from how I feel. If you can't say what you believe, then what's the point of being a pundit? The BBC, for instance, could get an ice cream salesman off the street to say more than Alan Shearer does on Match of the Day on Saturday nights. Gary Lineker also lives off his 'Mr. Clean' image and has a 'I'm never going to say anything controversial' aura around him. That's fine if you can get away with it, but it's not for me.

I have always tried to be 'real' because that is who I am. As a player I tried to be different, using the skills God gave me to create a feel-good atmosphere. Football crowds like to be entertained, not sit through ninety minutes of dross. If the players on the pitch are not enjoying the game, then how can the fans? I took that attitude into the television studio and was always determined to be me. I'm appalled when you hear stories of some pundits being warned off subjects because it might damage the image of the company. When a manager signed me he knew what he was getting, a Loose Cannon. When I was employed as a TV pundit, they knew they would get honesty and sometimes controversy: that's the mix. I have always been one hundred percent spontaneous. I have never thought "Let's stir things up here." What comes out of my mouth is how I feel. I react to situations quickly, just as I did on the pitch. Even if it didn't always work, and I have not always been right, at least I can say I've been honest. There is also knowledge there, and whatever people may think, I care about doing the right thing and giving value for money. I have always loved football.

It's interesting, because I often lie in bed thinking back over my career, about the things I have said and done as a player and pundit. I think long and hard before I drift off to sleep, but there is never a moment of regret. I have never woken suddenly in the middle of the night thinking, "That was a mistake," or "I wish I hadn't said that." My life in football, television and radio has been Rodney in the raw, me, my thoughts and I.

When I was sacked by Sky it was a moment of madness, the Loose Cannon striking once more. I absolutely never had any intention of causing offence to anyone but knew it was inflammatory. I was appearing on Sky's nightly phone-in programme, 'You're On Sky Sports,' days after the Tsunami had caused devastation in Thailand. A Newcastle fan rang in and was talking about David Beckham joining them. Beckham had been linked with a transfer to the North East, and the Daily Mail newspaper had even run a story saying the deal was on. I answered the call by saying that Beckham would never sign for Newcastle because of all the trouble the Toon Army (how the Newcastle supporters are described) had caused in Asia. The moment I said it, I hadn't sat there thinking, "I must use a Toon Army joke," it just came out. It was a joke that was on the internet for days before. The actual comment about Beckham was spontaneous. All hell broke loose. The producer of the show, Mike Curry, came rushing in with a face like thunder, worried sick about the repercussions. "We'll have to do something," he said, "make an apology, anything." By the time we went back on air, the emails were flooding in, so I faced the camera and said, "If any of you were offended by my little joke about David Beckham I apologise. There was certainly no offence meant." And there wasn't. I didn't mean to upset the families still affected by the problems in Thailand, Newcastle fans or anyone else for that matter.

I will not discuss the terms of my termination but it was one pun too many for Sky, and I was sacked soon afterwards. Andy Melvin, the Deputy-Head of sport, called me and said that they were terminating my contract because it had caused too much controversy. "You have been brilliant for Sky Sports, Rodney," he said, "That comes from Vic Wakeling (former Head of Sport) and I. Vic wants to take you out to lunch. There have just been so many complaints that we couldn't go on with you." I respected him and Vic Wakeling for that. He told it how it was and that has always been my life's motto: don't hedge around the truth, tell it how it is. Wakeling and Melvin were as good for me as I was for Sky Sport. No regrets? Not in the slightest.

The Beckham situation just followed the pattern of my career. Just when everything was going well, my mouth took over and along came another Loose Cannon moment. It was the same at Fulham when I fell out with Vic Buckingham, at QPR with Gordon Jago, I never saw eye to eye with England manager Sir Alf Ramsey, and my fallout with Tony Book at Manchester City was such that he ended my career in England by refusing to play me. So, the Sky sacking followed a pattern and I don't blame them. I don't blame anyone for what has happened in my career; I did it and I stand by everything.

My breakthrough with Sky came when I stood in for George Best on a Sports Saturday show. The person negotiating with and encouraging Sky was Mary Shatila, George's partner at that time, who had dealt with Sky when organising all of George's appearances. Everything was done through that little phone sitting on the pub bar at The Phene Arms. Amazing, really, when you think that a huge television company communicated with the greatest player that ever lived through a pub phone, with people ordering drinks in the background. After my first appearance with Paul Dempsey and Sue Barker, Mary took me to see Vic Wakeling. He said he'd enjoyed my performance and would like to sign me for more shows. That was great for me; it led to me appearing with Sky's number-one superstar pundit and footballing genius, Andy Gray, in the Boot Room programme when Andy analysed tactics and formations, and I was also a regular on the mid-week Footballer's Football Show. It's public knowledge now and well documented that the big breakthrough for me and Sky, was when one of the back-room boys, Andy 'Buzz' Hornet, and Vic Wakeling came up with the idea of having four guests and a presenter sitting behind monitors, telling the public what was happening at the big Saturday football matches around the country. There was also a running results service. The first idea was to make it look like a burger bar, and one of the first panels that sat and discussed what was happening in football that afternoon was Alan Brazil, George Best, Clive Allen and me. I admit that when we initially heard of the idea, we all looked at each other and said, "This won't work. How can we sell something that the public can't see?" How wrong we all were! The show, Gillette Soccer Saturday, has been one of the great success stories in sport. No pictures, just former players telling it how it is. I'm very proud that I helped to turn the programme into the iconic success story it became, and indeed remains.

Since the very beginning, the presenter has been Jeff Stelling, and I can honestly say I have never worked with anyone so brilliant at what he does. The job is perfect for one of his personalities. His ability to pick up the mood of the games and the pundits, and to then transfer it into the homes of the watching public is just great. He and I became friends, sort of. I say we are friends even though there were times when I feared that he really disliked me. What was important is that we were professional on screen, and I hope that we respected each other for the jobs we did.

I have to say I was disappointed with Andrew Hornet, who at that stage was young and bright, inventive and a risk-taker. I believed he had a great career ahead of him, but somehow he lost his way and was never the driving force behind the programme I expected him to be. I thought he would go to the top and become a big player, like Vic Wakeling or Brian Barwick, the former Head of Sport at BBC and ITV, and Chief Executive of the Football Association. Yet he disappeared, became a partner in a football agency and eventually moved to the doomed Setanta Television, which churned out total garbage in my opinion, and is now, I believe, an assistant producer or something at ESPN. He was replaced as producer of the show by Ian Condron, who was better for the job, and what we, the pundits, needed. For me, the show had to be as if we were all sitting in a pub, disagreeing, debating, telling stories and making fun of each other. That is how it became, and the public responded well to our banter.

One of my favourite partners on the show was 'Uncle' Frank McLintock, the former Arsenal captain and centre-half who led them in their first double year. "You didn't say that last week," was a favourite comment of mine to him. Frank would always respond by becoming indignant, and it just got funnier and funnier. We had a big argument one Saturday about why forwards got paid more than defenders. Frank was furious, especially when I told him that the late Alan Ball made five times as much as him at Arsenal when he joined them from Everton. Frank always seemed to be eating a sandwich or a biscuit when the camera went to him and that just added to the frivolity of the show. It was natural and real, great television. I always thought Sky dropped Frank from the show too early because he was a great character.

I always sat next to Jeff Stelling on the show and became his foil. If the producer said in his ear, "Let's keep this going," or "We can't go to a break yet," he would turn to me with a question and I would waffle on until everyone was ready. I got used to this and, in the end, would call Jeff's bluff. If he turned to me and said, "This is a cracking game Rod, isn't it?" I would say, "Yes, Jeff, it is," and add nothing else. He would look at me like thunder, pleading with me to keep talking. All good fun and the public were not aware of the games I played. But there were also many times when he was under pressure and I knew I just had to ramble on for thirty seconds until he cleared his head. I know as a professional he appreciated that.

After four or five years, I felt the show had changed and become tired. Jeff had become guarded and there were signs that they were uncomfortable with controversy. I wasn't happy, and so took it upon myself to create what I thought was a feel-good atmosphere to give the show an edge again. I wanted to be provocative although, again, I didn't say things just for the sake of it and was simply honest in my way. Vic Wakeling even sent down a message with instructions to allow me to do what I liked, because the show was working. That simply gave me encouragement to be me. Funny, isn't it how things repeat themselves? Vic's support is exactly what I got at QPR, although there were not many other times when anyone gave me free range to do my own thing. It is important to know your strengths and what you have at your disposal, and Vic Wakeling was brilliant at both those things.

With the green light to do my own thing, my role in the show became more controversial, if that was possible, and I did rub a few people the wrong way. When Jeff turned to me one Saturday and asked how I thought Liverpool manager Gerrard Houllier was doing under the pressure, I answered, "Of course he's under pressure, he's had a heart attack hasn't he?!" I thought it was a perfectly reasonable thing to say, but the reaction we got from the viewers suggested they didn't agree! They accused me of bringing up the subject of Houllier's heart attack when I had no right to. I wrote a letter of apology to the former Liverpool manager, explaining that it was just a comment and that I hoped he hadn't been offended. I was delighted when he communicated back to me to tell me that he found what I said amusing and, no, he wasn't offended in any way. He added that he knew the French had a reputation for not having a sense of humour, but that he loved the show. One of my phrases I use all the time, especially on television, is, "This is my opinion, and my opinion only," and he actually used it himself.

It is well-documented that Jeff Stelling once had to make a written public apology for me after I said on air that Sir Alan Sugar, the hugely successful businessman, former Spurs owner and now TV personality with his 'Apprentice' programme, didn't understand football, because he talked about money more than about the game. Sugar was quoted in the press as saying something to the effect that Spurs had signed Les Ferdinand and that he was not worth £3 million or something like that. Jeff did his "please accept our apology" moment, and I'm happy to report that much later, Sugar was one of the many people who contacted me to say how much they enjoyed the show and my comments. I thought he showed he was a big man when he did that.

Then came the now infamous saga that was to become known as 'The Bradford Head Shave.' It all began at the start of the 1990 season, when I said that Bradford was the worst team to play in the Premier League. "Useless," I said, "They can't defend, won't score goals and will definitely go down. No doubt about it, they will go down." The following week I had a phone call from their Chairman, Geoffrey Richmond, and he started waffling on at me. "Geoffrey," I asked, "What is your point?" "It's not what you say, it's the way you said it," he said, and he asked why I'd been so dismissive. With my tongue firmly in my cheek I said "The trouble with Yorkshire-men is that you are always complaining and whinging." Again I asked him what his point was. He said the fans were all screaming and shouting things about me. "Geoffrey, what is your point?" I repeated. He finally asked me if I would travel up to Bradford, and go face to face with him on a live radio phone-in. "No problem," I said, it sounded like good fun. Indeed, just up my street. I got slaughtered, absolutely slaughtered. As soon as the guy in charge said, "Rodney Marsh is here to take your calls," their switchboard lit up like a Christmas tree. At the end of the show, Richmond had one more question. "What happens if Bradford don't go down?" "You will," I said. I backed my judgement, and he challenged me to shave off my long silver locks if Bradford survived. "Tell you what," I told him, "if Bradford don't go down, I will come up on the first home match of next season and have my head shaved in front of the crowd, live on Sky, sitting in the centre spot of Valley Parade." Richmond said, "We won't go down," but I still said they would and we argued some more. It became a massive story and fantastic PR for Sky.

Stelling loved every minute of it as the results ticked away on Saturday afternoons, and the banter between us got to fever pitch. He poked fun at me and the others joined in. I was the butt of haircut and shaven head jokes. But that was me, and I didn't mind it one bit. The Bradford population went on a crusade of anti-Marsh feeling. There were t-shirts made, radio stations kept up the attack with phone-ins, articles were written, and the chant they sang at games as they pinched a point here and there was "Are you watching Rodney Marsh?" It was great for Bradford, good for me and sensational for Sky. With eleven games to go, they were still adrift while Wimbledon, fourth from bottom, looked out of reach. "I told you so," I repeated on the show, while Jeff and the rest kept warning me that it wasn't over.

Then Wimbledon went on an incredible run of failure, picking up only one point from a possible thirty-three, mad! It came down to the last game of the season with Bradford needing to beat Liverpool at their Valley Parade Stadium. How it came to that, I will never know. I still couldn't believe Bradford would survive, especially with something resting on the game for Liverpool. Then, out of the blue, from nowhere,

David Weatherall rose like a salmon at the far post to brilliantly head the only goal of the game. Bradford had survived and I was heading for the razor.

Fast forward to August and the new season, and picture the scene. Valley Parade packed, cameras, radio and the media waiting in anticipation, plus a bloodthirsty crowd. I had made the bet and was never going to back down. I did think, when they plonked me down on a chair in the centre circle that I was going to have a 'number two' shave. I didn't know that Sky producer Ian Condron had told them they could go to the bone. Thanks Condo! One of the stipulations was that, on the day, there would be a charity collection, and the good people of Bradford threw what they could afford in to buckets passed around the stadium. We raised £20,000 for the 'Burned Children's Club' charity. You can imagine how, back in the studio, Jeff and the panel pissed themselves as my locks came off. It was a brilliant promotion, and people still say to me "See the hair has grown back Rod." Surely that's what being a pundit is all about, saying what you believe and holding your hands up when you get it wrong.

I screwed up again when West Brom were promoted and had only spent around £750,000 on new players, while other clubs had invested millions of pounds on their teams. Again I said they had no chance of surviving, and when Jeff went through the signings they'd made, I described it as "putting lipstick on pigs." Again, I got slaughtered and West Brom even sold 'Lipstick on Pigs' t-shirts at their club shop. Good fun, good television, which can only be created by someone who is prepared to say what they think. Today, there is too much blandness on the box, and for me it's not what the fans want to hear. They want honesty, the truth and a bit of fun.

Eventually, I became disillusioned with Gillette Soccer Saturday and believed the show had lost its edge. By the time I was sacked, I feared it had lost its spontaneity, humour and banter. George Best was long-gone – one Saturday he left the make-up department for the studio and never arrived. They eventually found him a hundred yards away at the pub, and the regulars became Phil Thompson, Alan McAnally, Gordon McQueen and Charlie Nicholas. I had trouble listening to Charlie because I found what he had to say had no final point, and I often day-dreamed as he waffled on. The same with Clive Allen, who spoke sense but without passion. As I saw it, it had become just another football show, and that was sad.

So, I was sacked by Sky after the Newcastle row, and of course it was down to my reputation as a Loose Cannon. It has been the same throughout my career, just when things get to a certain point I have to do something. It is like my mind is programmed to do something shocking, and my thoughts often return to that meeting I had with the psychiatrist in America and the things he told me about my state of mind. Things can play on my mind, and I recall receiving a phone call late at night while I was in America from Terry Venables, whom I hadn't spoken to for years. He told me that he didn't want me to find out the shocking news from anyone else, that Dave Clement, a smashing lad from my QPR days, had just committed suicide. I was gob-smacked and didn't get back to sleep that night. Why would such a lovely boy with a lovely wife and family, and an England international fullback, want to do that? What went on inside his head, I'm sure I could apply to certain points my life. What problems did he have to make him want to throw everything away? I had three sessions with my psychiatrist, and he described me as having a sabotage mentality, saying that when things are going well, I self-destruct. Do I? Is that not just saying it like it is?

I often think back to the things I have done. If the Newcastle fan hadn't rung in, if Jeff Stelling hadn't asked me about Gerrard Houllier or Bradford, then I would not have answered honestly, or with my sense of humour. I don't sit there thinking, "I must be controversial," these things just come out of my mouth, my inner feelings and what I believe in. People said after I was sacked by Sky that I must be devastated, but I always answered "no, absolutely not. I did my best and the fickle finger moves on. Onwards and upwards," is what I say, and I truly believe there is always something else. That's life. I have nothing against Vic Wakeling and Andy Melvin, two professionals who did what they believed was best for Sky. I have no problem with that.

I am proud of what I achieved at Sky and what I helped create for them. Perhaps the show had become a case of "What's Rodney going to say next?" and maybe that was a problem for too many people. Of course I rubbed people up the wrong way, but that's me, isn't it? I am what I am and it is what it is. It's just what Loose Cannons do. Ask Eric Cantona why he flew two-footed at a Crystal Palace fan on his way to the dressing room after being sent off on January 25, 1995. He didn't think he was going to do that, it just happened, a spontaneous moment. I've had millions of them. His subsequent quote at his disciplinary hearing, "When the seagulls follow the trawler, it's because they think sardines will be thrown into the sea," could have come from me, couldn't it? It sounds like one of mine. That is what we do, surprise people. He never apologised for what he did. No regrets.

I was delighted by the response I got when news broke that I had been sacked by Sky. Almost everyone involved with the shows I did phoned me to say thanks and goodbye. All except Charlie Nicholas that is. He must have sensed something. I'd received a lot of calls along the way from the most unexpected people, people who appreciated my honesty and comments, even if some of them were cutting towards them. Bryan Robson contacted me out of the blue, and as I have already mentioned, so did Sir Alan Sugar, now Lord Sugar, of course. Once, as I remember, just before we went on air, he told me he that wanted me to understand the background to the Sol Campbell transfer from his club Spurs to Arsenal, and he gave me permission to reveal it on the show. David Seaman, Geoffrey Richmond, Gerrard Houllier and the West Brom Chairman and many more, all took the trouble to phone in for a chat during my career at Sky. Over the years, a lot of good things came out of what I said and did. It was heart on the sleeve stuff, and I like to believe that I always said what other people were thinking.

Was I really that controversial in my eleven years on the panel of Gillette Soccer Saturday? A year after I was sacked, I did a guest appearance at a dinner in Epsom. It was a question and answer session, and three international goalkeepers were on the top table. There were about seven hundred people at the function, and half way through the evening a guy stood up and asked one of the keepers a question. He coached twelve year-old kids, and wanted to know what was the best piece of advice he had ever received. "Never have sex with a retarded midget!" was the answer. "It's not big and it's not clever!" Everyone was aghast and horrified. "Wow," I thought on my way home, "that was far, far worse than anything I said or did at Sky."

I experienced a harsh reality check about my time at Sky when I was the Master of Ceremonies at a charity golf day I put on at the Wildwood Country Club in Sussex. Some of the boys from Sky were asked to come down, and they all responded. Among those who turned up were Jeff Stelling, Paul Walsh, Chris Kamara, Alan Smith, Alan McAnally and even Charlie Nicholas turned up. The 'stars' played for different teams, with the punters paying for the opportunity to go out on the course with some of these household names. Before we teed off, I did my stuff on the mike and introduced the guests in my tongue in cheek style. "Charlie Nicholas is on team A," I announced, "so be careful, because he won't buy a drink in the bar afterwards." Everyone laughed as it set the mood of the day, and I went through the others with some funny stories.

"Stelling can't play," I said, "he's a bit of an old woman, and will be moaning and groaning and boring you stupid about Hartlepool." Kamara will be "Unbelievable Jeff," and then I got to Alan Smith. "Stand up and introduce yourself as 'Mr. Personality', Alan." More laughter and banter. It was a craic and good fun. Smith clearly didn't think so and approached me before play. "Can I have a word, Rodney?" he asked, and I said, "Sure, fire away," but he would only speak outside. As soon as we moved outside, Smith turned on me and screamed, "What the fuck do you think you're doing? How can you say that about me when you don't know me?" "Hold on Alan," I said. "This is a bit of fun, we're raising money for charity, and I am not only taking the piss out of all you lot, but myself too." He then delivered a never to be forgotten line. "Rodney, don't you know that there are people around you who hate your guts, but we don't say it, do we?" I said, "Alan, that's the difference, what I said is to your face, all that stuff is behind my back."

I was taking the piss out of myself all day too and the personality jibe was just a bit of fun, but he couldn't see that and took it the wrong way. He just walked off after our brief exchange. I did have respect for Smith in calling me outside and telling me to my face.

It was also Alan who, on Soccer Saturday, delivered one of the most hilarious lines ever. He was a remote reporter from a game and while describing a player who had been forced to play out of position, said of him "He's like a fish up a tree." Jeff and me were crying by the time they threw it back to the studio. Brilliant!

If some of my colleagues did hate me, so be it. I believed Smith, because he said it with such passion he could not have made it up. Hate is a strong word, but that is what he said to me. He had said something that clearly had been festering, and now it was out in the open. I didn't have a problem with that, and don't look back in anger. I did what I did, said what I said and moved on to the next stage of my life.

I was immediately picked up by TalkSport radio on a two year deal and it was while I was working for them that I had an incredibly intimidating experience. I have mixed with some dodgy characters over the years, but nothing compared to the day former World Heavy Weight boxing champion Mike Tyson came into the studio. Programme Director Bill Ridley had told us that Tyson was going to do an interview. "What, via the satellite link?" we asked. "No," he said, "In the studio." I couldn't believe that Tyson would bother to come into TalkSport. Sure enough, the following week he turned up, along with fifteen minders. You have never seen such hoods in your life, all of them bursting out of their suits with sunglasses on, and scowling faces. And they all insisted on going into the studio with the man they were being paid to protect. It was a scrum to say the least, and you could have cut the atmosphere with a knife. It was as if they were waiting for me, or fellow presenter Paul Breen Turner, to make one false move. Tyson sat next to me, his huge tattoo decorating his face and with a sneer on his lips. We were worried about our questions to him. Paul asked the first couple of questions and you just didn't know what might trigger off something nasty. You couldn't be controversial for fear of upsetting them, and Tyson, after a few minutes, had a look on his face that said, "What am I doing here with these two numpties?" He hadn't a clue who I was.

Tyson was in the UK to promote one of his tours, so I gambled on getting his attention and interest. "Mike," I said, "I'm a bit of a student of sport and love my boxing, how much do you know about it?" He looked at me sideways and I asked him a question, "What was Rocky Marciano's nickname?" He didn't blink and answered correctly straight away. For the next ten minutes we quizzed each other and he relaxed, much to my relief. It lightened the whole atmosphere, and by the end of the interview we had seen a different side to Tyson. He was human after all! Just joking Mike! Now, this guy is proper tough, and when we did some photographs together afterwards, he almost crushed my fist with a handshake. He seemed to enjoy it even if the minders didn't. They kept their stare in place until they left. If anyone doesn't need a minder it's Mike Tyson! Who pays fifteen bodyguards to follow the main man into a radio station? Madness, really, but that is their world.

TalkSport radio is the only job I left on my terms, when I'd eventually had enough of the way they manufactured controversy. Now, I know I'm controversial, but everything I say comes from the heart and I mean and feel it. At TalkSport they would criticise anyone, or say anything to get a reaction. Presenter Adrian Durham is brilliant at it, and one day he called Liverpool's Jamie Carragher a bottler for refusing to play for England again. Within two minutes, Carragher was on the phone demanding to know what Durham's problem was. "Listen," Carragher said, "'I will be at Liverpool's training ground all next week, and if you think I'm a bottler and want to come and talk about it." Durham could only stutter, "but, but, but." Good luck to Carragher; if anyone's not a bottler, it's him.

I do want to add at this point that I do completely respect one show on Talk Sport. Hawkesby and Jacobs. Not everyone's cup of tea but I found them to be fresh, creative and on the cutting edge of original humour. Long may they continue.

Shortly before the World Cup, I made a series for NBC Television in America, interviewing players, managers and coaches. It was called Countdown to the World Cup, and one of the men I sat down with was Bob Bradley, the coach of the US team. Soon into the interview, I asked him whether, when he first heard the draw for South Africa that USA were England's first opponents, he thought that this was the biggest match of his career? "Biggest match?" he said, "it will be the defining moment of my life." He spoke deeply and passionately about the game, and said that if he were to mastermind a victory over England, in fifty years they would still be talking about it and, more significantly, him. "I will go down in history," he said, and there was a silence for a short period afterwards as he contemplated the enormity of the game for his country. That is what football does to people; it draws out the inner feeling, the desire and the wanting. I had no idea my question would trigger such a reaction and that, I suspect, has happened to many, many interviewers. You don't quite know what to expect. I have been interviewed thousands of times in my career, and can now understand what a 'good interview' means. I hope I always gave good value during the time I spent with newspapers, television and radio people. I can assure them I was always myself.

So, what is good pundit? In my view, it is someone who tells the truth and is not scared to tell it how it is. If you're not scared to give your opinion when talking football in a pub with your mates, then that is how you should be on television. You are paid to give your opinions. If you upset people along the way, tough, if some don't like it, tough. If it leads to the sack, so be it. If you feel you have to be protective to others, then don't take the money and go on. You will lose respect.

Many of the pundits I have worked with, one in particular who is highly thought of, talk about football totally differently off air than they do once they go 'live'. I think that's patronising and insulting to the broadcast audience.

People in power have to make decisions, and I have rubbed those in authority up the wrong way throughout my life. From schoolmasters, to the England manager and heads of sport, I have been a nuisance to them. But you get what you see and I believe that over the years, this Loose Cannon has given entertainment and value for money.

14

Into the Jungle

When I finished playing I had no idea what to do. Most footballers ask themselves "What next?" but I have never been worried about the future. Something always turns up and my cup is always half full, not half empty. I had no idea, for instance, that I would become a Manager and then Chief Executive in America. Who could have predicted that I would join George Best for a multi-year road show, work for Sky Television for eleven years, and then go to TalkSport Radio for two years? Companies have approached me to do things for them, to advertise their product, and I have appeared on the successful TV show 'Come Dine With Me,' when actress Lesley Joseph and I hit it off so well, people thought we were having an affair. I have appeared on shows like 'The Alan Titchmarsh Show,' and not a day goes by when I don't think of a new project. My mind races with fresh ideas.

Nothing, however, beats the persistence of ITV executives to get me on the hugely successful 'I'm A Celebrity, Get me Out of Here' show. It went on for three years before I eventually agreed to go into the Australian jungle, during which time the fee increased yearly until I agreed in 2007.

Why have I always been in demand and why do people want me? These are good questions. Loose Cannon characters have the curiosity factor I suppose. People don't quite understand what makes us tick and, therefore, they try and find out. Most managers didn't have a clue how I operated on a football pitch. Game plans went out of the window and tactics were ditched because I did my own thing. I have always said and done what I feel is right. I have met some wonderful people, and at times have got involved with others who I didn't understand or want anything to do with, but I learnt from them all.

It was wonderful to meet Sir Henry Cooper in a TV series I did with famous people. One of the questions I asked him when we sat and chatted in his Thomas-a-Beckett gym in London, was "What do you consider the greatest boxing venue of all?" He hardly hesitated before he answered, "Highbury, the old home of Arsenal." They were his favourite football team; he watched them as a boy, so to box in front of the fans gave him his biggest thrill. I had expected him to say Madison Square Garden in New York or the MGM Grand in Las Vegas, but no, it was Highbury. It is the link with football that constantly inspires people and brings all different classes together. I'm happy to say I have been in the middle of it all my life.

I could tell Lesley Joseph liked me as soon as we started recording our cookery programme. We hit it off, two oldies together and the chemistry was there. You can just tell, can't you? There is no reason why she and I should not work together in the future. You can't manufacture chemistry on television, can you? It just happens. Also on the show were Abi Titmuss, Paul Ross and Linda Lusardi and it was great fun, something completely different for me. I'd also appeared on 'Ready Steady Cook' and I do enjoy cooking. I used my daughter Joanna's place for my stint of entertaining on 'Come Dine with Me' and took advice from a number of people before I went live in preparing a three-course meal. Who knows what the future might bring. A cookery book perhaps, who knows?

The Jungle was certainly the biggest project I'd done away from football. Did I want to do it? Not really. But I was flattered they chased me so hard and, in the end, the money was too good to turn down. My entry into the Aussie outback came about when I was working with Ram Sports, a company I had formed with Melissa Chappell. We formed the company as equal partners. She had other clients like Sky's Helen Chamberlain, and Kirsty Gallagher. Ram eventually merged with Merlin Sports and I went with her. Richard Thompson, the owner of Merlin, had been talking to various companies and had promised to bring me ambassadorial opportunities. They eventually arranged for me to meet ITV about going into the Jungle and they kept me waiting for an hour, so I walked out. Many people misunderstand my honesty for rudeness, although one thing I'm not is late for appointments. I pride myself on punctuality. If you want me somewhere at ten o'clock, I will be there at ten to. There was no apology from ITV and I was pissed off.

At that point I had retired and had returned to the USA.

The following year, my daughter Joanna, who had taken on managing my diary, was talking to ITV about something else and they brought up the subject of the Jungle. "Didn't we get close to your father? Why not let's have another chat?" they said. There was a meeting in London and, to be honest, because of the way they treated me the previous year, I wasn't bothered. They offered me a fee and I spoke to Alex Best when we bumped into each other one evening in Wimbledon Village. She had also been on the show in a previous year, and I asked her how much she got. When she told me £25,000 was a normal fee, I realised the money was good. I still wasn't sold on the idea and said no to ITV. They came back with an improved offer and I said no again. A fourth and fifth time they asked me and each time I said thanks, but no thanks. Finally they came up with an offer that was commensurate with my position in the media and I agreed to go into the jungle and make a fool of myself. Then, when I thought about it that night, I became sceptical again and rang them the next morning and said no. Clearly, this time they were pissed off and got someone else.

Incredibly, the next year they were back again, calling Joanna. We messed up the first year, they said, last year was your fault, how about third time lucky? For some reason they wanted me, and the offer was still on the table. I said, "Let's do it," so a contract was thrashed out. I'd seen the show, watched in horror as stars ate all sorts of weird, wonderful and disgusting things and laughed as they did the trials. What ITV didn't know as I signed the deal is that I had no intention of swallowing a kangaroo's bollock or anything like that. The timing was good for me because I had just left TalkSport Radio, a company that bored me to tears in the end and I was up for a new challenge.

Also with me in the Jungle for series seven were Anna Ryder-Richardson, the interior designer, TV presenter, pantomime dame and TV personality Christopher Biggins, Welsh singer-songwriter Cerys Matthews, English actress and glamour model Gemma Atkinson, singer Jason 'J' Brown, American model and fashion photographer Janice Dickinson, chef John Burton-Race, English reality TV contestant and journalist Katie Hopkins, public relations consultant and commentator on women's issues Lynne Franks, and soap opera actor Marc Bannerman, and me. What I was doing in the jungle with ten strangers? I had no idea. The money was decent and I have always been someone to open up new doors and discover.

Everything about this show is first-class with no expense spared. There is a production team of more than six hundred, and the presenters Ant and Dec are brilliant, professional and generally super, and ITV made a fuss of us with great hotels and first-class travel. I didn't know who else was on the show until I got to Australia and we all met up. The only person that knew was Janice Dickinson, who had demanded to know who she was up against. After a first-class flight to Sydney there was an initial meeting, during which they tell you what you can and can't do. They prefer you to have done some kind of fitness exercise, so with my regular tennis matches, I was okay. Indeed, compared to Biggins, I was an Olympic athlete.

They also organise a meeting with a psychiatrist who has to establish whether you are mentally stable enough to cope with the stresses and strains of the jungle, so they know that you won't do anything stupid if the pressure gets too much. Now, this was just up my street, dissecting the mind and trying to find out what makes people tick. I'm sorry to say I made her cry when I told her, soon into our conversation, that I didn't trust her. This led to she and I talking for more than two and a half hours and my daughter Joanna, who came with me to Australia, thinking something was wrong as she waited outside in her car. "No, nothing wrong," I said, "just playing games with the mind." No change there then.

By the time they fly you into the jungle by helicopter, you have already met the other contestants. I immediately hit it off with Katie Hopkins, who is a real person. I loved her company and she was good fun. From what I saw and given how they were with each other, I suspect Cerys Matthews and Marc Bannerman were more than friends and if they weren't they would have liked to have been. I thought Anna Ryder Richardson was a complete doughnut, and Lynne Franks was an awful woman. First impressions are often the best, aren't they? I have no idea what they all thought of me, and you know what I thought about that.

There were two camps of five, and Biggins was the odd one out as he came onto the scene later. We were six hundred miles into the jungle so there was no going back. Anyone who thinks the whole thing is a set up and that you don't live the life of someone marooned in the jungle should think again. It's real and it's difficult. Ant and Dec had their own living unit and came in and out of the camps with results, but we were right in the heart of the bush. On the first day I kept thinking "Rodney, what are you doing?" but then I decided it was a good opportunity to have a little bit of fun. I liked and got on well with Bannerman, even though he started to make a bit of a dick of himself by making it clear that he would like to 'bonk' Cerys Matthews. Bannerman was like a young version of me, bit cocky and confident, and on one trial we did together he asked if he could ask me a question. We covered up our mikes in case it went out on the show, and he asked me whether I thought he was making a prat of himself with Cerys. I told him that he had a girlfriend, and that they were thinking of getting married, yet here he was flirting like mad in front of six million people. "Work it out for yourself," I said, and he admitted, almost sadly, "Yes, I suppose you're right." He was the first celebrity to be voted out.

I had some trials to do, some underwater swimming thing that I didn't find a problem. Then I was in some kind of bubble, which was okay, but I was useless when put out on a balancing wire, which I found hard. The only thing I knew I wouldn't be able to do was eat the slimy body parts of animals. Fortunately, I was never presented with that kind of challenge.

There wasn't enough camaraderie in our camp for me. At one stage I thought

John Burton-Race was going to do something mad. I woke once at four in the morning because I was cold, and he was sitting over the fire carving a piece of wood with the big knife they give you to cut the wood for the fire. He'd decided it was his responsibility to keep the fire alight, so was carving away when I woke, but he had the knife-blade aimed towards him. "Any minute now," I thought, "he'll slice his hand off," so I asked him what the matter was. "My fucking wife," he said, "She's sold the restaurant and all sorts of things are going on at home." I feared for him and hoped he wasn't on the brink of doing something stupid.

The only communication you have with your family is a letter after ten days, and I got one from Joanna, although the stipulation is that they are not allowed to talk about what is going on in the outside world. You are literally cut off from everything. When I asked them if they could find out the score of England against Croatia in the big European Championship decide at Wembley that night they said "No, not a chance." What happened next was so fortunate. The next morning I got an injury by falling down a hill face – yes, another dive, but I was good at it after years of practice! – I told them my knee was knackered. They carried me out of the jungle and popped me into a hospital for treatments and tests. I got someone to find out the score and what had happened, then limped back into the jungle. When I heard that England had lost 3-2 and not qualified for the 2008 European Finals, I'm not sure whether the injury had been worth it. Steve McClaren, I later found out, was sacked that day, and what a waste of time he proved to be. For England not to be at a major final was ridiculous.

I thought Christopher Biggins, who eventually won and was crowned King of the Jungle, was sensational. Good company, funny and a great character. One night in bed I heard him sobbing, got up and asked him what the problem was. "They won't let my boyfriend out," he cried, "His company says he can't leave England to come over here and be with me. They just won't let my lover come and it's awful, really awful. I so want him to be there when I come out." I gave him a hug and he sobbed some more. Picture the scene, Rod, the most heterosexual man in the world, cuddling a pantomime dame in tears, asking for his lover. Couldn't make it up could you? I was surprised they didn't use that scene in the show, and there were other situations that were not screened, like the games and exercise routines I organised. For the first five days I had all my colleagues doing exercises and then organised a baseball-pitching contest. It was good fun and helped to ease the boredom, but they didn't show any of it. They clearly didn't want me to be seen as an organiser or ringleader, which I find interesting. The more I spoke to the organisers, the more I realised that the contestants are hand picked to be the character the producers perceive them to be.

Did they see me as a troublemaker, and was that the reason they paid me so much to finally accept the invitation?

I just tried to be myself throughout but after I came out, I discovered more and more that they wanted me to be trouble rather than to allow my true character to unfold. Why did they invite me in, and was I a disappointment to them? Did they see me as an anti-feminist and a chauvinist pig? When you put me up against Lynne Franks, that's probably how I came across. What a nightmare she turned out to be. Is that what they wanted?

Have you ever had moments when you just know you are not going to get on with someone, that you are so different and far apart it simply isn't going to work? The best thing to do is to retreat and distance yourself from them, although in the jungle, of course, that isn't possible. I took an instant dislike to Lynne Franks and hated everything she stood for. You could have cut the tension between us with a knife, and I'm sure at times it looked nasty. She just wanted to dominate everything, made it clear that whatever she said was right, and she kept trying to control us with orders like "This afternoon, we are going to do this," and "Now, we are all going to feel good about ourselves." Fuck off Lynne; we don't need you to preach what is wrong and right.

She had this habit of dancing in the afternoon. This seventeen-stone lump would parade in front of us, arms waving as if in the wind and, to my surprise, others copied her. "Lynne," I said, "How did you become to be so graceful, and where did you learn to dance so well?" She didn't realise I was completely taking the piss, even though Bannerman was killing himself laughing while she told us that it was while she had once visited Native India. "You're amazing Lynne, so nimble on your feet," I added as she stumbled through another set of dances.

It was just a wind up, and she was an easy target for my kind of humour. I asked her if she thought women were second-class citizens, why there had been no great female inventors, and if she got on a plane and there were two female pilots, would she get off? I thought she was going to explode with rage! Eventually, she realised I'd been taking the Mickey out of her for days. This led to rows and confrontations, and I'm not sure the show did justice to how much we disliked each other. She and her feminist preaching, and me with my cockney wit and humour. When she was selected to do a trial, she asked the entire camp to meditate for her. Lynne, will you please fuck off.

I didn't get on with Janice Dickinson, either. I thought she was a complete arsehole who was only there to try and further her career. One night by the fire, she told me that she'd lost so much weight just to look good for the camera. "How?" I asked, and she told me she'd undergone a tummy tuck, lifting up her shirt to show me a huge bright red scar with staple marks. Again, the ITV producers decided not to show that scene.

There are no washing facilities in the Jungle, just a waterfall where they give you organic soap because it flows away easily downstream. The toilet is a bucket under a hole in the ground. We had to change it every morning, and John Burton-Race, who was clearly a self-loather, did it every time. "My job," he said. Extraordinary. "Hey, go for it" I said.

It's interesting that when it was obvious that we were getting really hungry, the trials to win good food became easier. The moment we ate well and the frustration and bitterness had decreased, they made the tests harder again. The mental card was played a lot. Some can cope, others can't, and I managed to hold on for as long as I could. I am mentally tough when it comes to things like that. Mind games I can play.

After each day, the votes came in from the public for which contestant they want to kick out of the Jungle. They make the decision by phoning in on our individual numbers. You are asked to nominate a charity before the series begins, with a percentage of the money taken on the phone calls going to the charity of your choice. I put forward 'The Burned Children's Club' charity, which has become something close to my heart. Jamie Redknapp is the patron and my physio Kevin Lidlow is a contributor. When children get burned and are treated, there is not enough follow-up treatment and help for them. There is no programme to re-build faces and body parts, not enough psychological help to send them back into the world, not enough counselling, and I was keen to raise money for this cause. I asked the producer how much was normally raised, and he told me somewhere between six and eight thousand pounds. I was delighted when my charity, 'The Burned Children's Club,' received £38,000. It made it all worthwhile.

I got voted off after seventeen of the twenty-four days, and it was definitely a relief. The experience was good for the powers of self-control and mental toughness, but I can't say I enjoyed my stay in the jungle. I told the public to vote me out a few days before I went, although there was one stipulation: don't vote me out before Lynne Franks! Thankfully, she did go before me, ghastly woman.

I have to say the show is brilliantly organised and handled. It is a work of art, with so many people behind the scenes pulling it all together. Presenters Ant and Dec have no more involvement than what you see on television. They come and go and talk to us for only the amount you witness sitting at home. They are good operators who have a great sense of humour. Those celebrities who go out early have a life of luxury, being put up in a seven-star Versace hotel, all expenses paid, while waiting for the show to end when the King or Queen of the Jungle is crowned. This time it was Biggins, who was overwhelmed and full of emotion when he was chosen. I met Biggins for lunch a few weeks after the show; he is a delightful guy and we have kept in touch. I also went out to dinner with Katie Hopkins, and I stayed in contact with John Burton-Race.

The Jungle was another box to tick for me. Another experience. I have always enjoyed testing myself and, like everything in life I have done, don't regret the experience. I met interesting people, some I got on with, others I didn't. I'm sure those I shared the campsite with have not all been complimentary about me. I don't care about that, and they should not worry what I think. If you allow too many negatives to stay in the brain, the only person to suffer is you. I have always approached everything I have done with a positive attitude. It's the only way.

15

Captain, Manager and Chief Executive

I don't believe in role models. What does that even mean? That you try to be something and someone you're not? My motto in life has always been 'just be yourself.' I have never wanted or tried to make others follow me just because I had a successful career in football.

Rodney Marsh is not a role model; I have never wanted to make people look up to me. What I believe to be most important is to try to be true to myself. I failed many times and I admit I haven't always followed that through in certain situations, but in football I have attempted to give the public what they wanted. However, if others choose to follow or to copy you, then that is an entirely different matter. You have responsibility as a celebrity, even if that doesn't necessarily make you a role model.

For instance, apart from England, I captained every team I played for when, deep down, I know I should never have been given the honour. When I was told that I would be captain of Queen's Park Rangers, Manchester City, Fulham and my teams in America I didn't think, "Right, now I'm the leader I must change and be different." I was ALREADY different, and I believe that is why they made me captain. I played as I played and being captain made no difference to me.

I always took the responsibility of scoring goals, taking penalties, creating chances for others and, in America, winning the shoot-outs, and I suppose others could judge me on that. I don't think I was a good captain, and I'm sure the only reason my clubs made me the skipper was because they felt that if they couldn't beat me, then they had to join me. I was always going to do my thing, have my say, be critical and possibly controversial, so they probably thought, "We might as well make him captain." Life and football is not a popularity contest and if my team mates didn't like me as captain, that was their problem, not mine.

The first captain I played under when I began my career at Fulham in 1963 was Johnny Haynes, then Alan Mullery. At QPR it was Mike Keen and Terry Venables, then at City Tony Book and Mike Summerbee. With England, it was a privilege to be led out by Bobby Moore, but when he didn't play it was Emlyn Hughes, who I did not respect. When I went back to Fulham, Alan Slough was the captain. Apart from Moore and Haynes, I didn't hold any of them in particularly great esteem, although Mike Keen was QPR's greatest ever captain. Others didn't mean that much to me. I just did my own thing and that's probably why I was a bit of a manager's nightmare. I never applied myself to the job and was always the one to forget the instructions from the manager. I was a leader in many ways, but mainly as an unorthodox character, not as a captain.

I never had any problem taking on responsibility, even if I didn't believe in those in authority. Taking penalties, for instance, came naturally to me. I loved the challenge of one against one, the feeling of the two men, the goalkeeper and the taker, trying to double guess each other. The look into the eyes and the coldness of the moment, I thrived on that. Taking penalties is a hundred percent about mental attitude. That is why England has failed so badly in the past at major tournaments. It's all in the mind. Put Frank Lampard, Steven Gerrard, or any of England's other regular penalty takers into their club situation or onto the training pitch, and they would blaze away into the corners of the goal. Drop them into an international situation and it all changes due to the pressure and fear of failure. England have messed up so many times in the past that the players will have been dreading another shoot-out in the last sixteen matches onwards at the World Cup.

I had a mental block in the end, and after scoring eighteen penalties on the trot, I changed my mind at the last moment and missed. It was never the same after that. I'd second-guessed myself and that is dangerous. The only player I would have complete trust in today to score a World Cup winning penalty is Wayne Rooney. I compare myself a lot to the Manchester United star, but it is in mental attitude only. He has a toughness about him that stems from the heart. He was a born a passionate winner.

I have already said I would not want England to win in South Africa because an Italian, Fabio Capello, is in the top job, and will go further than that to say, that at the time of writing this, I don't believe they had a chance. Everyone pinned so much hope on Wayne Rooney, and he is not super-human. The way England play is just not conducive to success at the highest level. We want to play at one hundred miles an hour, but that is impossible through a World Cup.

Two things I would love to have done in my career is play for England at a World Cup, and take part in an FA Cup Final. Sadly, it never happened and I don't look back with regret, more a tinge of sadness. I've previously mentioned that I did play for Manchester City at Wembley in the League Cup Final, and was so disappointed at losing to Wolves that I refused to accept my loser's tankard. My request to the F.A. a few days later for my tankard was declined - my punishment for not conforming and doing the right thing on the day. How many times have I heard that levelled against me?

One thing always aimed at me is that I was a maverick. What the fuck does that mean? I have been coupled with players like Frank Worthington, Eric Cantona, Stan Bowles, Tony Currie, Peter Osgood and Alan Hudson. It's like being called a role model. If people want to see me as someone who did his own thing, fine. Is that a maverick? It's how others see you, nothing else. I read a recent comment by Bowles who, like me, was a star at Queen's Park Rangers because he did things others couldn't do. In the comment he criticised me and was very negative, and I was surprised because Bowles, for me, was one of the most talented, brilliant players England has produced. He won nothing and people might look upon that as a failure for him, but I don't because he provided such entertainment. You went to Rangers to watch Marsh and then Bowles. It seems that if you are even a little bit away from the norm, the game labels you as a rebel, a maverick or, most significantly, a failure. It's crazy, really.

I ran onto the pitch so many times believing that I was superior and better than the opposition. I used to look at some of them at kick-off time and think that I could destroy them. They knew that too, and it made me a target, which was a compliment. I recall one player who played for Doncaster, confronting me in the tunnel just as we were going out and saying that I would go off with a broken leg. He made it very clear he was out to get me. He was a big centre half with a bald head, not someone you'd want to meet in a dark alley at midnight. It was an inferiority complex that triggered his threat, the fact he knew he shouldn't have been on the same pitch as me. I was brilliant that day and destroyed him and Doncaster, but his comment did affect me.

What is a hard player? He is different today from when I played. Men like Norman Hunter, Tommy Smith and Ron 'Chopper' Harris just went through you at every opportunity. They were allowed to and had a different mental approach to others. They didn't have the individual skill of their opponents and instead just used their 'couldn't care less' attitude to destroy. That's what they did, to stop the likes of me playing and doing what I was good at. I used to look at the team sheets before games against Chelsea and Leeds and groan to myself, "Another kicking coming." How there were not more serious injuries back then, I will never know. They would not get into teams today because they didn't have the skills. I laugh when I hear some players today called hard men. There aren't any in football now because the game has changed so much, for the better I might add. John Terry, the Chelsea captain, is tough not dirty, and is a throwback, an old-fashioned player. He gets stuck in and leads his team with his 'never say die' attitude.

When the time was right to finish playing, I had no idea what would come next for me. I didn't want to be a manager, a coach or a Chief Executive. Indeed, not a pundit. I knew that I was approaching a slight dilemma, an unprepared moment. You know that you should give up when the legs will no longer allow you to do what the mind tells them. Funnily enough, I didn't really care what was next. "I might do this, might do that," I thought, and I stepped off the edge that all footballers reach without having a real target. That's just how I am, always Charles Dickens' figure, Mr. Micawber, thinking, "Something will turn up." I'd earned good money in my time, invested it relatively wisely and had enough to drift for eighteen months.

It was Manchester City and Tony Book who brought my career in England to a close at thirty-one years old. With a different manager, indeed, a different type of person, I might have stayed and played at home for a few more years. After three months at City, I was the fittest I'd ever been. It's a great feeling when you are a sportsman, to be a hundred percent fit and in control of everything, mentally and physically. One game against Derby, I was right in the zone and we destroyed them. I could do no wrong and that was down to a combination of fitness and mental strength. I believe I lost the First Division title for City in the season I arrived, that a lot of it was down to my lack of fitness in the first three months. The only other time I've felt the same was at Tampa in 1978 when I was thirty-three years old. We played a lot of indoor football, which I combined with weight training and two hundred metre pile-offs, when you run two hundred metres flat out, then walk one hundred, and do you it again and again. I lost twenty pounds in that period and felt so good.

It is no good trying to cheat when you know your legs have gone. I believe a great example of that was Alan Shearer towards the end of his career at Newcastle. He could hardly run, couldn't get away from defenders, and could only muscle opponents out of the way, but he wanted that club goal-scoring record and hung on until he got it. David Beckham knows in his heart that he should not still be playing for England. He plays with inferior players in Los Angeles, and then travels nine thousand miles to play ten minutes and get another cap. I'd have said "Okay, that's me done," long ago. You know you're finished professionally when you just can't make the runs anymore, and it is a huge barrier to overcome when playing, scoring and being a hero has been your life.

Paul Gascoigne is a classic example of someone who couldn't cope with retirement. Some people are born to do one thing and one thing only; Gazza's only lifeline was being a footballer, and what a brilliant footballer he was. To see him hanging on and dropping down the leagues was sad. It was an embarrassment, and I can never understand great players wanting to play the equivalent of pub-team football. I believe that all the problems Gascoigne has created and faced in recent years are down to his inability to cope with not being able to carry on with what he was born to do, play football. It is a difficult situation for many outstanding players: heroes one minute, forgotten the next.

My first job as a manager was with New York United in 1980. My reaction was a bit like when I was invited to be a captain. The question was "Why me?" They were semi-professional, and I joined them first as a coach and then took over as manager. You won't be surprised to know that, from the start, I was like Kevin Keegan. It was all attack, attack, attack, no defensive tactics, plenty of goals, excitement and fun. I wasn't your man for nil-nil draws. I enjoyed the experience. Someone must have enjoyed it too, because after one year I received a call from an executive in Charlotte with an offer to manage Carolina Lightnin'. "Come over and talk to us Rodney," he said, "We want some fun too." I asked my boss at New York, and he gave me permission to travel to talk to them. "Oh, I'm that important to you, am I?" I laughed. The first year was remarkable and we won the whole Championship and the playoffs in the first season. After three years in Charlotte, I went back to Tampa as coach/manager before becoming Chief Executive.

The biggest problem I had as a manager was asking players to do things that I had found easy as a player. The fact that many players didn't understand, or couldn't carry out my instructions frustrated and annoyed me. I have heard other former players say this, and it certainly is a big problem. Malcolm Allison and Terry Venables were not great players, but they were great coaches and perhaps that is their secret, why they were so good at coaching. At forty years old I couldn't cope with it, even if in my first year in Charlotte, we won the whole thing.

Managing is the art of getting the balance right; man-management in one corner, and getting your team to work together as you want them to in the other. I had an ongoing problem with it. After four years I went back to Tampa, my first love in the US, where I became all-powerful. It was a period during which I learnt so much about the other side of football, the running of a club, even if some of the other owners talked to me as if I had three heads! In return, I soon got to know that there are a lot of people out there with power who know absolutely nothing about the game.

One year I went to represent the Rowdies at an annual meeting of the Soccer League. Every year, they discussed possible rule changes, like no off sides, shoot outs, the thirty-five-yard line, whether there should be no more draws, replaced instead by a Golden Goal, and everything else that might introduce new excitement. At this particular meeting, they came up with an absolute beauty. It was suggested that FIFA should be told that America would introduce a rule that allowed one outfield player, wearing the number nine shirt, to handle the ball. "Let him punch the ball into the net," they said. At first I thought it was a wind-up! I couldn't believe it when I looked around and only a couple of us shook our heads in disbelief. "It'll be exciting, just like basketball, get the crowds going," they said. "Let the number nine be allowed to out-jump the 'keeper and punch the ball into goal." The more they talked about it, the more I wanted to crawl away in embarrassment. This idea was actually put forward by a committee, and no doubt they'd taken hours to come up with such drivel. After the presentation, I had to say something and upset the majority by telling them that if they put this forward, then FIFA would look upon the US as if we were all dressed in Mickey Mouse costume. "They will not take us seriously ever again," I said strongly, and added that I wanted no part in it.

One guy, Lee Stern from Chicago, got up to argue the case for, saying that it didn't seem such a bad idea. "We might get some 5-4 games," he said. I butted in and said that it was a joke idea, so we eventually agreed that it would go to a vote. There were twenty-four teams represented, with the Chairman having the deciding vote if necessary. The vote was close, thirteen against and eleven for. Had it been twelve against twelve, the Chairman would have voted to accept. Can you believe that eleven grown men actually thought it was a good idea? I was relieved, if still worried, that I was getting involved in something I might have no control over. It just proved to me that, right across the world, there are men in power controlling committees and making big decisions, who do not have a clue. We can relate this to all walks of life and business. How do they reach such positions of power? I have always been in favour of change and doing oddball things but please, I ask you, a number nine scoring goals with his fist?

Whatever you may think of me, I love football, always have, always will. I would not make any changes to the rules, apart from to try and create a situation that would see an end to football's obsession with money. The game itself is brilliant. I recall watching Arsenal take on Manchester United two years ago, and the match was a wonderful advert for everything that is good about football. Free flowing, loads of chances, great skills and individuals doing their stuff. It was a privilege to be there, watching. It had everything, and produced everything I love about football.

What I don't like is to see the fans so far-removed from the game. They have been pushed aside in the relentless pursuit of money. Every decision today is based around one thing, money and making a profit. Take agents, for example, do they really deserve the obscene amounts of money they take from the game? They do not love the sport and are only in it, only attach themselves to players for one reason, and that is to enrich their own lifestyles. Please don't let anyone defend them. The vast majority are parasites and I hate the damage they do to the game. Football used to be ninety percent love and passion and ten percent money, but now it's the other way around.

Let's get it right, some footballers are also parasites and are only in the game for what they can take from it. Robinho kissed the Manchester City badge during his third game, but it wasn't long before he was shipped off to Santos because he didn't actually fit in or like English football. My feeling is he would rather have played for Chelsea. In some games he didn't try or seem to care, yet he was supposed to be a man of the fans. It's bollocks isn't it, and in my opinion, players like Robinho give the English game a bad name.

It will never return to the days when players gave everything for the shirt and the pride of playing. The fans turn up week in, week out, while players come and go. Loyalty? Don't make me laugh! I don't feel part of what is happening today, and I blame the Football Association for allowing this to happen. The day they allowed Manchester United not to play in the FA Cup was the day that supporters came last in football's way of thinking. Testimonials are a thing of the past, because players don't hang around at one club any more. The days of the Manchester United kids under Sir Alex Ferguson not moving on have gone. There will never be another Ryan Giggs or Paul Scholes, one-club men who still try and prove that loyalty remains in the game. Steven Gerrard and Jamie Carragher at Liverpool and Chelsea's John Terry are other great examples.

Money? Is that what football has really come down to. Surely not? To think that I once argued with Queen's Park Rangers Chairman Jim Gregory over a few quid rise, and today players are earning £150,000 a week. It doesn't make them any better. I don't look back over my career with any regrets or sadness, but instead feel sorry for football and the money-obsessed sport it has become. As a player, captain, manager and Chief Executive I have witnessed many changes and the biggest is money. What concerns me as the big clubs chase the prizes on borrowed money, is that so many others are trying to keep up when they can't afford to. I just hope that football doesn't one day implode!

If that ever happened, how many players or agents would feel devastated? You could probably count them on one hand. Football will always be football. The fans are the ones who would be the big losers.

16

I Told You So

I hate to say I told you so, but I told you so. England's awful showing at the World Cup was no surprise to me. The difference between club football and international football is staggering. Earlier I said that I hoped England didn't win the World Cup because of the appointment of an Italian by the F.A..

As much as I think he has an outstanding club resume, I never wanted Fabio Capello as England manager and didn't believe he had a chance of bringing success to the country. How can an Italian, who has no direct knowledge of our game, know the mentality of the English player, understand what makes them tick and be able to communicate properly with them. South Africa represented England's worst showing at a World Cup tournament and it saddens me. I saw it coming for so many reasons and have been shouted down about this over the last couple of years.

There is a chasm between being a top club manager and being an international manager.

My criticism of Capello and the FA for appointing him were not just 'Loose Cannon' comments made for the sake of it. There is no one who loves football or England more than I do and this just didn't feel right to me. I watched the Algeria game with some American friends and I squirmed with embarrassment when I watched the way England played in South Africa. It was awful; we are light years behind the world's best.

The FA has retained Capello's services again. That doesn't surprise me because it was the easy, safe option and that is typical of the FA. For me, the fact that he has a period left on his 'no cut' contract without compensation, is the determining factor in their decision. Pathetic!

Go back years and years and you will find comments from me that were dismissed as rubbish, with people saying that it was just Marsh sounding off once more. No, I say these things because I care and believe in them. A long time ago I was pilloried for suggesting that, at the very top, what the FA needed were people in authority with football minds. Real football people. I said that Sir Bobby Charlton should have been used as a voice of authority and was laughed out of court. They signed Adam Crozier as CEO, enough said! In my opinion, the FA don't make football decisions, they make convenient ones. Public relations and marketing decisions.

The result is years of waste and you saw how far we are behind World Cup finalists Spain and Holland in South Africa. Watching England scramble around reminded me of the saying 'Can we have our ball back, please.' We need someone to keep the ball, to love it, but where are the young players with good habits? Where is the next Bobby Moore who can hold the ball in defence and use it sensibly? Rio Ferdinand came close at one stage but was always short of the great man, and there is no one now.

I watched Mathew Upson, Jamie Carragher and John Terry sometimes whacking the ball forward aimlessly and asked myself why? Why panic when things don't go right, as England always do? Capello's excuse that the players were tired is nonsense. Good players don't get tired at big tournaments. Why didn't Capello change his tactics; so many questions and not enough answers?

The system in England is all wrong, and it is not the FA that runs the game and makes the significant decisions. The Premier League is all-powerful and we are geared towards club football rather than the international set up. That is fantastic for the Premier League and I love watching it. But foreign owners, foreign managers and foreign players are stifling the life out of any production-line English football needs. If one of the big clubs gets an outstanding English talent they usually farm him out on loan to a smaller club for experience; e.g. Joe Hart from Manchester City to Birmingham and Jack Wilshire from Arsenal to Bolton. Why not play them and groom them at the highest level? Look at the millions Manchester City threw at success during the summer; most of it was on more foreign talent. They are not alone.

How do you change the system? You don't, because the club Chairmen are all-powerful and they don't want change. They don't want to give up what they have got. Go back twenty years and we were saying the same things after a tournament failure. We must go back to grass roots, develop young English players, play less football, and have a winter break and so on and so on.

Nothing changes and it never will.

English football is like an upside down pyramid. All the wealth, the big players and millionaire owners are at the top while underneath and out of sight there is nothing growing. A scramble for survival.

If you and I can see that, then why can't others? Maybe they don't care? Have we become so obsessed with club football in England that the England team no longer matters?

Capello and the players rightly take criticism for what happened in South Africa, although others should also stand up and be counted. The FA escapes every time and the Premier League just carries on creating a monster to the detriment of the National side.

Four matches we played at the World Cup. The disappointing performance against the USA was camouflaged by Robert Green's mistake. England were desperate against Algeria, who out-passed us and had more control. The sheer relief of victory over Slovenia hid times when we were hanging on. Germany were far superior and embarrassed us. Once again the nation had got sucked into the hype, expectation and ridiculous words of promise from the coach and the players.

All around England at the World Cup there were players more comfortable on the ball, defenders who knew what to do with it in possession, eleven men who gelled like a team and who didn't run out of ideas. England were a shambles and it saddens me to say it. I didn't want an Italian to win it for England but I certainly dreamed of a much better showing. But how can we win the World Cup when sometimes we play like a struggling lower league side!

From the moment he got England to the finals everything went wonky for Capello. The online game. Are you kidding me!! What was that all about? Whatever it was, I hope the team weren't distracted by it. Then he tried to bring Paul Scholes out of retirement at the last minute. He took injured players to the World Cup and then came the stories of unrest and unhappiness inside the camp. Take Wayne Rooney. Not once did he play with a smile on his face and we didn't see him react to situations like he does for Manchester United. At Old Trafford if he loses possession around his opponent's area, Rooney chases back. At the World Cup he gave up the ghost. It was clear for all to see that he was an unhappy player and in my opinion the management have to take some responsibility for this.

Capello's reaction to the win over Slovenia was that of a relieved man. As he raced onto the pitch to celebrate with surprised players he looked like a man who had no idea how the win was coming, but who was just so excited to get it. It was quite a pathetic sight.

England needs a new era and yet where is it coming from? The Premier League is alive and kicking again, ready to capture the imagination in a new season. Capello has no option but to select a majority of the same players, like Frank Lampard, Steven Gerrard, Gareth Barry, John Terry and Ashley Cole, because there in no others to pick; just a few youngsters who have never been given a chance by their clubs.

The biggest indictment against Capello the FA and the deterioration of English football came in the final twenty- five minutes or so of our 2010 World Cup campaign. When all was lost and we were staring the biggest embarrassing defeat in our history, who did Capello throw on to bring us some pride back? If it had been me managing that day, looking along the bench, which young, eager fiery English youngster would I have put on?

England is a country that has run out of players and ideas. We are lost in club football and foreign money.

My attitude towards Capello hasn't changed. I don't want an Italian running the England side and, when the European Championships comes around in two years, I will not want him to win it. Roy Hodgson or Harry Redknapp should be the England manager today, not after we fail in 2012!

The definition of insanity is continuing to do the same things in the belief that the outcome will eventually be different. That is England. Never learning. Always second best. Never changing.

As a proud Englishman it saddens me. So where to now for England? Nowhere, I'm afraid.

17

Where Do I Go from Here?

There was a lovely little wine bar in Wimbledon Village close to my England home called Volley's. I loved it in there, and often sat on my own sipping a cold beer or glass of wine watching the characters come and go. It attracted all sorts of personalities and during Wimbledon fortnight, Volley's would be packed out with tennis stars. Agassi, Steffi Graff, Becker, Chang, Gabriella Sabatini and loads more loved it. In the 90's it was my summer local when I was in the UK.

One man who visited Volley's as regularly as me was George Carmen, the famous barrister in the seventies and eighties who made a name for himself by successfully defending former Liberal leader Jeremy Thorpe, who was charged with conspiracy to murder, and comedian Ken Dodd with his tax evasion charge. George loved the ladies and if, when he strode into Volley's, there were a couple of attractive women talking at the bar, he would always say the same thing, "Two bottles of Dom Perignon, please, and give one to the ladies." He would then spend the evening chatting to them and entertaining them with stories of his favourite court cases.

He was a great character, and he and I were often the last to leave after a stimulating evening spent discussing life in general. During one such night, he told me that he'd only lost one case in his whole career. "Do you know what that was?" he said, "Bloody George Best on a drink-driving charge when he was at Manchester United. I took on the case and lost. Couldn't believe it! I'll tell you something else about George Best," he added, "Never forgave him for sleeping with my wife!"

Just one of the wonderful moments of my life, once again you couldn't make it up. I have been blessed and privileged in that football has allowed me to mix with so many wonderful characters and personalities. You can't orchestrate nights and moments like that with George Carmen, they just happen.

Carmen was not a friend, he was someone I occasionally drank and chatted with. At one point the most respected legal mind around, here he was chatting about

Manchester United and why they should get rid of Eric Cantona; you see in football, everybody has an opinion. In my opinion, there is a huge difference, and I will admit again here that I do not have a 'blood brother' in my life and am not anyone's blood brother. It's a Cheyenne Indian thing, where once they make that connection it's there for life. I don't think there is anyone, in fact I know there isn't anyone, I have ever really completely confided in. If that offends people who thought they were much closer as friends, it is what it is. Maybe my definition of a friend is off base too. What is a friend? Someone who knows you well, doesn't judge you and who is always there for you, especially in times of trouble. Someone who tries to understand you, forgives you, and who is constant. I am probably the worst friend in the world, nothing like the person I have just described. However I don't judge anyone. No one should unless they have been in the shoes of that person and even then unless asked, should mind their own business. Opinions are different than judgement though and if anyone has an opinion of Rodney Marsh, hey… knock yourself out. Maybe I never wanted a 'blood brother,' and all the countless lovely people I have come across have simply been passing ships.

I always kept my family away from football so they have never been part of it. I always looked at my playing mates as just that, playing mates.

The only person I would say at one time was an exception to all that is Willie Donachie, my old Manchester City team mate and former number two to manager Joe Royle. But even Willie has disappeared into oblivion now. Is that his fault or mine? I don't know. I'm not one to make calls or send letters or bother people. Fundamentally, I think people can't be bothered and give up on me. I feel Willie did that. You know the person you are and what you need back. I am who I am and I know what I stand for. I have probably revealed more about myself in this book than I wanted to.

Willie Donachie and I used to room together at City and lived in each other's pockets for four years. We became close, and in him I found someone to talk to. There were a lot of deep conversations that went on behind closed doors, and he used to give me books to read and thoughts to consume. When I was at my lowest point in 1975 he bought me Siddhartha by Herman Hesse. It changed my thinking. If you read my book, please read Siddhartha.

Many years later I read somewhere that Kurt Cobain from the rock band Nirvana used it like a Bible.

Willie and I used to challenge each other about life and football. I once said to him that I thought I'd never played in a football match where I'd given the full hundred percent. He thought about what I'd said for a long time and it led to us doing a spot of ad hoc research with managers, coaches and players we knew. They all agreed with me, that it was impossible to give a hundred percent for the entire ninety minutes. Players simply can't perform to exhaustion every time. Some games I gave sixty per cent, while others I performed at forty, or seventy. When everything was going well and I was in good form, then the percentage became higher. If we were away from home and losing 4-0, what was the point in giving a hundred percent? It would have been chasing a lost cause. When you hear a manager or player saying that he gave one hundred and ten percent, it is absolute bollocks. Don't believe him.

Yes, there have been times when I have deliberately not tried, when games were out of reach and meaningless. There were many times I was sent out onto the pitch by a manager knowing I was injured and unable to give everything. I once played at Cardiff for QPR when manager Alec Stock knew I was injured, but he wanted me to play and so I did. It was a mistake and I'm sure there are a number of players today who are either injected to perform, or go out when they know they shouldn't.

These are the kind of things that Willie Donachie and I used to discuss. There were many subjects we covered, and unfortunately we moved apart when our careers went separate ways. I hadn't heard from him for three years when I received a text message out of the blue a few Christmas's back. It simply read, "Love you Rod." I sent one back saying, "Me too." There has been nothing since, but we have a bond because we shared intense moments, and there is still a part of me that thinks of Willie with great affection. I listened to him for hours, talking about life and football and when that text came through, I had no idea where he was or what triggered him to message me. "Funny old life," Alec Stock used to say, and he was right.

People thought I was close to Malcolm Allison, but he was always a passing ship. I'm impossible to know and I know some people think I'm an arsehole because I can't communicate. They are entitled to that opinion and I'll defend their right to have it, but if that's what you think, I'd prefer it to my face. Willie Donachie achieved more than others in breaking down the barriers. The defence mechanism was formed as a kid and remains there today. I have never been a completely open book. Now, when it came to socialising, having a few drinks and enjoying a bit of a rave up, that was a different matter. I was your best friend for the night.

I have let many people down and maybe that's the reason I don't let people in, because I'm afraid I'll get hurt. If there are any psychologists reading this please feel free to give me a call.

Willie was younger than me and I'd say I treated him as a friend more than as a footballer and team mate. We had this incredibly close relationship in terms of certain things, mainly centred around the psychology of life. A conversation went on for hours one day, when Willie said that losing as a footballer could be a good thing.

He said losing was good and he still believes that. He said you had to learn to lose to enjoy winning. Maybe, over the years, he got used to it.

Every man is alone with his own demons and now, when I look back over my career, I admit that I could have achieved more. I have just played the cards life dealt me. My cards have caused me all sorts of problems and I have faced up to them and worked through things, climbing mountains and running down hills. Life is for living, and on and off the pitch I played for fun and enjoyed myself.

As a footballer I don't believe I ever compromised myself, probably because I have never given a fuck what people thought or, indeed, think of me today. On the pitch, the other players were just the supporting cast. It was my show and I was centre stage. "Give me the ball, and I will do something with it," was my motto. When it worked and all went well, it was fantastic. When it didn't, oh well, there was always the next game. I have lived my life as if looking at a deck of cards; some hands were good, others dodgy. I just picked them up, had a gamble and carried on. Could I have been a better player? I have been asked that many times. What I will say is that I could not have been a better Rodney Marsh. Had I been, I would have been Colin Bell!

I have no football regrets whatsoever. I have done things in football that made me the person I am, although a lot of people just look upon me as being arrogant and a loudmouth. I don't care. What they say is possibly true, but I only say and do what is in my heart.

I have made mistakes, many of them and, yes, there was regret when I once broke an opponent's leg. Manchester City were playing Rochdale and we were 6-0 up and cruising. I was playing out of my skin, really enjoying myself when the ball bounced between this nineteen-year old kid and me. I was late and high with my challenge, and while I wanted to be physical and make a firm tackle, it was a bad one. I didn't mean to hurt him; his leg was clearly broken, and it affected me badly as I watched him being carried off on a stretcher in such pain. In the dressing room after the game, I said to Willie Donachie that I had to go and see the kid and say sorry. We both went to the visitors' dressing room next door, but he'd already been taken to hospital. Their manager was fuming and swore at me as I said to Willie that I needed to go to the hospital.

Willie drove me and when we got to his room, he had already been operated on and his leg was in plaster. I leant over him and explained that I was sorry and never meant to hurt him. He looked at me, propped himself up and produced a match programme. "I'm your biggest fan," he said, "would you sign this?" I felt like a complete prat and I still think about that incident to this day. It damaged me for a long time. It is ironic that I was so upset, when there had been so many opponents in my career who set out to break my legs. I still carry the scars and threat in my head.

There were loads of people who had an influence on me, like Johnny Haynes, and Dennis Law because he was such a showman and I loved to watch him with his one finger in the air goal celebration. My dad influenced me too. He loved his football and, after watching the great Hungarian, Ferenc Puskás, help destroy England 6-3 at Wembley, he had me juggling a ball on my left foot for hours on end. I can still do it fifty times today.

There were highs in my career that not many people get near to. At one sportsman's dinner George Best and I were talking one day about the best goals we scored. The trouble is that there were not enough videos around in our day to do justice to the skills and goals scored by so many players. I got one against Tranmere for Queen's Park Rangers that defied logic. A pass was struck to me at shoulder-height as I strolled around the halfway line. I got it quickly under control, and as it dropped to the ground, one defender flew past me and I moved slightly forward. From about thirty-five yards out I struck a shot that swerved, bent and then skipped on the ground before it got to the goalkeeper. It suddenly skipped even higher, went over his head as he dived and into the top corner of the net by the angle. Two goalkeepers wouldn't have stopped it and I still don't know why I shot from so far out. It was not on camera. Had it been scored in a World Cup Final it would have gone down in football history, but it was against Tranmere.

For someone who never looks for a row, I was sent off five times in my career, mostly for head butting or punching in retaliation. Can you believe that? There was one at Southampton, another at PSV away. Memphis in the NASL was another, when former Everton player Jimmy Husband deliberately went down the back of my legs with his studs, and another was against Glasgow Rangers in a pre-season friendly.

It was always retaliation that got me into trouble. When you saw two opponents come together in anger, I was always the one who led with his head. Why? I have no idea and was always so sorry afterwards, but it was too late. Loose Cannon? Yes, I suppose I was.

There is a great picture somewhere of me being held back by QPR coach Jimmy Barrett in 1969, when we played Glasgow Rangers before the season started. I had clashed with Kai Johansen, their Danish right-back, who had kicked lumps off me all afternoon. He kicked me again on the running track when we rolled out of play and I retaliated. The referee got involved and Jimmy, seeing the red mist, jumped on the pitch and held my arms behind my back. "It's okay Jim," I said, "its over." With that, this great big ginger-haired defender called Jock Watson, I think, came rushing over to confront me. He was foaming at the mouth, completely gone, and as I stood up, still with Jimmy holding on, I was completely vulnerable so just butted him. I was fined £500 by QPR, another £500 by the FA and suspended, and this was not even a proper match, just a pre-season friendly!

The following week in the post to the club, someone from Glasgow had written to me saying that he and his mates were coming to London to beat up my wife and kids. "You don't do that to one of ours," it read. Amazingly, it had the guy's name and address on the top of the letter and the club handed it over to the police, not believing anyone could be stupid enough to make such a threat and reveal his identity. Sure enough, when the Scottish police went around to his house, there he was still sounding off about me. The Police warned him off, but couldn't do anything else because apparently the law states that if someone says he will cut off another person's head, he cannot be arrested unless caught in the act of trying. Madness, but it showed the passion that football generates.

I have never been able to stand people who whispered things behind your back and threatened me through others. I always prefer a face-to-face chat and telling it how it is. I got to hear from others, including Manchester City captain Mike Summerbee, that team mate Mike Doyle was rubbishing me and stabbing me in the back. To my face, he said that I was fantastic for Manchester City and that I had attracted more fans, which had brought everyone else more money in crowd bonuses. Behind my back, he was saying that I was lazy and a liability. So, one day in the showers after training, I remember confronting him. "Do we have a problem Mike," I said, "If you have, just tell me to my face." "No, no, Rod," he squirmed, "No problem."'

Who would have thought I would have lived this extraordinary life, my life, after such an upbringing in the East End of London. From an era when men went down the mines for twelve or fourteen hours a day and emerged, their faces blackened, to go home for tea and some sleep before starting again. An era when football was an escape for the working classes, when the man of the house worked on Saturday morning and then went to his football match after lunch to scream and shout and let off some steam. I was frustrated as a child because I knew there was something else to come, there had to be. When it was all kicking off around me, I used to lie awake at night and think, think hard about life and about people. I dreamt of a different world, and there was never any doubt in my mind as I fought sleep that one day it would come.

I was blessed with being able to play football, and that has taken me on an amazing roller-coaster ride. Like at the fairground, I have been up in the sky and down in the depths. Mentally, it has sometimes been difficult, but physically, I have enjoyed every minute of my career and I wouldn't change a thing. I have been surrounded by stars and by interesting people, by great players and good ones, by others I respected, and by a lot of people I had no time for.

I mean what I say when I reveal that, through it all, no one has come with me. Not someone I can call a 'blood brother'. My family has been wonderful and I thank them from the bottom of my heart. Through all my shortcomings and all the nonsense they have always been there. I'm probably the hardest person to love and I have to live with that.

It is often in a book like this that people like me say how much they regretted doing certain things, or that they look back and wish they could rewind the clock. Not me, I've got to this point by being Rodney Marsh, the Loose Cannon, and that is how I will end.

I don't suffer fools, so a person can say something to me that will put me off instantly, and make me not want to be in his or her company. For example, I hate it when someone says things like, "In the grand scheme of things,' or "All things being equal." What the fuck does that mean? If all things were equal then every game of football would end 0-0. We'd get nowhere. Life and football is not equal!

The title of this book is, 'I Was Born A Loose Cannon,' chosen because it probably sums me up perfectly. I have been asked many times how I would like people to label me now that my playing career is over and I have finished with the other side of football too, the media career and as a Chief Executive. You have to believe me when I say I really don't give a toss. I really don't.

When managers were raving at me for not following instructions, deep down I was laughing at them. A bollocking at half time would often end up with a second-half hat trick and all smiles in the dressing room at the end of the game. That was me, ride the downs and enjoy the ups.

These days, when I'm in America, I spend my time with my little grandson Addison. I help my son Jonathan with Marsh Group Inc., his property development company, and I do occasional broadcast/media work in Tampa.

I am also an Executive Ambassador to Optimum Business Solutions, which is a Manchester based procurement outsourcing and consultancy company, and the parent corporation of my publisher. In that position I get to see many Manchester City games when I'm in the UK, which is a huge bonus.

I have never done something I didn't really want to, or needed to do. I have made mistakes, plenty of them, and they have all been my fault. I have never been one for appeasing people. In football and in the media I am not the guy who hides his true feelings; I say it and get everything out in the open.

It used to do my head in on TV or radio when someone would be describing a missed open goal, saying, "he'll be disappointed with that." When I missed an open goal, I didn't think, "I'm disappointed with that." Instead, I would say to myself "You twat, how could you miss that!" When Kanu missed that sitter under the bar when he was playing for West Brom, he would have felt like a prat, not disappointed. So why do we try and pull the wool over the eyes of the public? You should tell it as if you were in the pub with your mates, just tell the truth.

Another classic I hate is, "They're getting beaten badly but they're working their socks off," and Alan Shearer uses this one a lot. No Alan, they are shite, get over it!

The only thing I wanted was respect from people I myself respected. When Bobby Moore told me to my face that I was behaving like a prat, I took it on board; thought about what he had said and made an effort to change. I took it from him because he was the greatest. I didn't want to be rude to Sir Alf Ramsey when I made that sarcastic comment before my last appearance for England; to me it was only a joke. What is a joke to some people is an offence to others. Alan Smith is testament to that, but like me he should have had a bit of a laugh at himself and moved on.

I meant no disrespect.

When I criticise the FA for appointing Fabio Capello it is not because I don't like him or respect what he has achieved in his career, it is because I did not want him as England manager. I don't believe it to be right, and I don't want England to win the World Cup with an Italian in charge. That's how I feel so I say it. What's the point in thinking something but being too afraid to say it?

I have done so much in my career and there isn't one thing that I regret or still want to achieve. I am happy and content. I don't have a 'blood brother' from all the people I have come across and spent time with. Everyone has just passed through my life.

In football, George Best, Bobby Moore, Malcolm Allison, Terry Venables: all passing ships. Incredibly, Venners turned up at a lunch around my sixty-fifth birthday out of the blue, we chatted for a couple of hours over a bottle of champagne and he was on his way. Funny ol' game.

I am sure many have said the same about me. How do you get close to Rodney Marsh? It's definitely difficult. Willie Donachie probably was an exception, although he and I eventually sailed off in different directions too.

There were tears in Jim Gregory's eyes when I gave him my first England cap as a thank you for him being like a father figure and rescuing my career. I owed Gregory my career for what he did for me at Loftus Road, but it didn't make him a close friend. He was a tough, hard man, who lived his life on the edge, but I'd seen a different side to him and for that I was grateful. I'd gone to his house in Coombe, near Kingston in Surrey, to re-negotiate my contract and before we started talking, I said I'd like to give him something, then handed him my cap, all braided and tasselled, and he just welled up. Now, not many men will have seen that! My other England caps, by the way, are safely locked away in a cabinet at my Florida home. They are the only material things I have kept from my career, apart from a few early medals, which include the 1967 League Cup Final tankard. Everything else is in my head.

I will always have a soft spot for the teams I played for and I still always look for their results first. Was it really that long ago, almost fifty years, since I made my professional debut for Fulham? You could say a lot has happened since then. I've played at Rangers, Manchester City, and then moved on to America. I've embraced every minute and don't look back with anything other than joy.

I wonder what all those in football I have upset are thinking now, at this very minute? Do they ever think of me and reflect? What is Tony Book, the man who prematurely ended my career in England, thinking?

I have been blessed and done so much and achieved more than most. That is not a boast, just the truth. There isn't anything else I am desperate to achieve, although I know, I just know there is still another chapter to come. I can feel it in my bones. I don't know what, and I wonder with anticipation and excitement what it might be?

There are still things that will remain in my heart and in my head.

There is only one truth, but it's not the whole truth.

I'm now going to tell you something about myself that I have never revealed to anyone. Not one person. It has been a closely guarded secret. It's that . . . . . hmm, in fact, maybe I'll just leave that one for next time.